IDENTITY AND RELATIONSHIP

IDENTITY AND RELATIONSHIP

A contribution to Marxist theory
of literary criticism

JEREMY HAWTHORN

1973
LAWRENCE & WISHART
LONDON

Printed in Great Britain
by W & J Mackay Limited, Chatham

ACKNOWLEDGMENTS

Acknowledgments are due to Messrs Chatto and Windus, and William Empson, for permission to reprint 'Note on Local Flora', from *Collected Poems* by William Empson; to the estate of Robert Frost, Edward Connery Lathem, and Messrs Jonathan Cape for permission to reprint 'Mending Wall' from *The Poetry of Robert Frost*, edited by Robert Connery Lathem; to Messrs André Deutsch and Geoffrey Hill, for permission to reprint 'September Song' from *King Log* by Geoffrey Hill; to the International Copyright Bureau Ltd., for permission to reprint extracts from *Six Characters in Search of an Author*, by Luigi Pirandello, translated by Frederick May and published by Messrs Heinemann Educational Books Ltd.; to Messrs Faber and Faber Ltd., for permission to print an extract from 'Thirteen Ways of Looking at a Blackbird', from *The Collected Poems of Wallace Stevens*; to M. B. Yeats, Messrs Macmillan and Co. Ltd., and the Macmillan Company of Canada Ltd., for permission to reprint 'Sailing to Byzantium', part of 'The Second Coming', and part of 'Easter 1916', from *The Collected Poems of W. B. Yeats*. Acknowledgments are also due to the holders of copyright of other works from which brief quotations have been made; a full list of these will be found at the end of the book.

Parts of Chapter 8 appeared in a different form in 'Marxism Today'. I am grateful to the editor for permission to reprint this material.

I must also express my thanks for financial help received from the Pantyfedwen Fund of St. David's University College to cover costs incurred in the publishing of this book.

J. M. H.

CONTENTS

Preface

This book is an attempt to suggest ways forward in two areas of knowledge which seem to me to share common problems—Marxism and literary criticism. In a sense the final push to writing it came from my feeling that certain works which were just becoming available to English-speaking readers contained within them solutions to some of the problems which critical theory within the tradition of Anglo-American literary criticism has been grappling with for some time. I refer to those Marxist writers who have attempted to regain and develop the dialectical element in Marxist theory during the present century, in particular the Lenin of the *Philosophical Notebooks*, György Lukács, Antonio Gramsci, and Lucien Goldmann. Certainly without the work of these writers—and their translators—this book would never have been written. I hope that my obvious dependence upon their thought will lead the reader to a direct acquaintance with their work where this does not already exist.

It struck me that within the works of these writers there existed ways out of a number of debilitating log-jams that seemed to have developed in the field of Anglo-American literary criticism—recurrent cruxes of critical theory which one meets with in almost every second book on critical theory published at present. I have attempted to bring these two streams together, and to suggest ways in which they can be of mutual benefit. Because of the nature of this task, one possible criticism of what I have done occurs to me which I would like to take this opportunity of replying to in advance. It may seem that by taking those representatives of Marxist thought who seem to me to be the finest thinkers within this area, and relating their writing to various recurrent problems contained in the work of a number of literary critics, I run the risk of being accused of what I have referred to as 'Aunt-Sallyism' later on in the book. I am conscious of the truth of Gramsci's point, that unlike military battles, in intellectual battles there are no real advances to be gained from attacking one's opponents at their weakest points, as victories so gained mean little or nothing.

I have not, however, been primarily concerned to win battles, but to try to find examples of particular critical problems in the work of certain critics, and examples of a clear and 'pure' nature. This is why in dealing with formalism I have taken works which do to a certain extent represent extreme positions, some of which were written some time ago, and many of which have been superseded by more subtle presentations of formalistic literary criticism, often by the same writers. I hope that it will not be thought that I have been looking for easy victories here. In my defence, I should point out that my debt to a number of non-Marxist critics should be apparent from the extent of my reference to them.

As a result of the reference to two areas of knowledge—Marxism and literary-critical theory—which this book makes, many readers may find that parts of the book present problems for them. Marxist readers may find that too much attention is paid to critical theorists who seem to them merely to concern themselves with minor problems which are insoluble because of the isolation of such problems from a social and political context. Non-Marxist readers may feel that the references to general Marxist theory—particularly in the opening chapters—are somewhat heavy going and are of dubious relevance. I hope that readers belonging to both categories will be as tolerant as they can of the fact that the book does move out of conventional subject-divisions, and will accept that the author has moved away from these divisions because he feels that they restrict and impede adequate study of the problems that have already been mentioned. I think that much Marxist writing in the recent past has been too ready to be dismissive about non-Marxist writing in a manner that seems alien to Marx's own approach. Similarly, I feel that the comfortable rejections of Marxism made by many literary critics after the Second World War, although not entirely without justification, have worn somewhat thin in the past decade or so, and I think that many non-Marxist readers should be prepared to consider what Marxists say about literature in the same way that they are prepared to consider what most critics say about literature —with a willingness to accept what they agree with and reject what they do not, rather than with the aim in mind of accepting or rejecting a complete system once and for all.

My debt is not one that is limited to books, but which extends to my friends, colleagues and students. Without their help, knowledge and encouragement this book could hardly have been started, let alone completed. As is usual in such situations I am too much aware of the discrepancy between the largeness of the debt and the inadequacy of the finished product to be happy with a direct association of anyone in

particular with this work other than myself, but I hope that those concerned will accept this sincere, if anonymous, appreciation.

J. M. H.

Cellan, Cardiganshire.
April 1972.

I. *Identity and Relationship*

> Briefly, metacriticism is centrifugal, intrinsic criticism
> centripetal. The one is concerned with a work's relation-
> ships, the other with its identity; the one with its signifi-
> cance, the other with its meaning. In short, the one moves
> *from* the work, the other inwards *to* it.
>
> > ALLAN RODWAY.[1]

It is well known that critical approaches to literature have tended to
group around the two main theoretical positions that Allan Rodway
calls 'metacriticism' and 'intrinsic criticism'. Many different names have
been given to these two approaches; the former being referred to as the
sociological, the mimetic, the moral approach, and the latter the autonomous, the formal, and the formalistic approach. In particular usages
these terms have of course assumed different shades of meaning, and
individual critics have been able to distinguish between, for example,
moral and sociological critical approaches. Nevertheless, many critics
and critical theorists have recognised that the distinction made by
Rodway is not only valid and meaningful, but one which is more
fundamental than many other such distinctions. Wellek and Warren
extend the distinction to all aesthetics, and express it as follows in their
Theory of Literature:

> In a sense, the whole issue in aesthetics might be said to lie between
> the view which asserts the existence of a separate, irreducible
> 'aesthetic experience' (an autonomous realm of art) and that which
> makes the arts instrumental to science and society, which denies
> such a *tertium quid* as the 'aesthetic value'. . . .[2]

Given the general acknowledgment of this distinction, an obvious
question is raised and has to be considered: what is the relationship
between these two approaches? Are they complementary, or are they
mutually exclusive? Is there room for both approaches in the theory and
practice of the ideal critic, or must the latter inevitably make a choice,
choosing one and rejecting the other? Some believe that the critic
must choose between these two theoretical approaches, that he cannot

be both a 'metacritic' and an 'intrinsic critic', examining both the irreducible aesthetic experience and the relationship between the work of art and other areas of experience. For example, in his book *Character and the Novel*, W. J. Harvey writes:

> We may call the two systems I am . . . isolating the theories of autonomy and mimesis.
>
> . . . .
>
> I suspect that if one manoeuvres a critic into such a situation he will ultimately have to make this either/or choice, to commit himself finally to one or other of these theories.[3]

Allan Rodway, however, leads on from the quotation given above to examples of the two approaches which are clearly capable of peaceful coexistence—on the one hand, studying the Bible and seventeenth-century history as a way into Dryden's *Absalom and Achitophel*, and on the other using the same poem as a way into seventeenth-century history, or as part of a course in Biblical Studies. Put in these terms, it would seem probable that not only are the two approaches capable of being subsumed into the same critical theory and practice, but that it would be hard, if not impossible, to separate them absolutely and produce a 'pure' piece of intrinsic criticism of *Absalom and Achitophel* which did not in some small way contribute to our knowledge of seventeenth-century history.

For this reason I find Rodway's terminology helpful, for it does not imply the sort of mutual exclusiveness that Harvey argues must be recognised by the critic. This of course is not to suggest that there are not many, and fundamental, irreconcilable elements in the theory and practice of many metacritics and intrinsic critics, and I hope to be able to consider some of these in due course. I would not wish to maintain that in their conventional forms these two approaches can be fully integrated with one another, thus allying myself with those who make it their life's business to demonstrate that in reality nothing ever disagrees with anything else. There are, for example, items of critical faith held by Marxist and formalistic critics which cannot live together in a consistent and logical critical system. What I want to argue is that important and fundamental parts of these two critical approaches are not only reconcilable, but imply one another and must be combined to produce a full and adequate critical theory. It is true that it is impossible to simultaneously approach the work of literature both as an 'autonomous whole', and also as dependent upon a context which includes the writer, the reader and society seen in a temporal dimension. What I do believe is that a literary theory which seeks to combine as much as possible of value from past critical theory and practice must in a sense be both metacritical and intrinsic, and must be capable both of seeing the work of literature as a distinct 'whole' and also of perceiving that this 'whole' exists in and is defined by a complex of relationships of which it forms a part.

In practice, the word which militates most effectively against a view of the two approaches as complementary is the dangerous 'autonomy'. In view of this I propose to drop the use of this word except in the context of stated critical disagreement, and to substitute the word suggested by the quotation from Allan Rodway—'identity'. My use of this word necessitates an initial definition, for it does not have a simple unambiguous meaning. The two main dictionary definitions of 'identity' are (1) 'The quality or condition of being the same'; and (2) 'Individuality, personality'. It is identity as individuality or personality, the identity *of* something, rather than the identity of something *with* something else to which I refer when I use the word in connection with the work of literature. My contention is that in fact many of the undoubted successes of formalistic criticism have rested upon a successful isolation and description of the identity of a work of literature, rather than of any alleged autonomy it may possess. My use of the word obviously suggests various analogies between the work of literature and the individual human being, which I shall return to.

The attempt to demonstrate that elements of formalistic criticism can be used to enrich and broaden a metacritical—or more specifically a Marxist—literary criticism, is by no means an original undertaking, although it is a rare one. One very significant example of such an attempt can be found in a speech given by N. I. Bukharin at the first Soviet Writers' Congress. Bukharin's approach is important because it contains certain theoretical justifications for such an attempt at integration, and rises above a merely eclectic desire to make Marxist criticism the repository of all other critical systems. Unlike Zhdanov—whose speech forms an instructive contrast to Bukharin's—Bukharin recognises that although one of the basic premises of formalism, that the work of art is a totally autonomous whole, is false, it nevertheless draws attention to an aspect of the work of art's mode of being to which Marxists could and should devote more attention. The formulation Bukharin uses is that of what he calls the 'specific nature' of the art work, which I would argue has a similar reference to my term 'identity'.

The most creative part of Bukharin's argument is his insistence that far from being irreconcilable, the investigation of the identity of the art work and the investigation of its relationships with that which is extrinsic to it are complementary procedures which of necessity define and imply one another. The work can have no identity without existing within a complex of relationships nor can it be related to anything outside of itself without having a distinct identity. Bukharin accepts the formalistic contention that diverse elements join together to form a unified artistic 'whole' which is more than the sum of its parts, but moves on from this position to a conclusion different from that of the formalists:

> Evidently we must draw just the opposite conclusion (*to that arrived at by a formalistic writer*, J.M.H.) . . ., namely, that since all the elements enumerated here have entered into some synthetic whole—a work of art—then, in order to understand this whole in all its aspects we must go beyond its borders and reveal the sources of the entire morphological process. One cannot understand law without going beyond the borders of legal formulae.[4]

The implication that it is only 'sources' which need be investigated if one goes beyond the borders of the 'synthetic whole' of the art work may be questioned, but the basic implication of Bukharin's argument seems to me to be valid—that only by going beyond a thing can one understand what that thing is. As W. C. Brownell said over fifty years ago in his book *Criticism*: '. . . no one knows his subject who knows his subject alone'.[5] In his insistence upon seeing the art work as a 'synthetic whole' which can be fully understood only in a context larger than its own being, Bukharin presents the theoretical basis for a genuinely creative and dialectical alternative to the equally sterile poles of dogmatic, Zhdanovian mechanical 'Marxist' approaches to literature, and self-referential formalism.

What Brownell says of a subject can also be said of an object, which those critics who insist on seeing the work of literature as a 'thing-in-itself' tend to forget. Bukharin does not suggest that any neat or mechanical equation between the work's 'specific nature' and that to which it is related can be made; he is careful to distinguish, for example, between '. . . the ideological source of the content, and . . . its artistic transformation',[6] in a way that stresses both the uniqueness of the art work and the nature of its relationship with the world outside it. He neither rejects as irrelevant a consideration of the 'ideological source

of the content', nor does he neglect to note that the significance of this
is different in the art work from its significance outside the art work.
His use of the word 'borders', which has a less absolute ring about it
than T. S. Eliot's use of the word 'frontiers', implies a distinction, but
not necessarily a fixed and eternal division between the art work and the
rest of the world. Bukharin's final comment on formalism, written
before most of the debates between Marxist and New Critics familiar to
Western readers had taken place, is still one of the tersest and acutest
Marxist summaries on this subject:

> Formalism in literary theory . . . is closely linked up with formal-
> ism in art itself. Its most glaring error is that it attempts, on principle,
> to tear art from its vital social context. It creates the illusion, or the
> fiction, of an entirely independent "series" of phenomena in art. The
> specific nature of art it confuses with its complete autonomy. As
> for the laws of art's development, it sees them only in the immanent
> laws of its morphology, quite devoid of any connection with the
> most important problems of social life in general.[7]

It would be misleading to suggest that Bukharin is alone in having
suggested that Marxist criticism could profitably concern itself with an
investigation of the positive aspects of the formalistic insistence on
studying 'the work itself' rather than its relations with other areas of
life and experience. What distinguishes Bukharin's contribution to this
debate is the firm theoretical basis on which he attempts to build a
synthesis. This is the basic principle of dialectics, that the identity of a
thing and its relationships in time with other things are opposites which
belong to and define one another. It is perhaps ironic that an individual
so effectively, and justly, attacked by Gramsci for an undialectical and
mechanical approach to Marxism in one sphere, should have escaped
from mechanism and dogmatism so successfully in another.[8]

To talk of these two approaches as interdependent is to lay the
theoretical foundation for a more genuinely dialectical Marxist aesthetics. One critical discipline which recognised this early on was
structuralism. Jan Mukařovský, in an article on 'The Esthetics of
Language', distinguishes between the 'esthetic function' and the
'esthetic norm' in a manner that recalls our initial distinction, and he
realises that their interconnection and interdependence is a dialectical
one. He insists that between them 'there is a direct opposition in the
nature of a dialectic antinomy of related, yet opposing, forces', and
notes that the implication of this fact is that wherever one of them is

brought to bear, the other must also be present, at least potentially.[9] This is the conclusion to which we were led when considering *Absalom and Achitophel*, that it is not possible to use the poem as an end in itself without some appreciation of its historical significance, nor is it possible to use it just as a historical document, for its historical and aesthetic significance cannot be completely separated from one another. If the poem had little aesthetic value then its historical significance would also be changed—although not necessarily diminished.

Attempts to combine these two approaches on an eclectic and non-dialectical basis have had only a limited success. Although it may be possible to produce useful results in isolated critical instances, the critic must have a clear idea of the theoretical relationship between the two for any synthesis to be more than partial. The following two statements are representative. They are taken from the recently-published *Contemporary Criticism* anthology, and appear in essays by Graham Hough and Richard Hoggart. Taken together they can be seen as indicative of a growing need felt by many non-Marxist critics to achieve the sort of synthesis that I have already suggested can only be achieved on the basis of the acceptance of certain principles of dialectics.

> Criticism . . . both pays its tribute to the autonomy of literature and defines an area where it can speak with special knowledge. But the autonomy of literature is relative; and there is another requirement that seems to impose itself. Criticism should be able to give some intelligible account of the relationship of literature to the social order. There is a methodology for this, and so far as I know there is only one. To think on this subject at all requires some application of Marxism . . .[10]

> It is important that some critics continue to insist that a work of literature is an autonomous artifact. This reminds us that the 'coherent universe' of a work is, first and foremost, itself and not something else to be used for other purposes. It underlines the singularity of each work of art and the sense in which the expressive arts are free, pointless acts. The claim for autonomy has a heuristic value and in the last decade or two has done a great deal to sharpen and make more subtle our understanding of literature. But it is at bottom a limited and mistaken claim. A work of art, no matter how much it rejects or ignores its society, is deeply rooted within it.[11]

Hough's straightforward appeal to Marxists to undertake the theoretical work necessary for an adequate synthesis of the two approaches is perhaps no more convincing than the confusion which causes Hoggart to say that it is important that some critics continue to insist on something which he goes on to say is mistaken. This is eclecticism with a vengeance! Hoggart is surely on the right lines when he says that the claim for autonomy has to be dropped, and it is the use of the word 'autonomy' by Hough that causes what is needless heartache. Hough does qualify this use by means of the word 'relative', which has an importance to which I will return, but in the case of both critics one feels that the synthesis is more a case of 'on the one hand' and 'on the other' rather than a fully integrated synthesis, and the reason for this surely has to be sought in the lack of a theoretical basis for any uniting of the two approaches, only a perceived practical necessity.

I have already said that I feel that the positive aspects of the formalistic study of 'the work itself' can be retained whilst rejecting some of its negative aspects, by substituting 'identity' for 'autonomy'. Many Marxists, in the field of criticism and other disciplines have preferred the term 'relative autonomy', or, sometimes, 'limited autonomy'. In a letter to Conrad Schmidt, October 27, 1890, Engels wrote the best-known expression of this concept, although he did not use the phrase itself. Talking about the dependence of consciousness upon social existence Engels refers to the legal system (as did Bukharin) as an example of the dialectical rather than mechanical relationship which exists between the two:

> As soon as the new division of labour which creates professional lawyers becomes necessary, another new and independent sphere is opened up which, for all its general dependence on production and trade, still has its own capacity for reacting upon these spheres as well. In a modern state, law must not only correspond to the general economic position and be its expression, but must also be an expression which is *consistent in itself*, and which does not, owing to inner contradictions, look glaringly inconsistent. And in order to achieve this, the faithful reflection of economic conditions is more and more infringed upon.[12]

Several interesting theoretical points emerge from this statement. First of all, Engels's reference to the legal system as an 'independent sphere' is obviously not meant to be interpreted in an absolute fashion. The independence of any legal system can obviously only go so far; if it flirts with independence for too extended a period society can be expected to start divorce proceedings. In fact the passage quoted posits what can be described as a relative autonomy for the legal system which is obviously, in the last resort as Engels says, dependent upon the economic basis, but which has certain 'independent' characteristics built into it, and also in its turn influences the base.

Engels's formulation has not been without its critics however, and a brief consideration of one of the most cogent of recent ones is now called for. In the course of an article attacking Louis Althusser, Leszek Kolakowski has noted that many Marxists of the Second International were reluctant to admit this and other explanations of the non-absolute nature of the influence of the economic base.

> They believed, perhaps not without reason, that the idea of "many factors" enjoying "relative autonomy" deprives Marxism of its specificity, and makes of historical materialism a banal common-place, since the additional vague statement about the "determination in the last resort" has no meaning whatsoever in historical explana-tion as long as we are not able to define what are the limits of this "ultimate determination" and, similarly, the limits of the "relative autonomy" granted to other domains of social life, especially to various spheres of the so-called superstructure.[13]

It seems to me that one does not necessarily deal a death-blow to historical materialism by believing in the 'relative autonomy' of parts of the superstructure, for the implication of a belief in the ultimate sanction of the economic base is that this allows the investigator to distinguish between temporary and permanent causal factors in historical development, and to organise social practice accordingly. The final proof—as in everything—that the ultimate sanction of the economic base is not a vain item of religious belief has to be found in the realm of social practice; if such a belief allows those who hold it to change the world according to their predictions and efforts, then it can be said to be justified, and Kolakowski's assertions to the contrary notwithstand-ing, this would appear to have been the case.

The relevance of this to aesthetics is that the adoption of a belief in the relative autonomy of the art work does not destroy the scientific aspects of a Marxist criticism, for in practice the critic can retain an understanding of the way in which the art work is connected to the world outside it without necessarily having a dogmatic, mechanical adherence to a belief in the way literature, or art in general, reflects the economic base of the society which produces it. The concept of relative autonomy, or of identity, allows the critic to see that although certain dominant pressures are operative as much in the field of art as elsewhere, these pressures are transmuted into other forms in the art work (as

Bukharin points out), and in turn react back upon the economic base.

There is however a strong case for arguing that the term 'relative autonomy' is still a misleading one, for what is involved has in fact nothing to do with autonomy at all. It is true that in practice Marxists have realised that in a class-divided society the interests of the ruling class are often best served by concealing these interests, and thus (as Engels in effect points out) it is in the interests of the ruling class of a particular society that the judiciary, for example, should appear to be independent. To put it another way, the court which makes a specific decision that is at a certain point in time against the interests of the ruling class, may in fact be making a decision that, for the reasons I have suggested, is in their long-term interest. I have allowed myself to be diverted into discussion of this point here, because I feel that in the realm of aesthetics the term 'relative autonomy' as used to describe the art work may also do more harm than good, and that the substitution of a term such as 'identity' is therefore not a mere playing with words.

It is however significant that both Marxist and non-Marxist literary critics should be found using this term more and more frequently of late. On the part of the former this undoubtedly represents an aspect of a move away from the more mechanical and dogmatic formulations of Stalinism (which is one reason, I think, why Kolakowski's argument that an insistence upon the concept of 'relative autonomy' is related to Stalinism and dogmatism is only a partial one). On the part of non-Marxist critics a use of this term often suggests a desire to build up a literary theory which encompasses the positive achievements of formalism whilst rejecting some of its more obviously false elements connected with theories of the autonomy of the art work. Lucien Goldmann, in his *The Human Sciences and Philosophy* suggests another way of answering Kolakowski's accusation of meaninglessness in the use of the term 'relative autonomy', when he argues that dialectical material-ism as such has never denied the influence of ideological factors, but has combated attempts to separate them from concrete social life and to see them in autonomous or immanent terms.[14] There is, broadly speaking, no intellectual dishonesty or confusion involved in a distinc-tion between theories which suggest that there is a direct and immediate influence of all other factors by the economic, those which argue for the complete autonomy of certain 'wholes' or structures, and those which argue that economic factors do influence other aspects of social life, but not always in a direct way, and which insist that the economic struc-ture of a society, although in one sense primary, is influenced by non-economic factors. The latter position logically leads to an insistence that 'wholes' or complexes within society which are possessed of an equilibrium and an identity, have a certain limited self-determinedness, and are not necessarily immediately influenced by every fluctuation in the economic base of society, but are still subject to the 'last resort' dominance of such factors—just as a dictator may have *de jure* absolute power over a subject, but may not care, or find it necessary, to use such power all the time. Now Kolakowski is right that a mechanistic theory of the relationship between base and superstructure makes prediction much easier—which is why many dogmatists wish to retain their belief in such a relationship, as, quite simply, it makes life much easier in terms of thinking that you understand the world. What it has not proved capable of doing is making a real understanding of the world— involving the ability to change the latter—easier. What is now needed is constant application to the problems of defining what the real relationship between primary and secondary factors in historical change is, and, in the field of aesthetics, a far more subtle attempt to assess the ways in which the 'whole' of the art work can be examined in terms of itself, and the ways in which it must be examined in terms of other areas of life and experience. This, in brief, is why this book is being written.

Perhaps I can reinforce this point by returning to the analogy between the 'whole' of the art work and the 'whole' of the human individual suggested by a use of the term 'identity'. Certain obvious parallels with what has gone before become apparent in this context. Marxists have constantly argued that to demonstrate that human individuality or identity becomes meaningful only when given a location within a complex of social and economic relationships is not to degrade human beings, but to make them more comprehensible. The old anti-Marxist argument that Marxists 'reduce' human beings to mere responses to social and economic stimuli is as misleading as the parallel argument that Marxists similarly reduce literature to a sort of vague reflection of the economic health of a given society. This said, it must be admitted that just as in the field of aesthetics it has been seen to be necessary to reject over-mechanical attempts to relate a work of art to its social origin, so too in a wider area of dispute it has proved necessary to modify over-dogmatic attempts to mechanically relate aspects of human consciousness, or human actions, to their socio-economic causes. I say this because I feel that the task facing Marxist aesthetics at the present time is not an isolated one—a limited problem in a particular area of Marxist

theory—but is part of a much wider need for a bringing of less mechanistic—but no-less rigorous—intellectual effort to bear on certain recurrent problems. This will perhaps explain in part why I tend to refer
more to non-aesthetic Marxist writings in what follows, for I feel that
to a considerable extent Marxist writing on aesthetics has lagged behind
these. Thus the following comment on human personality from
Antonio Gramsci's *Prison Notebooks* has, I think, a direct bearing on the
problems Marxists face in reaching a more profound conception of the
mode of being of the work of art:

> . . . one must conceive of man as a series of active relationships (a
> process) in which individuality, though perhaps the most important,
> is not, however, the only element to be taken into account. The
> humanity which is reflected in each individuality is composed of
> various elements: 1. the individual; 2. other men; 3. the natural
> world. But the latter two elements are not as simple as they might
> appear. The individual does not enter into relations with other men
> by juxtaposition, but organically, in as much, that is, as he belongs to
> organic entities which range from the simplest to the most complex.
> Thus Man does not enter into relations with the natural world just
> by being himself part of the natural world, but actively, by means of
> work and technique. . . . one could say that each one of us changes
> himself, modifies himself to the extent that he changes and modifies
> the complex relations of which he is the hub.[15]

It is my basic contention that apart from the complicating factor of
consciousness, what Gramsci says about understanding man can also be
profitably applied to our attempt to understand the work of art. The
latter can neither be understood as completely autonomous nor, as
Gramsci puts it, merely 'in juxtaposition' with other aspects of social
life, which would suggest that the relationships between itself and the
outside world do not 'touch' the work of art. Both the human individual and the work of art can be understood only by means of a conception of the relationships within which individual identity comes to be,
and the relationships between this identity and the outside world. In the
latter part of this book I hope to simultaneously explore both, and to try
to arrive at a clearer perception of the nature of the identity of the work
of art *and* of its mediations with that which is outside it, distinct from it.

I hope that this analogy between the work of art and the individual
human being will be borne in mind by the reader even when I do not
explicitly refer to it, as I feel that it offers many possibilities of fruitful
cross fertilisation. W. K. Wimsatt's point that it is silly to see the poem

in a light in which the poet cannot be viewed, as somehow more hard and self-sufficient than him,[16] suggests that very often the critic does unconsciously base his theories about the nature of the work of art on his conception of human identity. Wimsatt's modification of formalistic insistence on the 'autonomy' of the art work comes when American society is being forced to modify many of the Cold-War rigidities concerning the complete autonomy and 'freedom' of the individual, rigidities which accompanied the most extreme formalistic insistence on the autonomy and 'self-ness' of the work of art. Ironically enough, the formalist often seems to be more influenced by changes in his society because he thinks that his consciousness is independent of them.

Perhaps this discussion can be brought nearer to flesh and blood by referring to a famous section of Henry James's *The Portrait of a Lady*, where two conceptions of the human personality are discussed in a way that is directly relevant to our initial distinction between the two main critical approaches to the work of literature. I was gratified, after writing a first draft of this chapter, to note that W. J. Harvey had already noted the relevance of this passage in a similar context in his *Character and the Novel*. In the passage, Madame Merle is talking to Isabel Archer:

> '. . . When you've lived as long as I you'll see that every human being has his shell and that you must take the shell into account. By the shell I mean the whole envelope of circumstances. There's no such thing as an isolated man or woman; we're each of us made up of some cluster of appurtenances. What shall we call our "self"? Where does it begin? Where does it end? It overflows into everything that belongs to us—and then it flows back again. I know a large part of myself is in the clothes I choose to wear. I've a great respect for *things*! One's self—for other people—is one's expression of one's self; and one's house, one's furniture, one's garments, the books one reads, the company one keeps—these things are all so expressive.'

> This was very metaphysical; not more so, however, than several observations Madame Merle had already made. Isabel was fond of metaphysics, but was unable to accompany her friend into this bold analysis of the human personality. 'I don't agree with you. I think just the other way. I don't know whether I succeed in expressing myself, but I know that nothing else expresses me. Nothing that belongs to me is any measure of me; everything's on the contrary a limit, a barrier, and a perfectly arbitrary one. . . .'[17]

Translated from the milieu of aesthetics to that of life itself, Madame Merle and Isabel represent the same two distinct ways of examining identity that we saw literary critics split unhappily between at the beginning of this chapter. It would seem that here the novelist has something to tell the critic directly about theory, for surely in the context of *The Portrait of a Lady* James is concerned to expose both of these views of human personality as partial. Madame Merle's concern only with her 'shell', disregarding that continuity of identity which in social terms manifests itself as honesty, and defensible pride, is hardly more severely dealt with, by implication, than is Isabel's inability to see that a full personality cannot be achieved merely through a private purity which fails adequately to come to terms with the realities of social life. Just as the person whose identity is to be found in her clothes can rest assured that so long as the latter remain immaculate and correct no moral criticism can be levelled at the person wearing them, so, too, the individual who sees everything with which she comes into contact as a limitation or barrier can console herself with a moral goodness that never manifests itself in social life. What is needed is neither one extreme nor another, but a balanced integration of social and individual elements into a healthy conception of personality, as is suggested by Allan Rodway in the article to which I have already had recourse:

> Literary works, like the people who create them, are born willy nilly into a pre-existing society; and far from necessarily preventing originality, these twin societies, of literature and life, are as necessary a condition for it as the laws of the game and the laws of physics are for gifted tennis.[18]

The conclusion here is an admirable one; identity and relationship must be seen as dependent upon one another both in the field of social life and literature, for to isolate the one from the other is to make both vanish.

Writers perhaps more than literary critics have shown an awareness of this fact in the past. The Father in Pirandello's *Six Characters in Search of an Author* would appear to be Madame Merle's spiritual cousin:

> My drama lies entirely in this one thing. . . . In my being conscious that each one of us believes himself to be a single person. But it's not true. . . . Each one of us is many persons. . . . Many persons. . . . according to all the possibilities of being that there are within us. . . . With some people we are one person. . . . With others we are somebody quite different. . . . And all the time we are under the illusion of always being one and the same person for everybody. . . .[19]

The Father is well aware that identity is dependent upon relationship here, although he does not fully appreciate that relationships are in their turn dependent upon a certain continuity of identity, which leads him to suggest that our relationship with one person is totally separate from our relationship with another. However, the Father's basic point, that we exist in terms of other people as much as in terms of ourselves, has an importance which there is a pressing need to stress at this particular time. In a brilliant book, *A Theory of the Classical Novel*, Everett Knight has demonstrated how a conception of human identity as fixed and immutable was adopted by the novelist as his 'lowest common factor'.[20] The individual 'character' could then be examined in various contexts, but uninfluenced, unchanged by them, separate even from the relationships which he or she formed part of. The Father in Pirandello's play is forced to realise the falsity of such conceptions when he meets his own daughter in a brothel, and discovers that what 'he' is to her normally is only a part of the complex totality of his identity.

As far as our ideas about what constitutes a human personality are concerned, people who hold such notions are often given a rude awakening through the experience of love, for a belief in the attractiveness of another person has to be understood in the context of that person forming a specific part of a complex of relationships, otherwise the change in identity that follows a change in these relationships is often both unexpected and unpleasant. This fact is expressed very well in a short story by Margaret Drabble entitled 'Crossing the Alps', where a man realises that the woman he loves will 'disappear' if he marries her, for that which he loves is brought into being precisely by her having an identity defined by a non-marital relationship.

> What was precisely desired, was so precisely denied: for what did he admire and love and want in her, but her dutiful and obstinate fidelity to her burdens, and what did she love in him, but his very infidelity to her, his alarming, unnatural, persistent loyalty to his wife? It was not that they loved each other because they could not have each other, in the true way of the Western world: they loved what they could not have because, if they had it, it would be so destroyed by possession that it would be no more.[21]

What is so well caught here, is the fact that one does not fall in love with an abstract individual, who somehow imposes him or herself and his or her unchanging identity on life come what may; one falls in love with a person who exists at a particular time, in a particular place, who is what he or she is in part because of these factors, and who is attractive because of what both partners are in that given context. Much the same point can be made about all human relationships, which are composed of innumerable factors which are interconnected, not separate from one another. In his book *Art and Morality* R. W. Beardsmore points out how absurd is G. E. Moore's method of testing the importance of friendship by abstracting it from the context in which it exists. As he suggests, if we try and imagine a world in which nothing exists apart from a man's love for his wife, then the result is a blank mind rather than a beautiful vision of a pure and isolated love.[22] This seems to me to be nowhere better demonstrated than in Arnold Wesker's play *The Four Seasons*, where the attempt to examine 'the four seasons' of love, through which it is implied all sexual relationships proceed, by abstracting the love from any defined context, merely makes it impossible to believe that the couple concerned are in love. We may also recall that in *The Return of the Native* Thomas Hardy shows how Clym and Eustacia's love starts to diminish when they move out into their little isolated house at Alderworth, and Hardy comments that the isolation in which they lived intensified their reciprocal thoughts, but consumed their mutual affections. It is as if they were living on the emotional capital of their previous immersion in a full social life, within which love can be born and enriched, but abstracted from which it dies.

NOTES

[1] Allan Rodway, 'Generic Criticism', *Contemporary Criticism*, ed. Bradbury and Palmer, London 1970, p. 92.
[2] René Wellek and Austen Warren, *Theory of Literature*, Peregrine edition, p. 239.
[3] W. J. Harvey, *Character and the Novel*, reprinted London 1970, pp. 11, 13.
[4] N. I. Bukharin, 'Poetry, Poetics and the Problems of Poetry in the USSR', *Problems of Soviet Literature*, London n.d. (?1935), p. 201.
[5] W. C. Brownell, *Criticism*, reprinted Port Washington, 1967, p. 20.
[6] *Problems of Soviet Literature*, p. 204.
[7] *Problems of Soviet Literature*, p. 207.
[8] Antonio Gramsci, 'Critical Notes on an Attempt at Popular Sociology', *Selections from the Prison Notebooks of Antonio Gramsci*, ed. Hoare and Nowell Smith, London 1971.
[9] Jan Mukařovský, 'The Esthetics of Language', *A Prague School Reader on Esthetics, Literary Structure, and Style*, ed. Paul L. Garvin, Washington D.C. 1964, pp. 31, 32.
[10] Graham Hough, 'Criticism as a Humanist Discipline', *Contemporary Criticism* ed. Bradbury and Palmer, London 1970, p. 57.
[11] Richard Hoggart, 'Contemporary Cultural Studies', *Contemporary Criticism* ed. Bradbury and Palmer, London 1970, p. 163.
[12] Karl Marx and Frederick Engels, *Literature and Art*, New York 1947, p. 4.
[13] Leszek Kolakowski, 'Althusser's Marx', *The Socialist Register 1971*, ed. Miliband and Saville, London 1971, p. 121.
[14] Lucien Goldmann, *The Human Sciences and Philosophy*, London 1969, p. 92.

15 Antonio Gramsci, 'The Study of Philosophy', *Selection from the Prison Notebooks of Antonio Gramsci*, ed. Hoare and Nowell Smith, London 1971, p. 352.

16 W. K. Wimsatt, 'Battering the Object: The Ontological Approach', *Contemporary Criticism* ed. Bradbury and Palmer, London 1970, p. 73.

17 Henry James, *The Portrait of a Lady*, ed. Edel, London 1968, p. 230.

18 *Contemporary Criticism*, p. 89.

19 Luigi Pirandello, *Six Characters in Search of an Author*, trans. May, reprinted London 1971, p. 25.

20 Everett Knight, *A Theory of the Classical Novel*, London 1970, p. 44, etc.

21 Margaret Drabble, 'Crossing the Alps', *Penguin Modern Stories 3*, Harmondsworth 1969, p. 82.

22 R. W. Beardsmore, *Art and Morality*, London 1971, p. 3.

2. A Note on Dialectics

> Achilles and Werther, Oedipus and Tom Jones, Antigone
> and Anna Karenina: their individual existence—their *Sein
> an sich*, in the Hegelian terminology; their 'ontological
> being', as a more fashionable terminology has it—cannot
> be distinguished from their social and historical environ-
> ment. Their human significance cannot be separated from
> the context in which they were created.[1]
>
> GYÖRGY LUKÁCS.

Lukács's comment, taken from his *The Meaning of Contemporary
Realism*, strikes a familiarly 'Marxist' note. 'Marxist', because for many
the main—almost the sole—distinguishing feature of Marxist literary
criticism is the insistence that to be fully understood the work of
literature must be seen in the context of its socio-economic origins. It is
however worth stressing that this insistence is in many ways secondary
rather than fundamental to a full Marxist aesthetic, being part only of a
fully dialectical approach to art and literature. Graham Hough, in his
An Essay on Criticism, quotes William Richter's comment that when he
hears the world 'dialectics' he reaches for Occam's razor, and there is
some truth in the assertion that the word in question—like most other
words—can be used in a meaningful or a meaningless way. It is certainly
true that in the context of previous Marxist writing on aesthetics the
word has often been dragged in as a piece of convenient window-
dressing, to conceal either an essentially metaphysical aesthetic, or else a
crude historically-biased mechanical materialist one. Lucien Goldmann
has argued that the most important contributions to dialectical theory
in the present century are to be found in Lenin's *Philosophical Notebooks*,
and in the work of Gramsci and Lukács.[2] It is significant that as far as
Lukács is concerned, this contribution is to a large extent to be found in
a non-aesthetic piece of writing—*History and Class Consciousness*.
Certainly many of his works of literary criticism are far from containing
a dialectical approach to literature; many of the essays in *Writer and
Critic* for example, written under the pressure of Stalinism, are mechanistic and undialectical, with their insistence on the 'reflective' character

of art, reflecting an objective world that is what it is independent of thought.

In *History and Class Consciousness*, Lukács argues that the two most important aspects of dialectics are, firstly, the dialectical nature of the subject-object relationship, and, secondly, the Marxist conception of totality.[3] These two aspects of dialectical theory seem to me to be crucial as far as aesthetics in general, and literary criticism in particular, are concerned. Lukács insists that it is the dialectical exposition of the subject-object relationship—a concept, he claims, ignored by Engels—which makes dialectics revolutionary. To fail to recognise the dialectical nature of this relationship, he maintains, is to imply

> . . . a failure to recognise that in all metaphysics the object remains untouched and unaltered so that thought remains contemplative and fails to become practical.[4]

It is this 'untouched' nature of the perceived object that is implied in Lukács's own, later insistence on the absolute objectivity of the external world, an objectivity which makes it independent of thought.[5] Goldmann has traced this mechanistic trend in Marxist thought from Lenin's *Materialism and Empirio-Criticism*, which is, he argues, rejected in essence in the *Philosophical Notebooks*, through to its adoption as a convenient tool by dogmatists in the Stalin era. The writers mentioned in particular by Goldmann—the later Lenin, Gramsci and Lukács—saw that such a conception of an independent and 'objective' world failed to take into account the dialectical nature of the subject-object relationship. In other words, it failed to take into account the revolutionising effect of man's perception of the world. Gramsci in particular consistently recurs to this point, and attacks very bitterly what he sees as the religious basis on which many mechanical materialists 'rejected' Berkeleian arguments. This is not to suggest that Gramsci was a Berkeleian, but that he saw that Berkeley's philosophical position with regard to the external world constituted a significant historical and theoretical advance which should itself be developed by Marxism.[6] The essence of Gramsci's position is that man is situated, and that his situation defines what he perceives, which is an aspect of a potentially infinite reality, rather than the 'absolute' truth. Gramsci and Caudwell use similar examples to illustrate this point, Gramsci noting that electricity 'is' what its relationship with man is, rather than an 'objective' thing,[7] and Caudwell making a similar point about man's relationship to the power of coal.[8] Writing this during a miners' strike, their arguments seem particularly apt. Man does not have a relationship to objective things such as 'electricity' or 'coal', but there is a changing complex of relationships between himself, other men, and the natural world. Gramsci summarises it as follows:

> The idea of "objective" in metaphysical materialism would appear to mean an objectivity which exists even apart from man; but when one affirms that a reality would exist even if man did not, one is either speaking metaphorically or one is falling into a form of mysticism. We know reality only in relation to man, and since man is historical becoming, knowledge and reality are also a becoming and so is objectivity.[9]

This seems to me a crucial point as far as aesthetics is concerned, for it is analogous to certain key arguments regarding the mode of being of the work of art. Rather than attempting to determine the latter's 'objective' nature, we should realise that we are situated in respect to it, and proceed to examine its identity in the context of our perception of it, rather than in a never-never land of objective truth. Just as Gramsci accuses mechanical materialists of allying themselves with those with a religious view of the world in positing an absolute objectivity of the material world, so too Everett Knight in his *The Objective Society* points out that Stalinist approaches to literature have often assumed the same 'scientistic' approach to the objectivity of the art work as was adopted as its fundamental world-view by the expanding bourgeoisie.[10] Such an approach is a godsend for dogmatists because it assumes that there is one unchanging truth, an 'objectivity' independent of human situation, which once discovered cannot be altered.

Knight, mainly as a result of the influence of Sartre it would appear, consistently attacks such conceptions whether on the part of the writer towards the 'truth' he is creating, or on the part of the critic towards the 'truth' he thinks he is discovering and merely contemplating. He insists that there is no 'Real' which is independent of the way we take cognisance of it, and that if we wish to make sense of things (the verb to 'make sense' has a revealing structure), we must examine not the 'Real in itself', '. . . but the whole cultural orientation which insists that this is the Real and not that.'[11] In this he goes beyond Sartre in insisting on the social nature of man's perception of the world. In *What is Art?* Sartre comments that when he is enchanted with a landscape he knows that he has not created it,

. . . but I also know that without me the relations which are established before my eyes among the trees, the foliage, the earth, and the grass would not exist at all.[12]

Knight's formulation insists both on the fact that it is man's situation that defines the 'real' that he perceives, but also that this situation is not just a private one, but is in part socially determined. Central to a dialectical-materialist aesthetics must be a recognition that the work of art is dialectically related to the world outside it—including the perceiver of the work. It is these relationships, in particular that between the perceiver and his society and the work, which define the 'Reality' of the work. A page unread by anybody is no more a page of poetry than an undiscovered deposit is a seam of coal.

This suggests that the literary critic should not try to examine the work of art with a view to isolating its 'objective' nature, but with a view to understanding what it is in a particular context, the context of its being perceived by specific people belonging to a specific society at a specific time, always remembering that as Gramsci says, man is 'a précis of the past',[13] and that what he 'is' at any given time involves the influence of man's social experience in time up to this point.

Lucien Goldmann has developed many of Lukács's early comments on this subject in the field of aesthetics. In an article entitled 'Reflections on History and Class Consciousness' he argues that as the subject-object relationship is not a static one, *it must always be made explicit*[14] (my emphasis). In other words, we have here a consistent theoretical basis for arguing that a work of art can never be discussed ahistorically, in 'purely aesthetic' terms, but must always be discussed in a defined context. Goldmann then goes on to posit a two-pronged approach to the investigation of all human phenomena, which coincides very closely to our integrated identity-relationship approach:

. . . all human acts . . . possess as such the quality of functional structures or significant structures. Their investigation involves therefore on the one hand an internal analysis aiming to *understand* them by revealing their immanent structure, and consequently the potential significance of the various elements of a given relationship, and on the other an external analysis, aiming to *explain* them by inserting the structure as a functional element in another larger structure.[14]

Writing about a similar topic in an article entitled 'Criticism and Dogmatism in Literature', Goldmann distinguishes between a dream, which has no immanent structure and can only be understood in the context of a larger structure (i.e. through psychoanalysis), and a work of art which has both an immanent structure which can be *comprehended*, and a place in a larger structure which can be *explained*[15] (his emphasis). It should be pointed out that Goldmann does not always bring out sufficiently either the interdependence of these two procedures, or the multiplicity of possible contexts within which the work of art can, and must, be viewed. Sartre, in his insistence upon the metamorphosing power of cognition, implies this dynamic, and therefore multiplying process more adequately:

> Man is the being towards whom no being can be impartial, not even God. For God, if He existed, would be, as certain mystics have seen Him, in a *situation* in relation to man. And He is also the being Who cannot even see a situation without changing it, for His gaze congeals, destroys, or sculpts, or as does eternity, changes the object in itself.[16]

Poets in particular have been quick to appreciate the nature of this process. Walt Whitman, in 'There was a Child Went Forth', writes:

> There was a child went forth every day;
> And the first object he look'd upon, that object
>   he became;
> And that object became part of him for the day, or a certain part of
>   the day, or for many years, or stretching cycles of years.[17]

Perhaps recalling Whitman, Wallace Stevens's lines in 'Notes Towards a Supreme Fiction' make a similar point:

> The partaker partakes of that which changes him.
> The child that touches takes character from the thing,
> The body, it touches.[18]

I said at the beginning of this chapter that the second 'most important aspect of dialectics' mentioned by Lukács was that of totality, and this too, it seems to me, is of crucial importance to a Marxist aesthetics. Like a Marxist use of the word 'autonomy', the concept of totality must be seen to be a relative rather than an absolute term. It applies to a particular complex of dialectically-related components which go to make up a particular totality in time and space, rather than an all-embracing totality within which the totality of interconnections is found. The latter, in spite of its dialectical sheep's clothing, turns out to be a metaphysical wolf underneath. Lukács, in *History and Class Consciousness*, argues that

the concept of totality propounds a more decisive difference between
Marxism and bourgeois thought than does the primacy of economic
motives, as it is fundamental to our conceptions of parts and components.[19] At this point it is worth noting that the concepts of totality
and of the subject-object dialectic are themselves connected; the latter
obviously precludes the possibility of a belief in the sort of all-embracing
totality which is somehow absolute, and within which, but not as an
organic part of which, the totality of interconnections are to be found.
Lucien Goldmann, in his *The Human Sciences and Philosophy*, also
stresses this interconnection:

> Dialectical materialism does not believe that the totality of indi-
> vidual states of consciousness is an arithmetical sum of autono-
> mous and independent entities. On the contrary: with Pascal, Kant,
> Hegel, and Marx it holds that each component can only be compre-
> hended in terms of the totality of its relations with the other
> components . . .[20]

and in this context he offers as substantiation the following words of
Pascal:

> The parts of the world have all such a relation and such a connection
> with each other that I believe it is impossible to know the one without
> the other and without the whole . . . I consider it equally impos-
> sible to know the parts without the whole, and to know the whole
> without knowing the parts.[21]

Before Goldmann, Lukács had also rejected a conception of totality as
either something 'above' its components, or as the mere mechanical
sum of the latter:

> . . . the category of totality does not reduce its various elements to
> an undifferentiated autonomy, to identity. The apparent indepen-
> dence and autonomy which they possess in the capitalist system of
> production is an illusion . . .[22]

I should note that Lukács's use of the word 'identity' here is not mine,
he is implying the identity of something with something else, not
identity in terms of a consistency of individuality or personality.
Lukács puts his finger on the issue which is of decisive importance in
any concept of totality—its effect on our conception of the relationship
between part and whole, between totality and component, and, from
this, the respective forms of identity, of modes of being, that the two
have:

. . . what is decisive is whether this process of isolation is a means towards understanding the whole and whether it is integrated within the context it presupposes and requires, or whether the abstract knowledge of an isolated fragment retains its 'autonomy' . . .[23]

It is however from Lenin that the classic and still, in my opinion, the best resolution of this problem comes. In his 'Once Again on the Trade Unions, the Present Situation and the Mistakes of Comrades Trotsky and Bukharin', he replies to Bukharin's polemic on the question of the identity of an object. Bukharin takes the example of a tumbler standing on a rostrum, and considers the problems inherent in defining what it is:

. . . two men ask each other: What is the tumbler that is standing on the rostrum? One says: 'It is a glass cylinder, and he who says it is not, let him be anathematised.' The other says: 'A tumbler is a drinking vessel, and he who says it is not, let him be anathematised.'[24]

Lenin characterises Bukharin's attempt to explain the dangers of one-sidedness as an eclectic one, and proceeds to argue for a dialectical alternative as follows:

A tumbler is undoubtedly a glass cylinder and a drinking vessel. But a tumbler not only has these two properties, or qualities, or aspects, but an infinite number of other properties, qualities, aspects, inter-relations and forms of "mediation" with the rest of the world.

Having given a long and amusing list of some of these, Lenin continues:

If two or more different definitions happen to suit the same object (a glass cylinder and a drinking vessel), we get an eclectic definition of different aspects of the object and nothing more.

Dialectical logic demands that we go further. In the first place, in order really to know an object we must embrace, study in all its aspects, all connections and forms of "mediation". *We shall never achieve this completely, but the demand for all-sidedness is a safeguard against mistakes and rigidity.* (My emphasis, J. M. H.)

The impossibility of ever achieving total knowledge is thus, far from being an argument for resting satisfied with partial knowledge, a continuous spur to perceptual regeneration. This offers a convincing answer to those who assume that criticism can ever arrive at a final critical placing of a work of art. There can be no such final solution because the identity of the art work can never be fully and finally perceived. In his book on Kant, Goldmann quotes a passage from the

Critique of Pure Reason which is remarkably similar to the passage quoted above from Lenin:

> . . . to know a thing completely, we must know every possible predicate, and must determine it thereby, either affirmatively or negatively. The complete determination is thus a concept, which, in its totality, can never be exhibited *in concreto*. It is based upon an idea, which has its seat solely in the faculty of reason.[25]

Thus, as Lenin suggests, the rational knowledge of the unachievability of such totality acts as a spur to the obtaining of as complete a conception of the object as possible, which in turn implies a dynamic and perpetually developing relationship between perceiver and object.

In the same passage Lenin continues:

> Secondly, dialectical logic demands that we take an object in its development, its "self-movement" (as Hegel sometimes puts it), in its changes.

Caudwell criticises formal logic for failing to do this in *Further Studies in a Dying Culture*, where he points to its failure to express 'the vital nature of reality'.[26] Lenin continues:

> In relation to a tumbler this is not clear at once, but even a tumbler does not remain unchanged, particularly in the purpose it serves, its use, its *connections* with the environment. Thirdly, the whole of human experience should be included in the full "definition" of an object as a criterion of the truth and as a practical indication of the object's connection with what man requires. Fourthly, dialectical logic teaches that "there is no abstract truth, truth is always concrete" . . .

My argument is that this exposition has an immediate relevance to the problem of defining the mode of being of the art work. The art work, even more than the tumbler, cannot be seen as a fixed, 'objective', autonomous whole, but must be seen in the context of its mediations with the outside world, as something with an infinite number of 'properties, qualities and aspects' which are manifested in an infinite number of concrete contexts.

A good illustration of this is the action taken in immediate post-war Germany in banning the film of *Oliver Twist* from public performance. Such an action did not imply that either the film or the book of *Oliver Twist* was 'objectively' anti-semitic, but that in the particular situation of the immediate post-fascist period in Germany the identity such a film might assume would have had anti-semitic associations which would have been undesirable. There was, and is, no suggestion that the film of *Oliver Twist* should be banned permanently, or should be seen to be an evil film for all time, merely a recognition that in a particular situation the identity which such a film might assume might be different from that which it might assume in a different situation. There is also an important sense in which such an action demonstrates that it is in man's power to *change* the identity that things have for him. To stick to the example of anti-semitism, one can argue that the man who, some time ago, conducted a one-man campaign to remove definitions of the word 'Jew' from dictionaries which referred to meanness and avarice was in an important sense aware that the meaning of things is not something that is objective and unchangeable, but is something that in a certain sense man *makes*. The campaign waged by this individual carried with it the implication that the dictionary should have an active as well as a contemplative relationship to the reality it attempts to order— which in a certain sense, of course, it has whether the compilers wish this to be so or not.

It is important to insist with Gramsci that a view of the unalterable objectivity of the external world is the cornerstone of a religious world-view, and one which was adopted as its own by the bourgeoisie. As far as aesthetics is concerned, Caudwell notes accurately this connection:

> The artist in bourgeois culture is asked . . . to regard the art work as a finished commodity and the process of art as a relation between himself and the work, which then disappears in the market. . . . The whole pressure of bourgeois society is to make him regard the art work as hypostatised and his relation to it primarily that of producer for the market.[27]

In similar vein Sartre remarks sardonically that it is a holiday for the critic when authors do him the service of dying, for the books written by them can then become less affecting and more beautiful—in other words, their life-giving mediation with the outside world can be more convincingly concealed.[28] A not-dissimilar attitude is frequently met with in our schools and colleges, where it is claimed that very modern literature is somehow like unhung game, and must be allowed to gather critical respectability over a certain length of time before being submitted to academic study. What this means in practice is that the real, dynamic connections with social life that literature has are pruned off, until a nice lopped aesthetically pure art work can be studied in rapt and unworried contemplation by all.

There was a story some time ago of a wrangle between the curators of the British Museum Reading Room and the publishers of a book of self-destructive poetry. The latter, impregnated with certain chemicals, was guaranteed to destroy itself within a limited space of time, and as the British Museum Reading Room requires a copy of each published work identical to that sold to the public, the publishers felt justified in sending a similarly impregnated copy to the hub of our intellectual world. Authority revolted however, and insisted upon having a lasting copy of the transitory work. Many critics argue from a doubtless similar basis that although the art work is not fixed and frozen, it must be regarded as such in order to be studied. There is a certain truth in this; man has to give a fictive fixity to transitory things in life so as to be able to conceptualise them—Caudwell notes that this is involved in reducing a changing thing to a relatively unchanging word—but it is a limited truth. For a certain period of time the art work may have to be regarded as fixed and frozen, as if its mediation with the outside world were constant, but this period of time must be kept as short as possible, for such ordering will carry with it sacrifices along with advantages, and although it may allow us better to understand one aspect of a work of art, it will conceal others. W. K. Wimsatt gives us a good example of the 'convenience' argument to justify the abstraction of the work of art from its relationships:

> The poem conceived as a thing in between the poet and the audience is of course an abstraction. The poem is an act. The only substantive entities are the poet and the audience. But if we are to lay hold of the poetic act to comprehend and evaluate it, and if it is to pass current as a critical object, it must be hypostatised.[29]

Now to a certain extent this argument begs the question which it answers, for if the poem is to pass current as a critical *object*, then of course it must be treated in a way befitting an object. But the implication that all perception of even an object is concerned with the same thing is the basic flaw which underlies this defence. I would not deny that the ways in which bourgeois aesthetics moved towards an acceptance of the necessity of seeing the art work as hypostatised object are extremely complex, and need to be examined historically to be fully understood. However I think that it is basically accurate to see this as one aspect of the whole process of alienation, or 'reification' as Lukács calls it, which substitutes a view of fixed and autonomous objects for a more fluid view of the primacy of developing human relationships. As

Caudwell's remark makes clear, the introduction of the concept of the market in man's conceptualisation of the relationships between writer, work and audience, led inevitably to a view of the art work as object, 'objective' and complete in itself, separate from man as commodities and their prices came to be seen as separate from their creation and function.

At this point it may be said that the distinction between a view of the work of art as hypostatised, and as having a relative autonomy, or identity, needs clarification, otherwise the justified suspicion might arise that the distinction is merely between value-judgements of much the same thing. I think that the important distinction centres around the question of whether or not the implied fixity is seen as something objective and eternal, or as something imposed upon the art work in order to make it receptive to analysis and study, but which is seen as temporary and is capable of constant modification. As Goldmann suggests, a fictive permanence must be given to changing nature in order to understand it, as man uses words to describe and understand things. The ways in which this process can be defended against misrepresentation, against dogmatism, are complex, and involve, I think, the adoption of a number of critical procedures which act as checks and correctives. Of these, the most important are a realisation of the temporary nature of all judgement and categorisation—all order, as Goldmann puts it—and also a refusal to abstract the 'identity' of the art work, or anything else for that matter, from its life-giving contexts. Caudwell, in his *Further Studies*, says that

> . . . any scheme which makes the material configuration of the environment the determining factor in civilisation fails because it does not see that the environment is not something fixed. As environment its very qualities depend on the subject, man, and primarily on his social organisation.[30]

In other words, to see the object—whether it be the environment or the art work—in the context of man's social and historical perception of it, is to safeguard against giving it a false and misleading fixity. The more the art work is examined within its life-giving contexts, the more investigation will be precluded from ignoring and denying its dynamic and fluid quality. This is why, in subsequent chapters, I wish to suggest ways in which this contextual investigation can be approached, by considering different aspects of the contexts in which the work of literature in particular exists. To give a brief illustration: when Caudwell, in *Illusion and Reality*, remarks that 'The poem is what happens when it is read . . .'[31] he is not just stating a truism but is reminding us of an aspect of the mode of being of the poem, of its mediations with the outside world which, given the subject-object dialectic, should prevent us from seeing it as fixed and 'objective'. The connection with my remarks earlier about the non-existence of the non-cognised world should be apparent here, although perhaps this connection is clearer in Sartre's comment that the work of art '. . . exists only if one *looks* at it . . .'.[32]

In his *The Verbal Icon*, W. K. Wimsatt touches on an area of debate which leads on from what I have just said. In the course of a discussion of 'The Concrete Universal' he notes that the difference between modern and classical systems of thought is that the latter tend to stress 'the similarity of the individuals denoted by the common term', which standpoint can lead to a belief in a real universality of meaning, whilst newer systems stress the difference in individuals, '. . . the constant flux even of each individual in time and space and its kinetic structure, and hence infer only an approximate or nominal universality of meaning . . .'.[33] Translated into the terms of our discussion of the work of literature, this would involve a distinction between those who argue that every reader (if not every reading) reads a different book, and those who argue that every reader reads the same, objective book which exists independent of those who read it. I think that both conceptions of identity are unsatisfactory, and would like to devote a little space to saying why. I have already criticised the latter formulation, and propose now to consider briefly the charge that if one denies that all readers of a poem read the same 'objective' poem then one is led towards a sort of aesthetic solipsism, with every reader reading something completely different.

Talking about the 'objectivity' of perceived objects, Everett Knight uses the example of two men travelling to the same village. One is returning to the scenes of his childhood, the other is a commercial traveller looking for business. Knight comments that for these two,

> . . . the village will exist in two entirely different ways; and it will be the same village only because it has a third form of existence—that which it has not for the individual in himself, but for the individual as a member of the collectivity.[34]

I do not wish to spend too much time on this point as I will be considering it in more detail when I discuss the question of aesthetic value in chapter seven, but I would like to make it quite clear now that I do not say that one's perception of a work of art is purely personal, although, as with the example of the village above, obviously personal elements enter into our perception of any work of art. It is this social dimension that is missing from the discussion of the meaning of words by the Father in Pirandello's *Six Characters in Search of an Author*, for he assumes that because any given word does not mean exactly the same thing to everyone who uses it, it must mean something entirely different to different people:

> How can we understand each other if into the words I speak I put the sense and value of things as I understand them within myself . . . while at the same time whoever is listening to them inevitably assumes them to have the sense and value that they have for him. . . .?[35]

What is obviously lacking from the Father's conception of language is the social dimension, and, in particular, the dimension of practice. Language can never become purely private because of its existence within the dimension of social act, which ensures that the purely personal use of language has, sooner or later, to be recognised by the individual to be impractical. In fact, ironically, it is just the uneasy feeling that adequate communication is not taking place which the Father describes, that is in effect a failure in the area of social practice, which constantly operates to prevent language becoming merely personal.

István Mészáros raises much the same problem as exercises both Wimsatt and Pirandello's Father, and argues implicitly that it is via the realm of social practice that the problem is solved—for us in theoretical terms, and for men in general in their day to day life:

> The great difficulty consisted in perceiving 'universal validity' in the actual, spatio-temporally limited experience of particular human beings. This necessarily appeared an insoluble dilemma so long as 'the universal' has been thought of as an ideal opposed to *the actuality of lived experience*. (My emphasis, J. M. H.)[36]

Mészáros argues that, as with our 'totality', as soon as the 'universal' is seen as *inherent in* particularity, and not *opposed* to it, the problem is solved. Likewise, as I argued before, it is only when metacriticism and intrinsic criticism are seen as inherent in one another rather than as opposed and utterly distinct approaches, that they can be properly comprehended, and thus integrated consciously into a working synthesis. Mészáros interestingly enough continues his analysis into a discussion of the identity of the work of art:

> Thus, the specific historical identity of, for instance, a particular work of art, could be recognized to be not the *negation* of 'universality', but, on the contrary, its *realization*. For the work of art could achieve universality only and precisely so far as it succeeded in grasping. . . the spatio-temporally specific characteristics of actual experience as significant moments of continuous social-historical development.[36]

It is social practice which enables us to unite conceptions of identity and universality, and to claim that a response to a work of art may be both unique, and socially accessible, without contradiction.

When we perceive a distinct 'identity' we are in a certain sense creating what we see, and this is precisely what is meant by the subject-object dialectic. When we name a thing we change it. The distinction Caudwell makes between the way a word 'fixes' a thing, and the way so-called formal logic does, is an important one. Language has developed mechanisms whereby this fixing is a temporary, a relative process—partly by means of the dialectical relation existing between words themselves, and partly by making language open to the pressures of social life and experience. Caudwell's objection to so-called formal logic is that it has built into it a protection against both these corrective mechanisms, as it claims to present absolute truths which are independent of social practice. Thus the distinction between 'identity' and 'autonomy' which I wish to develop in the field of criticism is, I feel, a very real and important one. In normal living this problem is dealt with in various semi-institutionalised ways. We assume that the wife seen at the breakfast table is the same person seen at the supper table the previous night, because in general such an assumption makes social life easier. If however our expectations are severely jolted we are prepared to say that she has changed, or that 'it is as if she has become a different person'. Our conception of human identity thus tends to be open to constant modification. Part of our problem in aesthetics is that no definition of the mode of being of the art work has proved equally amenable both to social mediation and to modification and change. We think of *Paradise Lost* as somehow more fixed, permanent and 'objective' than we think of the man next door or the woman we love. As Wimsatt says, this sort of distinction is not easily defensible.

Once again, I feel that if we turn to the practice of writers rather than critics we can find better precedents for a dialectical aesthetics. Wallace Stevens's *Thirteen Ways of Looking at a Blackbird* is an example of a truly dialectical vision of reality. In this poem what Stevens does is to put the blackbird into thirteen different contexts, demonstrating how in each one the blackbird *is* something different. We must learn to be able to regard the poem as Stevens regards the blackbird, as constant but changing, defined by its context and existing in many contexts. Section IX of the poem reads as follows:

When the blackbird flew out of sight,
It marked the edge
Of one of many circles.[37]

In this section all the contexts so far presented are fused into one, and this in turn is seen as one of many. I will return later on in this chapter to mention of the usefulness of a circular rather than a linear representation of dialectical interconnection, but would point out here how beautifully Stevens manages to make his blackbird both concrete and real whilst suggesting the fluidity and flexibility of the way in which we perceive—and thus define—it.

I think that one can compare this fluidity with the disastrous results of a misconception of the nature of the identity of literary characters, which is analogous to that of seeing the work of art as fixed and 'objective'. It has always seemed to me that the most important weakness in the Bradleyan conception of character in drama is that it rests on a conception of 'character' which is fixed and undialectical. The assumption is that if Macbeth at one point commits a murder, he must at some previous point of time have had some 'flaw' which was to develop into the eventual act of murder. L. C. Knights, in his attack on Bradleyan criticism in the famous *How Many Children had Lady Macbeth?* criticises Bradley for taking a speech in a play as indicative only of character, rather than comprehending its complex artistic role in the total context of the play. In other words Bradley sees the dramatic character as the hard core of autonomy in the play which is untouched by anything else in the play, but which makes its own fate independent of context. Such an approach of course ignores the fact that any character—real or literary—contains innumerable potentialities which will emerge or not emerge dependent upon the context in which this character is placed as well as upon these inherent tendencies themselves. G. M. Mathews has suggested that the doctrine of the 'tragic flaw' is one that has obscured the true nature of Shakespearian tragedy far more than any over-emphasis on 'character', although he does not suggest what seems to me to be likely, that the two are connected. He does however go on to make some very pertinent remarks on this subject:

> Indeed, it is only when a man's 'character' is pictured as a sort of hard, fixed core somewhere inside him (rather as the essential particles of matter were once pictured as miniature billiard-balls) that looking for 'flaws' in it makes any sense. . . . a man obviously cannot develop in any direction unless he is capable of doing so; but the theory is a nuisance because the potentialities of men are infinite, and whatever the greatness of a dramatic hero, any number of potential 'flaws' can be found, or invented, to account for his down-fall. Yet in all Shakespeare's tragedies except, perhaps, *Macbeth*, the determining 'flaw' is in society rather than in the hero's supposed distance from perfection. Tragedy does not occur in *Hamlet* because the hero has a bad habit of not killing people at once, but because the power of the Danish Court is founded on violence and adultery.[38]

I would disagree with this only to the extent that I feel that the actions of both Macbeth and Hamlet can only be understood artistically by considering both the 'given' identities of the two as well as the con-texts into which they are placed, and place themselves. The fact that the power of the Danish Court is founded on violence and corruption is not a sufficient exploration of everything that happens in the play; Hamlet's character has something to do with it.

That this is not just a family squabble amongst literary critics around the nature of a literary 'character' can be demonstrated by referring to an analogous misconception of identity in a non-literary context. Talking about the Moscow purge trials in his *The Meaning of Contemporary Realism*, György Lukács talks about Stalinist attitudes towards those purged, which are extraordinarily similar to those adopted by Bradley towards the dramatic characters he examines:

> These monstrous violations of legality and elementary justice were based on grotesque reasoning. All the difficulties and conflicts that arose during the building of socialism might have been avoided, according to this line of argument, if the security organs had done a better job and if Bukharin, Zinoviev, and the rest had been got rid of in 1917! In literature the adoption of this view led to a tedious schematism: difficulties in the building of socialism were invariably blamed on the activities of enemy agents. The exposure of these agents served as the denouement of the plot as well as the solution

of the conflict. Both before the agent's arrival, and after his exposure, there existed an idyllic state of non-conflict.[39]

With a few substitutions—Iago for Bukharin for example—the above could very easily be made to appear a criticism of Bradley's whole approach to Shakespearian drama. Both the political distortion described by Lukács and the literary-critical distortion involved in the theory of the 'fatal flaw' rest on an illegitimate creation of an autonomous 'character', existing in but untouched by a hitherto ordered world. Anything the character then does—whether it be Hamlet or Bukharin— is then explained in terms of that character alone in abstraction from his situation, and never in the particular, concrete context which called out some potentialities rather than others into the realm of action. In contrast to this Lukács's comments on Lenin's personality, made shortly before Lukács's own death, offer an instructive contrast. Lukács notes that Lenin did not consider people in terms of their being either totally perfect or completely defective, but that he saw the 'wise' people to be those who did not make serious mistakes, and who corrected their mistakes as soon as possible.

> Lenin demanded a concrete analysis of the concrete situation and this manifested itself also in human and political terms in his relationships. . . .[40]

Such a realisation that the identity of a real or a fictional character is dependent upon and defined by the complex of relationships of which it is a part avoids the related distortions of a view of character either as autonomous, or as mechanically conditioned by situation.

I would now like to pass on to a consideration of the problems involved in the transition from dialectical theory to dialectical method. Allan Rodway, in the article from which I have already quoted, reminds us of one basic problem which needs to be resolved.

> . . . you can't know the meaning of any part without knowing what sort of whole it is part of . . . But, since the whole is a sum of its parts, you can't know what sort of whole it is without knowing the proper meaning of the parts.[41]

Whilst disagreeing that the whole is merely a sum of its parts, there is obviously a genuine problem posed here which must be answered unless our theory is to hang in abstract and impractical limbos of pure knowledge. Rodway's answer to his own problem seems to me to be an admirable—and a dialectical—one:

We escape, so to speak, by edging out, tacking from evidence to hypothesis to further evidence to renewed hypothesis.[41]

Of course, it is important to stress that we actually get somewhere whilst tacking backwards and forwards, that we reach conclusions which allow us to come to terms with and change ourselves and our environment. However, Rodway's 'escape' reminds us of something that must be stressed, and to which I will return a number of times in the pages that follow: there is no final answer, no absolute truth which we arrive at, can parcel up and put under our pillows. As Goldmann puts it,

> (to) . . . the extent to which . . . the world is transformed and situations change, mental categories cease to be efficacious, lose their rationality, and must transform themselves in turn.[42]

As is implied in Lenin's comment about the practical value of trying to reach an unreachable totality of vision of an object, the search for truth, in aesthetics as much as in life, is constant and never-ending. Goldmann's description of his own critical method in *The Hidden God* is very similar to the one suggested by Rodway:

> There are several different ways of considering such a relationship between the parts and the whole. My initial assumption, however, is that as we fit the individual series of events into a wider context, we little by little improve our understanding both of the whole and of the parts.[43]

From this initial, simplified relationship between the parts and the whole Goldmann proceeds to a progressively more and more complex method of moving between isolated fact and incomplete whole, in a manner that gradually transforms both in a mutually beneficial way.

Goldmann stresses that '. . . one has to place the facts in the widest number of significant wholes', and that

> Any serious historical study must, in my view, have two starting points: the facts themselves, and a conceptual schematisation intended to make them comprehensible. And it is in the very nature of dialectical thought, that, as more facts are revealed, they will modify the original schematisation.[44]

This zig-zagging motion, or 'tacking' as Rodway calls it, is fundamental to a dialectical method, and its direction must itself be the result of a tacking between the larger pressures of social life and the forces exerted by the way the 'internal' logic of any piece of study leads. We must not picture this tacking process in a way similar to what Lenin characterised as the eclectic procedure of Bukharin—between two fixed points—but as something permanently repeating itself on different planes, renewing and changing the points between which the tacking takes place. I have already suggested that part of the context in which the work of art exists for us is the specific nature of our own perception of it. We cannot escape into the abstract, non-contextual truth of a mechanical subject-object relationship. Goldmann points out that the terms we use must be seen to have a relative and a temporary status; what, for example, is an *end* for the researcher (this book for me at the present time, perhaps) becomes a *means* for the social group (I hope), and much the same point can be made about the art work; an end for the writer, a means for the reader. If the art work becomes part of a different perceptual complex then its identity changes—a fact partly perceived by those critics who have argued that a work of literature is debased by being used as a means rather than as an end by the reader or critic. What such critics have often failed to grasp is that similar, if less profound, differences in the identity of the work result from its incorporation into *any* new complex of literary perception and appreciation. The student who reads *Tom Jones* as part of a course on the history of the novel reads something different from what he would read if the book were part of a special study of Fielding's work. It should always be remembered that terms such as 'whole' and 'part', not to say 'identity' and 'relationship', have a relative rather than an absolute significance.

A second objection to the practicality of a dialectical method can be found in a comment of Hillis Miller's, quoted in the *Contemporary Criticism* anthology by W. K. Wimsatt, who himself uses a comparable simile for the literary process in *The Verbal Icon*. The comment reads as follows:

> (the poem's) relations to its surroundings radiate outward like concentric circles from a stone dropped in water. These circles multiply indefinitely until the scholar must give up in despair the attempt to make a complete inventory of them. . . . as he proceeds in his endless quest, the poem . . . gradually fades into the multitude of its associations. . . . Instead of being a self-sufficient entity, it is only a symptom of ideas or images in the culture which generated it.[45]

An article in the *Times Literary Supplement* on Goldmann's criticism, which appeared to have been written for no good reason other than as an acknowledgement of Goldmann's recent death, made a similar objection to his critical method. The writer agreed that

> . . . a book can be understood only in terms of a context, and that every context possesses a super-context . . .

but he noted with some show of reluctance that, '. . . alas, every scholarly labour must stop somewhere'.[46] I feel that both of these criticisms involve an abandonment of the critic's responsibility, and encourage idleness and unmanly despair. Of course, any individual scholarly labour must stop somewhere, but it should be seen as a part of a continuing process, and as a part that contributes to future scholarly labours which can start where it leaves off. Understandably, the critic who has lived in comfortable cohabitation with his carefully-nurtured, lovingly-polished autonomous artifact of an art work will be conscious primarily of loss if he sees it becoming more inseparably connected with its associations and relationships. On a higher plane, W. K. Wimsatt's objections to what he sees as the twin fallacies of intentionalism and affectivism seem to rest on a similar objection to that made by Hillis Miller and the anonymous (scandalously anonymous, as F. W. Bateson would have it) *T.L.S.* reviewer. Wimsatt claims that the outcome of either fallacy is that 'the poem itself', as an object of specifically critical judgement, tends to disappear.[47] Now if he means that an isolable, autonomous and thoroughly 'objective' poem disappears, then he is probably correct, for the immediate result of any contextual approach to literary criticism is that critics no longer feel that they are looking at exactly the same 'object' that critics were looking at a century before when they looked at the 'same' poem.

The problem posed by these two objections is not, it seems to me, a real one in the last analysis. Because the ramifications of a poem's effect are infinite it does not follow that the critic must follow all of them. The critic need not seek, as Hillis Miller suggests, to make a complete inventory of the poem's associations and relationships; inventories are for shopkeepers and landlords, not critics, and even the former realise that they must limit their inventories to items which are relevant—and so must the critic. I stress again that the direction criticism of a poem takes is not determined totally by the poem itself, but should also be a response to the pressures of social life as well as to the internal logic of the poem's development. The critic must trace those associations which are important, and by 'important' I imply important to a particular individual or social group at a particular time and place. This insistence on importance need not result in a crude and immediate functionalism. In can be important for an individual to trace certain reverberations from a poem which have an immediately personal rather than social significance—and if not carried to excess there is nothing intrinsically dilettante in this. But some human importance there must be—otherwise the critic becomes what Caudwell refers to as a 'jackdaw', collecting material which he has no conception of ever fitting into any order which will benefit himself or others. The normal justification for such research is that very often discoveries assume an importance their discoverer never foresaw. In fact, most such discoveries were arrived at by a researcher pursuing a logical line of enquiry—perhaps following the 'internal' needs of a particular problem. It is rare for dustmen to find gold ingots in their load—and the value of the ingots found is insufficient to justify the expense of the collection. If we want to look for gold we must first consider where it is likely to be found.

In practice the critic must make decisions about which relationships are important and which are not. An investigation of new techniques in the novel—B. S. Johnson's interchangeable pages for example— might find that some have had enormous reverberations in the bookbinding trade. The critic should be able to distinguish between the importance of such associations, and of others more directly connected with the artistic importance of the works in question. As I have already suggested, diagrammatic representations of dialectical interconnections —like all representations—have their limitations. There is a strong case, however, for arguing that if diagrams there must be, the complex of eternally opening, closing, merging and separating circles is preferable to those clichéd triangles representing base and superstructure. Goldmann suggests that the central image dominating dialectical thought is that of the circle. Perhaps one of the most interesting discussions of the problem of limiting the infinity of possible enquiry in critical investigation comes in W. J. Harvey's *Character and the Novel*, where he writes as follows:

> Early on in *A Portrait of the Artist as a Young Man*, Stephen Dedalus turns to his geography book, on the flyleaf of which he has written:
>> Stephen Dedalus
>> Class of Elements
>> Clongowes Wood College
>> Sallins
>> County Kildare
>> Ireland

Europe
The World
The Universe.

This is an apt paradigm of the sense of plurality, of interlocking circles and multiple relationships, through which we move in our everyday lives. Reality in this sense is nothing but an incredibly complicated pattern of contexts, a pattern which moves in time and which ripples continuously outwards, as though from Stephen Dedalus to the Universe, until we can discern no pattern at all. Hence *any* formal limitation must be artificial and where to draw the line becomes a prime problem for the novelist. As Henry James puts it:

Really, universally, relations stop nowhere, and the exquisite problem of the artist is eternally to draw, by a geometry of his own, the circle within which they shall happily appear to do so.[48]

The problem is the same for the critic—for any human being—as for the novelist. Relations stop nowhere, but the human significance of relations both alters and diminishes. A practical awareness of this fact must guide the critic's investigations.

NOTES

[1] György Lukács, *The Meaning of Contemporary Realism*, reprinted London 1969, p. 19.
[2] In an interview with Brigitte Devismes in 'VH 101', Summer 1970, Paris, p. 35 et seq.
[3] György Lukács, 'What is Orthodox Marxism?', *History and Class Consciousness*, London 1971, pp. 3, 12, etc.
[4] *History and Class Consciousness*, p. 3.
[5] György Lukács, 'Art and Objective Truth', *Writer and Critic*, London 1970, p. 25 et seq.
[6] *Prison Notebooks*, p. 441.
[7] *Prison Notebooks*, p. 466.
[8] Christopher Caudwell, 'Men and Nature—A Study in Bourgeois History', *Further Studies in a Dying Culture*, reprinted London 1971, p. 136.
[9] *Prison Notebooks*, p. 446.
[10] Everett Knight, *The Objective Society*, London 1959, p. 114, etc.
[11] Everett Knight, *A Theory of the Classical Novel*, p. 11.
[12] J-P. Sartre, *What is Literature?*, reprinted London 1970, p. 36.
[13] *Prison Notebooks*, p. 353.
[14] Lucien Goldmann, 'Reflections on *History* and *Class Consciousness*', *Aspects of History and Class Consciousness*, ed. Mészáros, London 1971, p. 75.
[15] Lucien Goldmann, 'Criticism and Dogmatism in Literature', *The Dialectics of Liberation*, ed. Cooper, Harmondsworth 1968, p. 137.
[16] *What is Art?*, p. 16.
[17] *The Portable Walt Whitman*, ed. Van Doren, reprinted New York 1963, p. 168.
[18] *The Collected Poems of Wallace Stevens*, reprinted London 1966, p. 392.
[19] *History and Class Consciousness*, p. 27.
[20] *The Human Sciences and Philosophy*, p. 127.

[21] *The Human Sciences and Philosophy*, p. 128.

[22] *History and Class Consciousness*, p. 12.

[23] *History and Class Consciousness*, p. 28.

[24] V. I. Lenin, 'Once Again on the Trade Unions, the Present Situation and the Mistakes of Comrades Trotsky and Bukharin', *Selected Works* volume three, London 1961; p. 583. (I have altered 'anathemised' to 'anathematised' in this quotation.)

[25] Lucien Goldmann, *Immanuel Kant*, London 1971, p. 134.

[26] *Further Studies*, p. 253.

[27] Christopher Caudwell, *Studies in a Dying Culture*, reprinted London 1971, p. 45.

[28] *What is Literature?*, p. 18.

[29] W. K. Wimsatt, *The Verbal Icon*, reprinted London 1970, p. xvii.

[30] *Further Studies*, p. 136.

[31] Christopher Caudwell, *Illusion and Reality*, reprinted London 1958, p. 32.

[32] *What is Literature?*, p. 34.

[33] *The Verbal Icon*, p. 70.

[34] Everett Knight, *The Objective Society*, London 1959, p. 117.

[35] *Six Characters in Search of an Author*, p. 17.

[36] István Méstzáros, ed., *Aspects of History and Class Consciousness*, London. 1971, p. 1.

[37] *The Collected Poems of Wallace Stevens*, p. 94.

[38] G. M. Mathews, 'Othello and the Dignity of Man', *Shakespeare in a Changing World*, ed. Kettle, London 1964, p. 137.

[39] *The Meaning of Contemporary Realism*, p. 128.

[40] György Lukács, 'On the Personality of Lenin', *Marxism Today*', September 1971, p. 285.

[41] *Contemporary Criticism*, p. 94.

[42] 'Criticism and Dogmatism in Literature', p. 139.

[43] Lucien Goldmann, *The Hidden God*, London, 1964, p. 95.

[44] *The Hidden God*, p. 102.

[45] *Contemporary Criticism*, p. 76.

[46] 'The Times Literary Supplement', November 26th, 1971, p. 1465.

[47] *The Verbal Icon*, p. 21.

[48] *Character and the Novel*, p. 33. (The quotation from Henry James is from the latter's preface to *Roderick Hudson*.)

3. *Formalism and Marxism*

Lyrical subjectivity has to go for its symbols to the outside world; even if that world has been made by subjectivity itself, it is nevertheless the only possible one; subjectivity, as an interiority, never confronts in a polemical or negative way the outside world that is co-ordinated to it, it never takes refuge inside itself in an effort to forget the outside world; rather, it proceeds as an arbitrary conqueror, it snatches fragments out of the atomised chaos which is the outside world and melts them down—causing all origins to be forgotten—into a newly created lyrical cosmos of pure interiority.[1]

GYÖRGY LUKÁCS

Either the arts are passively dependent upon social reality, a proposition which I take to be that of mechanical material-ism, or a vulgar misinterpretation of Marx. Or the arts, as the creators of consciousness, determine social reality, the proposition which the Romantic poets sometimes advanced. Or finally, the arts, while ultimately dependent, with everything else, on the real economic structure, operate in part to reflect this structure and its consequent reality, and in part, by affecting attitudes towards reality, to help *or hinder* the constant business of changing it. I find Marxist theories of culture confused because they seem to me, on different occasions and in different writers, to make use of all these propositions as the need serves.[2]

RAYMOND WILLIAMS

I would like, in this chapter, to look in some greater detail at what I consider to be the flaws in critical practice which formalist and Marxist criticism has in the past often (though by no means always) contained. It is necessary to do this, I feel, in order to demonstrate that both critical disciplines have had both positive and negative elements in their critical theory and practice, rather than one having been the repository of received truth and the other of error and confusion. Of course, I must admit to a belief in the greater importance of Marxist criticism, to which in spite of what I see as its faults in the past I am committed. But this is not in any way to say that a Marxist must see truth to reside exclusively or consistently in those writings which are consciously and committedly Marxist.

The historical development of formalistic ideas in art and aesthetics is an interesting but complex subject, and one which it is possible to reduce to an over-schematised mechanical set of 'reactions' and 'counter-reactions' artificially abstracted from a much wider range of causal forces. As far as formalism in literary criticism in the Anglo-American tradition is concerned however, there is no doubt that even if it cannot be argued that it actually 'grew out' of Romantic poetic theory, it certainly owes the latter a considerable debt. Coleridge's comment that, 'Could a rule be given from without, poetry would cease to be poetry, and sink into mechanical art . . .'[3] is a favourite one for demonstrating at least the affinities between formalism and Romanticism. From this statement one can extract the theory that the poem conforms only to its own laws rather than to the laws of the outside world, as well as the implication, in the distinction between 'poetry' and 'mechanical art', that these two sets of laws are qualitatively different. Other references to the 'organic', self-referential world of the poem—about which, rather than novels and plays, most formalistic critics tend to talk—can be gleaned from the *Letters* of Keats and from Shelley's *A Defence of Poetry*. What I would like to stress at this point is that whatever the chances of pinning a paternity suit for formalism on to Romantic critical theory, there is one major difference between the two which is crucial to our present argument. Whatever was said by the Romantics about the 'organic', self-referential nature of the poem, they did not argue that it had to be seen as totally autonomous or as a completely ahistorical phenomenon. One can note, for example, that when Shelley replies to Peacock's attack on poetry in *The Four Ages of Poetry*, and writes in answer his *A Defence of Poetry*, he does not reject Peacock's essentially historical treatment. Peacock presents one historical view of the development of poetry:

> While the historian and the philosopher are advancing in, and accelerating, the progress of knowledge, the poet is wallowing in the rubbish of departed ignorance, and raking up the ashes of dead savages to find gewgaws and rattles for the grown babies of the age.
> . . . .
> A poet in our times is a semi-barbarian in a civilized community. He lives in the days that are past.

and Shelley presents another:

> . . . the connexion of poetry and social good is more observable in
> the drama than in whatever other form. And it is indisputable that
> the highest perfection of human society has ever corresponded with
> the highest dramatic excellence; and that the corruption or the
> extinction of drama in a nation where it has once flourished, is a
> mark of the corruption of manners, and an extinction of the energies
> which sustain the soul of social life.

Similarly, one could point to the highly-developed sense of historical
change in both the *Letters* and the poetry of Keats, which again militates
against a totally autonomist view of the art work.

What has been seized upon in Romantic critical theory by formalist
critics is its insistence upon the internal, self-referential harmony which
is to be found in the work of art. In addition to the statement of Coleridge's which I quoted earlier, one could in this context mention Shelley's
distinction, made in *A Defence of Poetry*, between 'poetry' and 'matter
of fact', which suggests that poetry has a different form of mediation
with the reader and the outside world from the isolated 'fact'. In the
implication here that the truth of the poem is to be differentiated from
the truth of 'matter of fact' Shelley obviously comes very close to a
central item of formalistic theory—which we will see expressed in its
basic simplicity by Elder Olson. What I would insist on at this point is
that there is a difference between seeing the poem as a 'whole' which
cannot be dissected without being destroyed, and which translates the
'facts' it contains into something qualitatively different from what they
were outside the poem, and a view of the poem as totally autonomous.
Further to this point, the concept of 'organic form', so beloved of both
Romantic and formalist writers, can be made to have a significantly
altered meaning by the latter. A number of critics—Raymond Williams
and Graham Hough spring to mind—have pointed out that the word
'organic' has such a number of different meanings in the terminology
of different writers that it should be used with extreme care—or not at
all. Monroe Beardsley, in his *Aesthetics*, suggests that the word is
redundant in the term 'organic unity'. In spite of these objections, I
think that a case can be made out for saying that the Romantics—
Shelley in particular—consistently use analogies for the poem or the
poetic process which can meaningfully be described as 'organic', and
that this usage differs in a number of important respects from what is
going on when formalistic critics refer to the organic nature of the art

work. As I have suggested before, formalistic theory tends to make certain apparently minor, but in fact highly crucial extensions of Romantic critical theory, and the concept of the organic nature of the work of art is a good example of this.

I would argue that in Romantic usage—and it is the concept introduced by specific analogies and examples rather than use of the actual word that one normally finds—the concept of the organic nature of the work of art refers to what the dictionary describes as follows: 'Of, pertaining to, or characterized by connexion or coordination of parts in one whole . . .'. This definition does not exclude all possibility of ambiguity or confusion, but it is arguably a meaningful one. Additionally, the concept of the organic as applied to the art work involves connotations of an analogy with the living rather than the inanimate. The living being—particularly the animal or human one—is obviously characterised by the coordination of parts in a whole, and Wordsworth's 'We murder to dissect' makes this analogy specific. In *A Defence of Poetry* Shelley constantly uses similes for poetry which point not only to the self-referential, 'coordination of parts in a whole' nature of the poem, but which also imply an analogy with living rather than inanimate matter:

> (the poet's thoughts) are the germs of the flower and the fruit of the latest time.

> . . . it were as wise to cast a violet into a crucible that you might discover the formal principle of its colour and odour, as seek to transfuse from one language into another the creations of a poet. The plant must spring again from its seed, or it will bear no flower.

Now I think that several very important distinctions can be made between a Romantic use of organic metaphors to describe the poem, and formalistic use of the word 'organic' to imply the total autonomy of the poem. Both of the comments by Shelley above, for instance, imply a dynamic, developing quality, which differs from the absolute fixity claimed for the poem by some formalistic critics. In addition to this, the very analogies used deny the possibility of total autonomy; a seed can only sprout into a plant and flower in a very precise context—left in total isolation it remains a seed. Similarly, when Keats argues that poetry should 'come as naturally as the leaves to a tree', he is not encouraging a view that the way to understand the leaf—or the poem—is to examine it in glorious isolation from its life-giving context. The opening of 'Hyperion' shows that he saw the leaf to be a different thing when separated from the tree. Perhaps the best example of the importance of the context within which the organic whole exists for the Romantic is Shelley's famous comparison of the poem with a child at play:

> A child at play by itself will express its delight by its voice and motions; and every inflexion of tone and every gesture will bear exact relation to a corresponding antitype in the pleasurable impressions which awakened it . . .

The solitude of the child, and the perfect relationship existing between the complementary parts of this scene should blind us neither to the essentially dynamic, changing nature of the picture, nor to its obvious dependence upon a larger context.

I have looked at Romantic ideas of the organic nature of the work of art not only because I feel that it is important to insist upon the fact that they do not offer a basis for arguing that autonomist theories of the art work have a historical legitimacy, but also because I think that they give a number of very fine descriptions of the nature of the identity of the art work, which, significantly for a Marxist, is not seen to be a unique phenomenon, but is seen as something to be found outside as well as inside the realm of art. If we turn to formalistic developments of this conception of the nature of the art work, the difference should be immediately apparent. Take, for example, the following comment by Cleanth Brooks:

> The poem communicates so much and communicates it so richly and with such delicate qualifications that the thing communicated is mauled and distorted if we attempt to convey it by any vehicle less subtle than that of the poem itself.[4]

From this it is only a short step to arguing that only the poem can communicate what the poem communicates, which is in one sense a truism, but which can be used to bolster up some rather more dubious critical theories and practices. There is an important distinction to be made between saying, as does Shelley, that one cannot translate a poem without destroying it, and saying that to attempt to convey what a poem communicates other than through the medium of 'the poem itself' is a vain task.

The implied analogy between poem and living thing—especially human being—that the use of 'organic' metaphors introduces in formalistic theory is again different from Romantic usage of the same analogy in as much as the formalistic critic tends to see the individual human being

in far more autonomous terms than does the Romantic, partly, as I
have suggested, for historical reasons. W. K. Wimsatt has observed
that

> The modern idea of the art work as a separate existant and in some
> sense autonomous or autotelic entity is closely tied to the idea of a
> vital organic form.[5]

In his essay on Keats's 'Ode on a Grecian Urn' Cleanth Brooks quotes
approvingly Macleish's dictum that 'A poem should not mean/But
be',[6] and in *The Verbal Icon* W. K. Wimsatt declares that this is
'. . . an epigram worth quoting in every essay on poetry.'[7] What few
formalistic critics seem to appreciate is that this dictum carries with it
some rather un-formalistic implications. Wimsatt himself, in the later
essay from which I quote him on 'organic form', notes that it would be
silly to expect a 'hardness and self-sufficiency' of the poem which its
author, the human person, does not have. It is surely this crucial implication of the analogy between the organic natures of poem and person
that the Romantics did not ignore, but which many formalistic critics
have missed. Macleish's dictum suggests that being and meaning are
irreconcilable qualities which either cannot, or should not, be united
in the poem. But being and meaning surely imply one another, and
cannot really exist apart; their relationship is analogous to the relationship between Goldmann's complementary processes of understanding
and explaining. To say that a poem means something is not necessarily
to detract from its being, its selfness or identity. Being and meaning,
like identity and relationship, belong to one another and cannot properly be separated.

The formalistic critic in fact often seems to commit himself to
critical theories which torpedo his own critical practice. The 'indivisibility' of the poem would not, in fact, leave much if any room for
critical analysis, and the total autonomy of the poem would, among
other things, appear to render critical discussion both pointless and
impossible. Brooks has tried to circumvent this difficulty by suggesting that there is a distinction to be drawn between examining a line of
poetry in the context of that poem, and abstracting a line of poetry and
looking at it in a different context. But the distinction is not a real one;
the critic who examines a line of poetry 'in the context of the poem'
is in fact asking his reader to look at this line in the context of the critic's
examination of it. When Brooks looks at the famous concluding couplet
of Keats's 'Ode on a Grecian Urn' he is in fact in a certain sense abstracting

it from the poem. It would seem difficult to draw a qualitative distinction between Brooks's examination of this couplet and Arnold's use of 'touchstones'—lines of great poetry carried around in the mind as a sort of intellectual smelling-salt to be used when mental uplift is required. There obviously is a quantitative difference—the level of abstraction in the latter case is much greater; but that is a different matter.

Not surprisingly the formalist is led into all sorts of practical difficulties through attempted adherence to such doctrines as the indivisibility and the autonomy of the art work. Writing about Keats's 'Ode on a Grecian Urn', Brooks talks about 'moving into the world of the urn', but not surprisingly has to keep moving back into our world to tell us what he has found there—in a manner which is reminiscent of the quotation from Lukács which I placed at the start of this chapter. Other illuminating contradictions can be found by comparing theoretical pronouncements from one essay with practice in another. In his essay 'What does Poetry Communicate?', for example, Brooks twice inveighs against the use of a dictionary to discover the poetic meaning of a word, claiming that the 'dew-drops' in the Herrick poem he is considering 'become a symbol heavily charged with meanings which no dictionary can be expected to give'. If we turn from this essay to two others, the one mentioned on the Keats ode, and another entitled 'Literary Criticism, Poet, Poem and Reader', we see a curious contradiction in his attitude to use of a dictionary to determine the significance of the same word—'green'. In the former essay he merely remarks that 'green' in the Keats's ode has connotations of naturalness, spontaneity, life, but in the second essay, in order to assess the significance of the word 'verdant' in a poem, he turns to a dictionary to discover that at the time the poem was written the word 'green' (and thus, probably, 'verdant' also) carried connotations of gullibility.[8] As Lukács puts it— brief raiding parties are sent out to snatch supplies from the outside world which then become part of a 'lyrical cosmos of pure interiority'.

As if realising in advance the nature of some of the pitfalls waiting for the unwary formalist, the Chicago critic Elder Olson tries to escape by positing a dual identity for the poem, distinguishing between the poem *qua* poem and the poem *qua* something else. Olson argues that a modern poetic should concern itself only with those questions raised

> . . . concerning it *qua* work of art . . . . . . a question relevant to the poem as an existant thing falls under metaphysics, a question relevant to it as productive of, say, social consciousness, falls under politics; lacking the proper peculiarity to poetry neither of these

would be poetic questions in the sense of which I propose to employ
the term *poetic*, . . . but on a community between poetry and
something else.[9]

Thus a clear distinction is made between a poem's identity and the
complex of relationships to which it belongs, and the former is abstracted
from the latter. For Olson, it would appear that our 'poetic' response
to a poem—say, Shelley's *The Masque of Anarchy*—and our 'political'
response to it, are two entirely different and separable things—which
I would have thought in common-sense terms was pretty obviously
not true. This formulation however allows Olson to agree whole-
heartedly with the sociological critic that a poem has a sociological and
political significance, whilst maintaining that it is not the job of the
literary critic to investigate this area of its significance.

However, even if one were to allow Olson his dual poetic identity,
this would not allow him to escape from becoming involved in a growing crescendo of contradictions. His desire to retain an autonomous
poetic artifact at all costs leads him on from the position quoted above
(from his essay on Yeats's 'Sailing to Byzantium'), to reject our two
crucial theoretical terms: totality and dialectic. The former, Olson sees
very shrewdly, would if accepted imply a degree of interconnection
between phenomena unacceptable to his insistence upon the autonomy
of the art work:

> . . . any attempt to furnish indices towards a poetics of the lyric
> can be significant only in a philosophy in which the arts and sciences
> are held distinct from each other; for, unless that is the case, the
> inquiry into principles as peculiar to poetics would turn on a non-
> sense question: if, in any sense whatever, all knowledge is one, then
> it must follow that the objects of knowledge must also be one in the
> same sense . . .[9]

Olson spots the danger very acutely, but fails to see the answer to it,
which could be abstracted from Lukács's comment that '. . . the category of totality does not reduce its various elements to an undifferen-
tiated uniformity . . .',[10] in other words, that the interconnection of
science and the arts does not imply that the arts—or the individual poem
—do not have a clearly defined identity which can be investigated.

Olson rejects the idea that 'in any sense whatever' knowledge is one,
precisely because he fails to perceive that the identity of the part is not
dissipated by its belonging to a larger whole. In like manner, Olson
rejects too any idea of a dialectical interrelation between the parts of

the poem. This at first sight is surprising, for the formalistic emphasis on analysis within the context of the art work might have been supposed a good basis for presuming that the relationship between the parts of a poem was a dialectical one. However, again displaying considerable, if misguided, shrewdness, Olson rejects this formulation too. His reasons for so doing are interesting:

> . . . a dialectic is necessarily regulated by the natures of things external to the dialectic, and must ultimately be evaluated, whereas the coordination of elements in a poem cannot involve reference to anything outside the poem.[11]

In others words, if Olson could give the poem or art work a sort of limited dialectical status, he would be happy, but he realises that the implication of the internal interrelation of parts in a poem is that the poem is itself dialectically related to that which is outside it. Olson certainly cannot be faulted here on grounds of consistency, but when his position is examined in terms of practicality its weaknesses are seen. The position has now been reached where not only is the poem to be considered as an autonomous whole, but its various components are also in their turn seen in like manner—for it is impossible to interpret Olson's rejection of an internal poetic dialectic in any other way. Why one should stop here—and not, for example, proceed until one has reached the autonomy of the individual letter—or beyond—is not stated. In fact Olson presents no argument for making the particular complex we call the poem autonomous rather than any other possible whole, other than saying that this is the case. Still following the same remorseless logic, he gives as a concluding argument the fact that if a dialectical relationship existed between this poem and that which is external to it, the poem would have to be evaluated, that is, seen in a larger context than itself, and this he rejects. Just a little more logical progression could have brought him to the point of seeing that the same could be said of just reading the poem, or thinking about it—or even being aware of its existence. All of these bring the poem into the context of something external to itself, and thus present the same problems from which he has been attempting to escape.

The words in a poem, Olson argues, do not receive their meaning from anything outside the poem, but from the poem itself.

> If the basic terms of a lyric poem do not receive their meanings from the chance associations of the reader, neither do they have their dictionary meanings; like terms in most discourses they take their

significance from their context, through juxtaposition to other terms with which they are equated, contrasted, correlated, or combined.[12]

This is a curiously self-referential explanation. 'Where does this word take its meaning from?' 'From the other words in the poem.' 'But where do *they* take their meanings from?' 'From one another.' And so on, and so on. Olson has already forgotten that he had previously implied that even the components of a poem were themselves autonomous, when he rejected the concept of an internal poetic dialectic. This would preclude any mutual definition on the part of the words of a poem, for as Beardsley says in his *Aesthetics*:

> If an object were intrinsically valuable, no reason could be given to prove it, according to the Instrumentalist, since the reason would consist in pointing out its connections with other things, but if the value depends upon these connections, then it is not intrinsic.[13]

Olson's use of the word 'context' is just as destructive to his basic position as would have been his acceptance of the word 'dialectic', for if we are to see a word in the context of the poem, why may we not see the poem itself in a larger context? Olson's logic is impeccable until it reaches the edge of his hard, gem-like poem, and there it falters. His description of the mode of being of a poem is comparable to the first, magical properties that a dictionary appears to have for a child; every word is defined by another word, which is itself defined by another word, and so on. It is of course only because language is a social phenomenon, linked to social practice, that we can make any sense of the dictionary at all, as otherwise the definitions of words given in it would be as useful as the instructions on how to open a sardine tin contained inside the tin itself. The same can be said of the poem. If it is autonomous, and every word gets its meaning only from other words within the poem, then the poem is not available to human cognition at all.

Josef Hrabák's definition of structuralism, in spite of its non–genetic and thus atemporal viewpoint, shows the way out from Olson's series of vicious circles:

> (structuralism) . . . starts off from the observation that every concept in a given system is determined by all the other concepts in that system and has no significance by itself alone; it does not become equivocal until it is integrated into the system, the structure of which it forms a part and in which it has a definite fixed place.[14]

Moving on from this position, Paul Garvin has pointed out that structuralism in general appreciates the fact that the principles used to determine the word's meaning in the context of the poem must also be used to determine the poem's meaning in the larger context of which it, in its turn, forms a part.[15] In passing I might note that by referring to this larger context as the 'larger social setting' perhaps Garvin lays too little stress on the multiplicity and dynamic interconnectedness of the various possible contexts into which the poem can be integrated.

In order to demonstrate that my objections to Olson's theoretical statements are more than just limited theoretical disagreements, but have an immediate significance in terms of critical practice, I would like to look briefly at Olson's treatment of Yeats's 'Sailing to Byzantium', which follows the statements of his to which I have made reference. To facilitate consideration of his analysis of the poem, I reproduce the full text of Yeats's poem below.

Sailing to Byzantium

I

That is no country for old men. The young
In one another's arms, birds in the trees
—Those dying generations—at their song,
The salmon-falls, the mackerel-crowded seas,
Fish, flesh, or fowl, commend all summer long
Whatever is begotten, born and dies.
Caught in that sensual music all neglect
Monuments of unageing intellect.

II

An aged man is but a paltry thing,
A tattered coat upon a stick, unless
Soul clap its hands and sing, and louder sing
For every tatter in its mortal dress,
Nor is there singing school but studying
Monuments of its own magnificence;
And therefore I have sailed the seas and come
To the holy city of Byzantium.

III

O Sages standing in God's holy fire
As in the gold mosaic of a wall,
Come from the holy fire, perne in a gyre,
And be the singing-masters of my soul.

Consume my heart away; sick with desire
And fastened to a dying animal
It knows not what it is; and gather me
Into the artifice of eternity.

IV

Once out of nature I shall never take
My bodily form from any natural thing,
But such a form as Grecian goldsmiths make
Of hammered gold and gold enamelling
To keep a drowsy Emperor awake;
Or set upon a golden bough to sing
To lords and ladies of Byzantium
Of what is past, or passing, or to come.

Bearing in mind Olson's argument that the poem cannot be understood except in its own terms, so that knowledge and experience of the real world are irrelevant to its appreciation and understanding, it is ironic that the poem is connected with a desire to escape from a world where transience and flux affect everything to one—like Olson's ideal poem— where unageing intellect can live in surroundings which do not mock it. It is ironic because however strongly the poem presents this desire, part of the poem's greatness lies in the way in which it suggests that such a situation cannot be achieved. The weight of the poem, ostensibly, is put on the side of the hard-done-by unageing intellect, but it is the dying generations, the young in one another's arms, the bird in the trees at whose song the salmon-falls and mackerel-crowded seas commend whatever is begotten, born and dies, which give the poem its extraordinary richness and density. The unageing intellect, to misquote Dr. Leavis, has all the arguments, but the young in one another's arms have all the life. The sheer pressure of fecundity, suggested in those composite adjectives, puts the unageing intellect—symbolised how ironically in that mechanical bird—completely into the shade. In this context the 'dying' of 'dying generations' assumes an almost earthy richness, especially when compared with the flat 'monument' of the intellect, and 'dying generations' sums up the force of so much of Keats's poetry, that the richness of life resides in its dynamic qualities, which are inseparably linked with death. The final achieved stasis of the poem stands in sad, sterile contrast to the lush energy of the first verse, and is itself betrayed by the song of the bird about 'what is past, or passing, or to come'—the very transience the poet claims to be trying to escape from. Like so much of Yeats (as I will argue in chapter eight),

the poem describes a love-hate relationship with life, coming implicitly
to the realisation that it is only life's totality—its movement and eventual
eclipse—which renders its joys possible.

In view of this Olson's attempt to see the poem as the poem attempts
to see unageing intellect—divorced from the movement of social life—
is ironic. His comments on the final verse of the poem are particularly
significant. The poet's desire to escape from a world of physical flux
and decay leads him to desire to be

> . . . such a form as Grecian goldsmiths make
> Of hammered gold and gold enamelling
> To keep a drowsy Emperor awake;
> Or set upon a golden bough to sing
> To lords and ladies of Byzantium . . .

One could contrast the adjectival richness and energy of the first verse
with the tired repetition of 'gold' and 'golden' here, which not surprisingly is not very efficient at keeping the drowsy Emperor awake, but
Olson, convinced that the words in the poem must be interpreted in
terms of their meaning drawn from other words in the poem, and not
from any connections they may have with the outside world, comments
on the final section as follows:

> . . . in stanza I a mortal bird of nature amid natural trees sings a
> brief song of sensual joy in praise of mortal things, of "whatever is
> begotten, born, and dies"; in stanza IV an immortal and artificial
> bird set in an artificial tree sings an eternal song of spiritual joy in
> praise of eternal things . . .[16]

It would be interesting for us to have Olson tell us how he knows that
the 'form' in the final stanza is supposed to be a bird—rather than, say,
an elephant or half a scotch egg. For the non-formalist, the answer is
simple. We know that the latter do not normally sit in trees and sing,
whereas birds do. But we are using our knowledge of things in the
external world, which Olson says cannot be used to understand what
goes on in the poem. Well, perhaps it could be argued that it can be
determined that the 'form' is a bird from internal evidence; a bird is
mentioned in the first verse after all. But Olson will not allow any
internal dialectical connection between the components of a poem, and
anyway, how do we know that the 'form' parallels the bird in the first
stanza? Or how do we know that it does not parallel the fish or the
flesh?

Now at a later point in his essay, Olson defends his assertion that the 'meaning' of a poem is unconnected with the outside world in a way that strikes me as spurious, but again is worth considering because it fastens on to what is I think a half-truth about the nature of poetic truth. Olson argues that

> . . . every poem is a microcosmos, a discrete and independent universe with its laws provided by the poet; his decision is absolute; he can make things good or bad, great or small, powerful, or weak, just as he wills; he may make men taller than mountains or smaller than atoms, he may suspend whole cities in the air, he may destroy creation and re-form it; within his universe the impossible becomes the possible, the necessary the contingent—if he but says they do.[17]

A man who can do so much can certainly turn a bird into a scotch egg if he so wills. And it could be objected that Yeats could have had an elephant or a scotch egg sitting on a bough had he wanted to—but he did not so want. The point surely is that we assume that the form is a bird because the poem can only be understood by importing our knowledge and experience of the world into our reading of it. Olson's half-references to *Gulliver's Travels* above remind us that the poet can present us with a world different from our own, although even here I would argue that if he wishes to be comprehended he must limit the extent to which he does this. What is important here is that where his artistic world diverges from our own Swift has to make this fact explicit, otherwise we assume that the artistic world is the same as our own. He tells us that the Lilliputians are small, and we accept this, but as he doesn't mention anything about the law of gravity, we assume that this operates on Lilliputians as it does on us. *Gulliver's Travels* is thus not an autonomous work in terms of its meaning, but even where its world diverges from our own it has to make a special effort to both exclude and use our knowledge of our own world.

There is also a more specifically linguistic objection to Olson's position, which I implied when talking about the non-self-referential nature of the dictionary. Kenneth Burke, attacking Olson's position in this essay, notes that part of his argument rests on an assumption that the reader or critic approaches the poem with a mind like a blank sheet of paper, to which he replies that in fact the critic does not begin his observation from scratch, but has a more or less systematically organised set of terms by which to distinguish and characterise the elements of the poem—even if these may be modified by his observing of a given

poem.[18] What we look for governs what we find—what, in fact, there
'is', and unless we approach a poem like Yeats's 'Sailing to Byzantium'
equipped with certain expectations, and certain organised ways of dealing with poetry which experience has provided us with, we will make
little sense of it. Further to this, we do not approach a poem merely
with a developed literary expertise, but with a knowledge and experience of social life congealed within the language with which we make
contact with the poem; as R. W. Beardsmore points out, the fact
that the language used in poetry is the same language that we use in
talking to our children or during the course of our job, runs counter
to the claim that art (and particularly literature) is isolated from the rest
of life—or, I might add, that it could be.[19] The only way I can envisage
by which the reader could be prevented from importing ideas, concepts
and experience into his reading of poetry via his prior understanding of
its language would be for the poem to be read in a language not understood by him, on which absurd paradox perhaps the subject may be
abandoned. We cannot perceive something that is totally self-enclosed,
for that which is totally self-enclosed cannot be perceived. This being
so, we might as well accept that contact with our perception to a certain
extent alters or defines the art work, and proceed to examine the nature
of our relationship with it so as to understand how this happens, rather
than pretending that, like the christian God, we can control things without changing their free-will and self-dependence.

If formalistic theories have been as riddled with inconsistencies as I
have claimed, why has it been that their criticism has been worth studying? Partly, I think, because formalistic critics have been prepared to
abandon the rigidities of their theory when engaged in the practical
tasks that criticism of specific works has necessitated. Helen Gardner
has drawn attention to the fact that many formalistic critics were only
'playing', as she puts it, at being ignorant of historical or biographical
facts, and in fact knew more about, say, Donne and the history and
literature of his age than they admitted, although, she adds, 'they might
have done better if they had tried to learn a little more'. But more than
this, I think that the formalistic fiction that an autonomous and self-
contained work was being examined independent of any social or
temporal or literary context often allowed the critic, unbeknown to
himself, to use that contextual knowledge which was relevant to the
investigation in hand, rather than drowning in a sea of irrelevant biographical or historical fact.

The least positive aspect of formalistic criticism, however has been the total rejection of all theories which suggest that the reader's role may be a creative one. Lowry Nelson and other recent critics have suggested that to see a work as communication is to imply some necessary collaboration on the part of the reader, and this may well explain why on at least one occasion Cleanth Brooks has rejected a view of literature as communication. In a similar way, Elder Olson too has reacted very strongly against the idea that the reader has anything other than a totally passive role to play, arguing that to allow the 'psychological connotations of readers', or the 'inevitable ambiguities of language' to enter into a literary response would be to admit

> . . . that the poem becomes a mere stimulus to independent poetic activities on the part of the reader—that is, the reader becomes the true poet . . .[20]

It is of course to admit no such thing, but again I will pursue this question further later. What these gentlemen lack, as Engels remarked of other gentlemen, is dialectic.

Unfortunately, other gentlemen resemble them in this respect, and have less excuse for so doing. Having, I hope, demonstrated by now that the work of literature must be seen in a wider context than that provided for the reader by itself, I would like to start to modify certain rather mechanical conceptions of the way in which this relationship between work and context should be seen. It would be innaccurate and unfair to claim that all Marxist criticism and critical theory in the Anglo-American tradition written in the thirties could be dismissed in a cavalier fashion. The fact that no developed Marxist aesthetic was available to critics at this time (in contrast, say, to Marxist economic theory), coupled with a number of local factors, meant that Marxist critical writing laboured under certain disadvantages. A historical account of the development of Marxist critical and aesthetic theory in the thirties would have to consider the short time span during which most of the important work was produced, the fact that most of those concerned in producing this work were those whose commitment to Marxism was not initially in the field of aesthetics, and the general influence of a world situation which was dominated by the rise of fascism, the apparently rapid degeneration of capitalism, and the influence of the Soviet Union. As a result of this, it can be argued that Marxist critics, in reacting strongly against atemporal, autonomist theories of art, and influenced by the doctrines of Socialist Realism propounded in the Soviet Union, tended to see the relationship between art work and socio-economic base in too direct and mechanical a manner, denying, in fact, that the art work was possessed of a distinct, though not auto-nomous, identity. I would stress that this is not to undervalue the very real theoretical and critical achievement of such critics as Caudwell, Alick West, and others—any more than pointing to the recurrent theoretical flaws in formalist theory and practice is to deny that critical works of genuine insight and value were produced by formalistic critics. But it is a critical responsibility, and one that a Marxist should feel a particular commitment to, to consider past achievements and shortcomings in a broad rather than a particularised way at a time when theory is being discussed. If this is done it can certainly be claimed that healthy as was the insistence of Marxist critics on the importance of the relationship between the art work and the society which produced it, the time has now come to consider other aspects of the mode of being of the art work, and to modify past overgeneralisations. Seen in the context of the thirties, Bukharin's insistence upon the distinction between the ideological source of the art work's content and its artistic transformation stands in a certain isolation.

I would suggest that a failure adequately to stress the fact that the art work has a distinct identity led Marxist critics into three recurrent critical shortcomings. The first of these involved an over-simplification of the nature of the relationship between the work of art on the one hand, and the society from which it emanated, or the author who wrote it, on the other. Parodying Marxist criticism in his book *The Pooh Perplex*, F. C. Crews suggests that Marxist criticism is concerned not so much to relate the work of literature to its society and to the socio-political position of the author, as to subsume it into the latter completely:

> Certainly there is nothing in Milne's background or reputation to encourage us towards optimism about his leanings. His origins were, I believe, thoroughly bourgeois, though I am not completely certain of this. I started reading his recently published *Autobiography* but was put off when I came across a reference to "our governess" on the third line of the first page.[21]

The parody is unfair of course—parodies always are—but if the above is compared with Caudwell's essay on Shaw,[22] certain embarrassing similarities can be seen. Here it should be said that one must bear in mind the intention of the critics concerned, for it is very probable that Caudwell's aim was not so much to attempt a critical analysis of

Shaw's plays, as to analyse certain aspects of bourgeois consciousness which he found in Shaw's life and art—an aim which is perfectly legitimate. This apart however, it is certainly true that the qualitative distinction between the man (or the time) and the work of art was very often lost sight of as the causal connections between the two were stressed. Such a stress on the relationship between art and society led to a number of problems, some of which I will take up in chapters seven and eight. For the moment, I would note that this led to serious problems regarding the evaluation of literature, a fact which Wellek and Warren point to in their *Theory of Literature*:

> There is a curious contradiction between this avowed determinism which assumes that 'consciousness' must follow 'existence', that a bourgeois cannot help being one, and the usual ethical judgement which condemns him for these very opinions.[23]

Leading on from this position, one finds that there is too often an assumption that the worth of an artist's work is directly related to—if not identical with—the worth of his consciously expressed opinions and allegiances. Now it is obvious that there is a connection, and an important one, between these two. But here, as elsewhere, the connection is often a lot more subtle than might at first appear. Just as it is not enough to dismiss any statement made by a reactionary on the grounds that he is a reactionary, so the relationship between an artist's extra-literary pronouncements and the value of his art is not to be reduced to a crude equivalence. A belief that it could be led to all sorts of curious contortions on occasions—often working backwards from a belief in the greatness of a particular work of art to a demonstration that the artist responsible for it must have had 'progressive' opinions on all the most important contemporary issues which faced him. Thus Jane Austen never mentioned politics because she wished to conceal her revolutionary sympathies, and Shakespeare sympathised wholly with expressions of lower-class discontent expressed in his time. This particular distortion is one which I find curious, and one that is not limited to the field of aesthetics. Marxists certainly seem to have a weakness for moving immediately from agreement or disagreement with an opinion, or an action, or approval or disapproval of a work of art, to an all-embracing moral approval or condemnation of the individual responsible for the opinion or art work. As Wellek and Warren point out, there is a particular curiosity about such opinions coming from those who insist on the extent to which the individual is conditioned and motivated by forces beyond his control. I feel sure that this phenomenon is not un-connected with the un-Marxist attitudes towards individuality based on conceptions of character-autonomy which I described in my previous chapter. Stephen Spender, in his autobiography *World Within World*, has described how social and personal estrangement from Marxists often seemed to result from political disagreement during the thirties. I feel sure that an interesting historical examination of such attitudes—certainly not shared by Marx or Lenin—would reveal some interesting connections between theoretical simplification and practical distortion. The problems of artistic reassessment necessitated by writers who changed their allegiances were the least of the embarrassments which followed from such a position.

The third weakness to which I would like to draw attention concerns the application of a narrowly functional evaluation of literature. Unless a work made a specific and successful appeal to immediate political action, it often ran the risk of being labelled passive, defeatist, or the all-embracing 'bourgeois'. There were again honourable exceptions here, and Alick West's treatment of Joyce's *Ulysses*,[24] which was in practice less rigid than his theoretical statements about value, could be cited here. Again, I would like to reconsider these problems when I examine the question of artistic evaluation later on. For the time being I would note that subsequent to the thirties a number of Marxist critics have pointed out that it is difficult if not impossible to measure the precise effect of a work of art, and that there are many different and complex effects which art can have on its appreciators. A work of art can have a multiplicity of different effects on different people at different times, many of which are not easily measured or assessed. Arnold Kettle, in his *An Introduction to the English Novel*, juxtaposes *Wuthering Heights* and *Uncle Tom's Cabin*, suggesting that although the former has never had the immediate and ascertainably positive effect within the context of a given society that the latter has, it is arguably a 'better' work. I wish to consider why this should be so in my later discussion of value.

The basis of any positive development of Marxist theory must be a firm perception of past achievements and past weaknesses, and I hope that it will not be thought that my insistence upon the latter implies an inability to perceive the former. To a large extent many of the impor-tant battles fought by Marxists in the field of aesthetics before the war have been won. University syllabuses now often testify to the fact that it is not only Marxists who recognise that art and literature should be examined in the context of the society which produced them—although

I would not claim that the situation was perfect and that there was not still far to go in obtaining general acceptance of this fact. Many of those who do accept this theoretical assumption, however, are asking for solutions to other, more complex theoretical problems. It is up to Marxists to attempt to provide these answers.

NOTES

[1] György Lukács, *The Theory of the Novel*, London 1971, p. 114.

[2] Raymond Williams, *Culture and Society*, reprinted Harmondsworth 1966, p. 266.

[3] *Biographia Literaria*, chapter 18.

[4] Cleanth Brooks, 'What does Poetry Communicate?', reprinted in *American Critical Essays*, ed. Beaver, London 1959, p. 256.

[5] *Contemporary Criticism*, p. 62.

[6] Cleanth Brooks, 'Keats's Sylvan Historian: History Without Footnotes', reprinted in *Five Approaches of Literary Criticism*, ed. Scott, London 1962, p. 231.

[7] *The Verbal Icon*, p. 81.

[8] Cleanth Brooks, 'Literary Criticism: Poet, Poem, and Reader', reprinted in *Perspectives in Contemporary Criticism*, ed. Grebstein, London, 1968, p. 104.

[9] Elder Olson, ' "Sailing to Byzantium": Prolegomena to a Poetics of the Lyric', reprinted in *Five Approaches of Literary Criticism*, ed. Scott, London 1962, p. 216.

[10] *History and Class Consciousness*, p. 12.

[11] ' "Sailing to Byzantium" etc.', p. 226.

[12] ' "Sailing to Byzantium" etc.', p. 225.

[13] Monroe C. Beardsley, *Aesthetics*, New York 1958, p. 542.

[14] *A Prague School Reader etc.*, p. vi.

[15] *A Prague School Reader etc.*, p. vii.

[16] ' "Sailing to Byzantium" etc.', p. 221.

[17] ' "Sailing to Byzantium" etc.', p. 227.

[18] Kenneth Burke, 'The Problem of the Intrinsic (as reflected in the Neo-Aristotelian School)', reprinted in *Aristotle's Poetics and English Literature*, ed. Olson, London, 1965, p. 129.

[19] R. W. Beardsmore, *Art and Morality*, London 1971, p. 50.

[20] ' "Sailing to Byzantium" etc.', p. 225.

[21] Frederick C. Crews, *The Pooh Perplex*, reprinted London, 1967, p. 17.

[22] *Studies in a Dying Culture*, p. 1.

[23] *Theory of Literature*, p. 107.

[24] Alick West, *Crisis and Criticism*, London, 1937.

4. *The Writer and the Work*

We are to visualize the English novelists not as floating down that stream which bears all its sons away unless they are careful, but as seated together in a room, a circular room, a sort of British Museum reading-room—all writing their novels simultaneously.[1]

E. M. FORSTER

The *Iliad* wasn't written by Homer but by another gentleman of the same name.[2]

Quoted by GRAHAM HOUGH

. . . the artist, by placing himself 'at a distance' creates . . . the identity he sets out to portray. Not being a *participant* in the reality which interests him, he is obliged to introduce from elsewhere some principle of intelligibility. If things and people are to be taken in isolation one from the other, then they must be supposed to possess a 'built-in', 'self-contained' identity. . . .[3]

EVERETT KNIGHT

The fact that the writer is directly and inevitably related to the work he produces is one that, like many such facts, is so obvious that its implications have often been ignored. Just as the excesses of sociological criticism have often provided fuel for those who have argued that the social background to the work of art should be ignored, so too the reliable escape-route for the bad critic—irrelevant biography—has convinced many that the critic can safely ignore most biographical information about the author of a given work of literature. I will go into more precise examination of different rationalisations of such a position shortly, but for the time being would argue that from a dialectical point of view the relationship between the writer and the work can never be totally ignored by the reader or critic, however many dangers lie in the way of the unwary biographical critic. One may well accept that, as Bukharin suggests, a comment made by an author in one context, and the same comment written by him in a work of literature, are, essentially, different things. Yet although they may be different, they are related, and it is by an examination of such relationships that the work of literature can be given a more and more fully developed identity. In practice the reader of a book builds up an area of reference associated with direct authorial responsibility, to which he may or may not give the name 'the author', and which he may or may not associate with the historical person who wrote the book. Additionally, even in the case of books whose authors are unknown, some consciousness of the experience of the writing process, and the figure of a person experiencing that consciousness, is present in the reader's mind. It is important that such, often shadowy, conceptualisations, are understood for what they are by the reader, for otherwise a number of misleading attitudes towards the 'author's presence' can be adopted by the reader. In the following chapter I would like to look at some of the problems which the reader faces in his conception of the writer-work relationship.

In his *Preface to Shakespeare*, Samuel Johnson makes what has become a famous comment on the relationship between the writer and the work he produces. He states that

Every man's performances, to be rightly estimated, must be compared with the state of the age in which he lived, and with his own particular opportunities; and though to the reader a book be not worse or better for the circumstances of the author, yet as there is always a silent reference of human works to human abilities, and as the enquiry, how far man may extend his designs, or how high he may rate his native force, is of far greater dignity than in what rank we shall place any particular performance, curiosity is always busy to discover the instruments, as well as to survey the workmanship, to know how much is to be ascribed to original powers, and how much to casual and adventitious help.

Johnson, it will be seen, neither rejects any investigation of the writer's situation and ability as irrelevant, nor does he claim that information about the writer has any bearing upon the worth of his book. Johnson's approach is basically a dualist one, involving judgements on the man and on the work which are related to one another one way but not the other. The book can be used as evidence to judge the man, along with other factors, but the man's situation is irrelevant in arriving at a judgement of the book, which is neither 'worse nor better for the circumstances of the author'. Now Johnson's critical schizophrenia here points to one of the recurrent problems involved in literary criticism, a problem which I believe stems directly from autonomist views of the work of art. Johnson is prepared only for a one-way relationship between author and work because his conception of the work here is an autonomist one, whilst his conception of the human author is not. He is prepared to see the author in the context of his situation, and to realise that his actions must be seen in this context because he rejects all idealist notions of human identity which do not place the latter in a concrete context of practical experience. On the other hand his conception of the work of art is a far less contextual one—although he is by no means to be seen as an early formalist—and thus his view of the art work's identity does not involve a view of its authorial context.

It can be seen, however, that such a distinction is both theoretically and practically riddled with contradictions. Like Elder Olson's suggested division of the poem into two distinct modes of being, Johnson's distinction can never exist in any practical form. If one really is to refer 'human work to human abilities', then some relating of the value of a book to the moral value of the writing of the book is taking place, a relationship which illogically is seen to define the moral value of the activity but not the artistic or aesthetic value of the work. One cannot have a sort of one-way dialectical relationship, where two related wholes are seen to be in a relationship which defines one of them but not the other. In more directly practical terms, it is difficult if not impossible to imagine one's reading of a book leading one to admire the author, without this admiration itself reacting back upon our aesthetic opinion of the book. I suspect in fact that terms like 'artistic' and 'aesthetic' very often carry a treacherous suggestion of an autonomous realm of response or value which is diluted or perverted by any infusion or influence from what is claimed to be non-aesthetic. We must, I think, understand that an aesthetic whole is composed of non-aesthetic components whose interrelationship creates a new identity, rather than something distinct and unitary which excludes and is not connected with the non-aesthetic. Certainly, one could point to Johnson's own practice in, say, *The Lives of the Poets*, where there seems no doubt that his final artistic judgement on a work of art arises in part out of his moral and other judgements on the person of the author.

It is important that this point be stressed, for it is very common for the critic to be prepared to admit the dialectical connections between the work and the society and the reader, whilst maintaining its absolute separation from the author. C. S. Lewis, in *The Personal Heresy*, in which he claims that study of a work of literature should not include a concern with the person of the author, commits himself to exactly the same position as does Johnson:

> Even the reports of two scouts in war differ, and that with a differ-
> ence traceable to personality: for the braver man goes further and
> sees more; but the *value* of his report by no means consists in the fact
> that the intelligence officer, while he receives it, has the pleasure of
> meeting a brave man. [4]

Both Johnson and Lewis implicitly suggest that the aesthetic value of a work of art is only part of its total value, a position not dissimilar to Olson's division of the poem into two distinct identities. It seems to me that such a division cannot in the last resort be justified, if only because no satisfactory way of drawing the distinction between aesthetic and non-aesthetic value has ever been found—a point to which I will return later on in this chapter, and in chapter seven. The 'value' of the reports of the two scouts and the value of a literary work are in this respect comparable. The former has a value in immediate military terms, and a value in terms of the testimony it bears to human courage, endurance, and so on. Lewis's position depends on his approximation of the purely military value of the report to the aesthetic value of the art work, both being only aspects of the total value of report and art work. Once achieved, this division allows one to declare certain of the relationships which the art work has to be irrelevant to its aesthetic value.

My own position involves a fundamental disagreement with the implications contained in the statements by Johnson and Lewis. I have said that I feel that the use of such terms as 'artistic' and 'aesthetic' to qualify discussion of the nature of literary and artistic value is treacher-ous, for they imply not only a difference between aesthetic and non-aesthetic (or artistic) value, but a total and absolute division. I do not think that any dialectical approach to aesthetics can accept such a division, and I feel that in practice too, our responses to literature and art will be found to involve no such feeling of 'aesthetic' value absolutely distinct and utterly separable from other aspects of the value of the art work. If a dialectical approach to an understanding of the mode of being of the art work involves placing it, as Goldmann suggests, into as many 'significant wholes' as possible, then one of these must be seen to include some reference to the creator of the work. In short, I accept that the art work has a distinct identity, and that this can be accorded a value, but I deny that this value can be subdivided into mutually exclusive parts. The value of the art work, I would argue, is equivalent to the *total* value of Lewis's scout's report, and not merely to its military value. And even here, a dialectical analysis of the value of the report brought back by Lewis's brave scout would have to point out that the different forms of value that it has are not utterly separable. Immediately, the military value of the report rests in its giving certain information that allows the army to act in a way that will lead to obvious advances. But such value is in fact connected to the bravery of the scout. The enemy army may not have expected the scout to be brave enough to venture so near, so the subsequent military action will possess the virtue of surprise; the commanding officer's morale and determination to win will be strengthened by his admiration of the scout's bravery, the scout himself, in his feeling of pride and satisfaction, will contribute to the morale of the army, and so on. Now admittedly, the military value of the scout's report is only infinitesimally increased by the fact of his bravery, but even an infinitesimal increase serves to demonstrate that the military value of the report is not an autonomous part of the total value of the report. Similarly, I would argue, no one aspect of the value of a work of art is absolutely unconnected with another; there is no totally self-referential area of autonomous aesthetic value, which a work of art can possess in addition to other forms of value. Different aspects of the value of the work of art are, inevitably, dialectically connected.

This said, it must be admitted that no simple generalisation about the relationship between the writer and the work can be made without involving oneself in immediate and apparent distortion. The extent and nature of our consciousness of an author when reading a work of literature, and the importance such consciousness has in our total response, vary from work to work, from reader to reader, from reading to reading. I would however like to make some general comments on the role played in our response by our consciousness of the author. Marx makes an interesting comment in the first volume of *Capital* which serves as a useful introduction to a general consideration of the relationship between creator and created product. He notes that

> . . . it is generally by their imperfections as products, that the means of production in any process assert themselves in their character of products. A blunt knife or weak thread forcibly remind us of Mr. A., the cutler, or Mr. B., the spinner. In the finished product the labour by means of which it has acquired its useful qualities is not palpable, has apparently vanished.[5]

Sartre makes a very similar point in his *What is Literature?*, noting that the man who uses a tool is engaged in a chain of means and ends whose scope escapes him, unless the tool should break, when the whole chain becomes apparent.[6] The relevance of such a fact to the field of aesthetics can be seen in Graham Hough's point that one is sent back to consider the intentions of a writer far more by an unsuccessful than by a successful work.[7] As Goldmann puts it in another context, '. . . it is the sick organ which creates awareness',[8] or, as William Empson puts it in his poem 'Your Teeth are Ivory Towers', 'The safety valve alone / Knows the worst truth about the engine . . .'. There does seem to be a sense in which if the relationships between an object and ourselves are as we want them to be, we forget about the relationships between the object and other things or people. Similarly, the truly satisfying work of art does seem to gather around itself an impression of totality, 'wholeness' and self-sufficiency, so that our thoughts and responses seem to be fixed on 'it', rather than on the chain of factors and circumstances which produced it. It is arguable that we would not be able to make sense of the world unless we were able to exclude a consciousness of certain relationships with the outside world which are not immediately relevant to us, or at least to consider them, in Goldmann's phrase, as 'constants'. But just as Marx shows that if we want to understand (and, more importantly, change) the world, we must understand the complex of relationships that constitutes our world, so too if we want fully to understand the art work and its significance for us, we must understand the complex web of relationships which make it what it is for us. Just as the economist must think of Mr. A. the cutler even when he has a sharp knife, so the literary critic must think of Mr. X. the writer, even if his work is a work of genius and offers the reader total aesthetic satisfaction.

I have said that I believe that when relationships are more successfully ordered, then the identity of those persons or things which are related seems to be more satisfyingly and completely defined. In social terms the man whose relationships with others are stable and satisfying is himself stable and satisfied; it is when the relationship between Pirandello's Father and the Daughter is confused—he goes to a brothel and finds his daughter there—when, in short, something 'goes wrong', that his identity seems most confused and ill-defined. But the well-balanced individual constantly examines his relationships, even when there is no pressing need so to do, to avoid taking as permanent those things which may only be temporary; and the reading of literature places the same obligation on the reader who wishes to maintain a healthy and full conception of the identity of those works he reads. I thus feel that E. M. W. Tillyard's reply to Lewis is the correct one, that our response to a work of literature involves both a perception of its origin in a human personality, and an awareness of the necessary relationship between our response to a work of literature and our extra-literary knowledge of the author, where it exists. Talking of Keats, Tillyard argues that

> . . . I believe we read Keats in some measure because his poetry gives a version of a remarkable personality of which another version is his life. The two versions are not the same but they are analogous.[9]

I do not believe it to be possible to exclude from our response to Keats's poetry that admiration of him as a man which is aroused both by our knowledge of his life through his letters and the records left by his contemporaries, and by our reading of his poetry. Of course, as Tillyard implies, this is not the only value the poems have (the poet is not the only person with whom the poem is related), but it is part of that value, part of our response to the poems.

Talking of the novelist's attempted 'objectivity', Everett Knight points out that

> We admit . . . that the novelist could never in real life know all that he puts down, but then we justify this liberty by supposing the truth to exist somewhere, and so the novelist has a right to suggest what in all probability it is. But once again, there is no such truth except from a non-human point of view.[10]

As I have already argued that non-humanly perceived truth does not exist, the 'truth' of the novel must reside in terms of some human cognition, and the only humans who can perceive such a 'truth' are the writer and the reader. Thus, I would argue, the truth of art is dependent upon and defined by its cognition by the writer, and the reader. However, most readers are aware that in practice some works send us back to their creators far more insistently than do others. T. S. Eliot, in 'The Frontiers of Criticism', suggests that the extent to which information about the poem's creator helps us to understand it is neither simple nor constant.

> Each reader must answer it for himself, and must answer it not generally but in particular instances, for it may be more important in the case of one poet and less important in the case of another.[11]

Does this cut across my previous argument that the writer's relationship with the work is always of importance to a full appreciation of the identity of the work of art? I do not think so, for the answer, I think, lies in the fact that some works of literature give us the information we require about their relationships with their creator more immediately than do others, and some force us to move outside our immediate experience of the work of art to find what we require. It also depends upon where primarily the value of the work resides, for some works, like sharp knives, are more fruitfully examined in the context of their relationships with the perceiver-consumer, than in the context of their relationship with the creator.

As an example of this, Eliot in the same essay refers to Wordsworth's Lucy poems. Eliot notes that Sir Herbert Read and F. W. Bateson have suggested that Wordsworth's relationships with, respectively, Annette Vallon and his sister Dorothy, are crucial in understanding his poetry and, in particular, the Lucy poems. Eliot's response to these claims is as follows:

> Well, he (F. W. Bateson) may be right; his argument is very plausible. But the real question, which every reader of Wordsworth must answer for himself, is: does it matter? does this account help me to understand the Lucy poems any better than I did before? For myself, I can only say that a knowledge of the springs which released a poem is not necessarily a help towards understanding the poem: too much information about the origins of the poem may even break my contact with it. I feel no need for any light upon the Lucy poems beyond the radiance shed by the poems themselves.[12]

It seems to me that what in fact Eliot's argument boils down to is an assertion that of the significant wholes into which the poems in question can be placed, that of their genetic origin is often the least important. We should not automatically assume that in this case Eliot is guilty of an autonomist position with regard to the Lucy poems—although his comment about the 'radiance shed by the poems themselves' needs some qualification. Although I would argue that the total value of a poem must always include some value which accrues from the reader's consciousness of its relationship with its creator, and a consciousness of his personality, this may in fact constitute such a minimal proportion of its total value as to be in practice not worthy of lengthy examination. In a different context, Leszek Kolakowski stresses this very point:

> . . . the question of whether or not the knowledge of genesis is indispensable in understanding the "structure" is wrongly put. It simply depends on what we are asking. There are many questions

which we can try to answer without genetic enquiry and many others
which require a genetic explanation. In trying to understand how a
contemporary combustion engine works, the knowledge of its
historical development is irrelevant. Similarly we can understand the
functioning of banks without necessarily knowing the history of
credit since the Middle Ages. But we cannot really understand contemporary painting without knowing anything about the history of
painting. . . .[13]

Although Kolakowski is getting at an important distinction, it seems
to me that he overstates his case, for even in the case of the internal
combustion engine, understanding in a full sense how it 'works'
involves some limited knowledge of the socio-temporal context in
which it exists. But it is true that different investigations involve more
or less concern with genetic origins. As before, the final test of relevance
involves a reference at some time to human experience and practice. A
gun made in a socialist country and one made in a capitalist country
have in one sense very different genetic origins, but for the freedom-
fighter these differences do not in certain limited contexts affect the
usefulness of the guns. In a situation involving the immediate necessity
of possessing a gun, one is not likely to make minute enquiries involving
genetic origins. Richard did not bother to specify the parentage of the
horse he was prepared to exchange his kingdom for. But such immediate, pressing contexts are never permanent; and the freedom-fighter
over a long period of time is brought to realise that there is a difference
between guns made in socialist and capitalist countries, often from the
starting point that his guns seem to fall into the former category,
whereas the guns fired at him fall into the latter.

What Eliot's example of the Lucy poems demonstrates is that for the
reader who discovers (as I do) that the most remarkable thing about the
Lucy poems is the way in which they capture and isolate certain recurrent facts about the experience of love, the question of how Wordsworth came to discover these facts, and with which particular woman
or women, is not immediately a relevant question. As the poems'
relationships with the reader are effective and complex, the reader is
not driven immediately to consider the poems' relationships with their
creator, although I would argue that, as in the case of Kolakowski's
internal combustion engine, he must have some hazy idea of what these
were. To revert to Marx's example of the knife, it is certainly not
immediately relevant to a police investigation of the murder of an
individual with a knife to know the detailed chain of connections that

produced the knife. But such knowledge is held in suspension on the off-chance that it might be useful, and until this time arrives a generalised picture of this chain of connections, what Goldmann calls a 'constant', is held in the mind.

We may examine the question of the Lucy poems from another direction. If, as I will go on to argue in chapter eight, there are certain aspects of man's cognition of the external world which have an absolute quality, then it does not always concern us how these facts are arrived at in any particular case if they seem to accord with our own experience of the world. It was not all that important whether Newton's apple was ripe or unripe, sweet or sour. If the Lucy poems capture and describe certain features of sexual love which within the context of certain forms of social organisation are always true, then it does not much matter to the reader how, and with which particular woman or women, Wordsworth came to an appreciation of these truths. If, however, Wordsworth had later murdered his sister, and I were engaged in trying to prove that he had, I would doubtless find Bateson's identification of Lucy with Dorothy both interesting and revealing. This I think explains why it is that the detective work of someone like Livingston Lowes is often irrelevant to the reader of Coleridge's poems; it casts more light on Coleridge the man than on his poems, and affects our perception of the poems' identity only to an infinitesimal degree.

Our conception of an authorial relationship with the literary work is thus a relevant context within which the literary work should be considered, but its relevance may be very limited. Goldmann has pointed out one of the problems relating to biographical criticism apart from the problem of immediate relevance—that biographical information about an author is difficult to obtain and often unreliable. He also points out that the author's consciousness of what he is trying to do varies from case to case, and in like proportion the relevance and helpfulness of biographical information varies too. His final conclusion in *The Hidden God* is that the personality of the author may provide a sufficiently autonomous whole within which context to understand the work, but that in most cases this will not be so and biographical information about an author will perform only the auxiliary role of supplementing other contextual wholes within which the literary work can fruitfully be studied. The 'law of large numbers', or the fact that generalisations can more fruitfully be made about a large number of people in a fixed context than about one, also suggests that information about an author's socio-economic background will tend to be less treacherous than private information about his own life when it comes to interpreting a literary work. There are other more subtle questions of literary value which I wish to go on to examine later, which also affect this question. Goldmann notes that when an author's aspirations and world-view have a more direct correlation with certain historical movements in his time then his work is more likely to achieve greater value, and this obviously affects our consideration of the relevance of different sorts of biographical information if true. Eliot in fact, in his essay 'Wordsworth and Coleridge', written some time before 'The Frontiers of Criticism', argues that without a knowledge of the revolutionary faith and social passions of the young Wordsworth, such early poems as 'Resolution and Independence' cannot fully be understood. Such an area of linked social and biographical information would seem to stand a greater chance of relating to aspects of literary production which are important and valuable, than purely personal and idiosyncratic items of knowledge about a writer, which will normally only serve to solve puzzles of incomprehension and confusion in a literary work.

In 'Wordsworth and Coleridge', Eliot rejects what he calls 'sociological' criticism, by which he appears to mean something other than what is normally understood by this term, but goes on to make an impressive comment on the impossibility of separating the literary work from the contexts—both personal and social—within which it can best be understood.

> I only affirm that all human affairs are involved in one another, that consequently all history involves abstraction, and that in attempting to win a full understanding of the poetry of a period you are led to the consideration of subjects which at first sight appear to have little bearing on poetry.[14]

There is little if anything here with which a Marxist should be able to disagree, and this suggests that by 'sociological criticism' Eliot has in mind a mechanical relating of literature to society which denies the fact that the work of literature has an identity which renders it qualitatively different from its social origin. What Eliot's rejection of a biographical approach to the Lucy poems amounts to when seen in the context of the above statement (whilst bearing in mind that Eliot is not always consistent in such matters) is not so much an autonomist position as an insistence upon the fact that detailed knowledge about some of the relationships with the author that the literary work may possess may not be immediately relevant to an understanding of the literary work's relationship with human experience of a more general nature. One of the key elements in Eliot's position as stated above lies in his insistence on the movement *from* the poem *to* other subjects which are relevant *to* the poem. Now I have argued in my chapter on dialectics that any genuine movement towards understanding a literary work cannot be a simple one-stage movement from work to social background, but must involve what Rodway has referred to as a tacking movement, to and fro between artistic whole and wider context, in the course of which both the art work and the context are more fully defined, and define one another. However there would seem to be a simple but valid distinction to be made between an investigation which takes the literary work as its base, and goes out on sorties to other areas of knowledge relevant to that work, and investigations which take a different base—biographical understanding of the author, for example—which will inevitably throw some light upon his work, but will do so to a lesser degree than will the former mode of procedure.

In a recent essay W. K. Wimsatt has argued that if a poet writes a 'red' poem, we may assume that at some time he has 'seen red'; in other words, that the description of a particular human experience in a poem is in itself proof that the poet has had this experience.[15] As one might expect, given Wimsatt's attack on the 'affective' fallacy, this ignores the possibility that the 'redness' might be in part the creation of the reader, but this aside, if one were to apply this to the Lucy poems one could question the relevance of Bateson's identification of Lucy with Dorothy as follows: You argue that Wordsworth had a particular sort of relationship with Dorothy, which allowed him to write of this experience in the Lucy poems. However, since the poems themselves prove that Wordsworth must in some form or other have had such an experience, you have only argued in a particular case what any sensitive reader of the poems should already have known. Your approach eventually leads the reader on a circular route through the following propositions: The Lucy poems demonstrate that Wordsworth understood a particular aspect of the human experience of love; Wordsworth was in some way sexually involved with his sister; therefore we end up by throwing light not on the poems but on Wordsworth, in our final conclusion that Wordsworth's relationship with his sister can be understood more fully by reading the Lucy poems.

Now such an attack would have some justice, but it is not totally fair to Bateson's case. He does move from his speculations to a conclusion

about the poems, arguing that it was Wordsworth's perhaps sup-
pressed fear of the potentialities inherent in his relationship with his
sister that caused him to kill off Lucy in the poems.[16] If this interpretation answered all the questions that Lucy's death arouses in the mind of
the reader, it would, I feel, be trivial rather than true or false, and would
demonstrate the point I argued a few pages back, that purely personal
information about an author can at best only solve minor problems in
our reading of a literary work, but cannot relate to their greatness in any
appreciable sense. It is quite possible, although not proven, that Lucy's
death in the poems did perform this function for Wordsworth. What
should be apparent is that if this were the only significance that Lucy's
death had in the poems—that of solving a problem for Wordsworth—
then readers of the poems prior to Bateson's suggested solution would
have found Lucy's death a blemish on the poems, a merely confusing
element in otherwise aesthetically satisfying poetry. As we know that
this is not true, we are led to the conclusion that whether intentionally
or not, Wordsworth has presented this death in such terms as give it an
important aesthetic significance within the poem for the reader who is
in love neither with his sister nor anyone else who is sexually out of
bounds to him. William Empson makes a very similar point about
various semi-biographical attempts to 'explain' Keats's 'Ode to Melan-
choly' in *Seven Types of Ambiguity*, where, after having detailed a
number of 'opposite notions' united in the poem, he comments that

> Biographers who attempt to show from Keats's life how he came by
> these notions are excellently employed, but it is no use calling them
> in to explain why the poem is so universally intelligible and admired;
> evidently these pairs of opposites, stated in the right way, make a
> direct appeal to the normal habits of the mind.[17]

The distinction, as usual with Empson, is brilliantly and convincingly
detailed, and could, I feel, be applied with equal accuracy to the biographical sources of Lucy's death in the Lucy poems. I have argued in
an article elsewhere[18] that it seems probable that Lucy's death performs
a complex function in the poems, one which is associated with her
virginity which is paradoxically preserved by her death, and with a
larger complex of common male fantasies which abound in the
Romantic period, where the death of a loved one offers a fantasy
method of achieving control over her, whilst at the same time mirroring
a perception of the independence she has of the male. My suggestions
may well be wrong, it is certain that at best they are only partial. What

distinguishes them in an important sense from Bateson's, however, is that they connect with the reader's finding Lucy's death aesthetically important in the context of the poems, which Bateson's explanation does not. To put it another way, I feel that my explanation attempts to take into account the identity of the poem as perceived by the reader, which involves consideration of the reader-work relationship, whilst Bateson's explanation concentrates on the relationship between Wordsworth's private fantasy-life and the poem, which impinges only marginally on the identity of the poem for the reader. Perhaps another quotation from Eliot's 'The Frontiers of Criticism', by describing the literary work in terms of an emergent, gives us a theoretical explanation for the relative irrelevance of biographical information which can be incorporated directly into a Marxist aesthetic:

> When the poem has been made, something new has happened, something that cannot be wholly explained by *anything that went before*. That, I believe, is what we mean by 'creation'.[19]

In other words, 'the poem' is not just the sum of its sources, is not just a part of the context of its creator's life and consciousness, but involves the totality of its mediations with the outside world, some of which are, *from the viewpoint of the reader*, more important than others.

It needs to be remembered that when it is said that a literary work has an identity or relative autonomy, this is not to imply that such an identity is fixed and unchanging. As I suggested when I considered the problems involved in arriving at a dialectical critical method, for every different context the work's identity changes in some way, and if an 'aesthetic' response to a literary work is seen to involve a placing of it in a number of different contexts, its aesthetic identity must be seen to be a multi-faceted whole. Eliot, again in 'The Frontiers of Criticism', seems to appreciate this point well when he notes that

> . . . the enjoyment of poetry can be a complex experience in which several different forms of satisfaction are mingled; and they may be mingled in different proportions for different readers.[20]

Just as a Marxist aesthetic must reject the idea of the autonomous, 'objective' art work, it must I think also reject similar ideas of the autonomy of the aesthetic response to the art work, or of any other part of the totality of the aesthetic process. The most common mistake made in the field of literary criticism relating to a confusion between identity and autonomy, is that which involves ignoring the necessary dialectic between the perceiver of the art work and the art work itself. I wish to treat this question more fully in a subsequent chapter, but would like to stress at this point that the art work can never be seen merely in the context of that 'autonomous whole' represented by its relationship with its creator, because such an autonomy would, as with the autonomous art work, exclude the perceiver. This mistake has been made by widely differing individuals concerned with widely different subjects. There is an ironic similarity between the arguments of the Chicago critic R. S. Crane, who states that

> . . . there can be no genuine refutation of a critical position except within the particular framework of concepts and rules of inference in which it has been asserted. . . .[21]

and Louis Althusser's assertion that it is only from within the particular problematic of the young Marx that the early writings of Marx can be understood.[22] Such a position would lead to acceptance of the assertion that it is only from within the ideology of fascism that one can understand and refute fascist arguments, whereas of course precisely the opposite is true. I have the impression that certain arguments advanced by linguistic philosophers who follow the later Wittgenstein are comparable to those of Crane and Althusser in this respect, although my knowledge in this sphere is only partial. To say, for example, that one can only talk about religious belief from within the language game of religion, seems to me to be asserting exactly the same sort of autonomy and self-determination in religious matters as Crane advances in literary matters and Althusser in political ones. I would have thought that Christians had as little excuse as Marxists for this sort of claim, as both systems include a conception of totality within which there cannot be autonomous, self-determined 'wholes' without bringing basic tenets of belief into question. The other implication of such a claim which again I would have thought Christians would needs be embarrassed by is that a Christian cannot convince an Atheist of the error of his ways except from within the language game of Atheism, which would involve the would-be evangelical Christian in certain major crises of conscience.

Attacking Althusser's position, Leszek Kolakowski points out that even in the domain of mathematics, which Althusser claims produces its own criteria of validity without recourse to "external" guarantees, the discussion of what constitutes a criteria of validity in mathematics proceeds in a manner which gives the lie to Althusser.[23] As Caudwell points out, the criteria of validity of any scientific truth is that it can be tested in the context of social practice by other men, and that it is in Marxism's rejection of any 'self-determined spheres of qualities' that its qualitative difference from other philosophies rests.[24] Althusser's 'scientific' examination of the early Marx turns out to be less 'scientific' than he claims.[25]

I said earlier on in this chapter that the extent to which the author was *conscious* of the relationship of what he was trying to achieve with his personal and social situation was important, and was related to the extent to which biographical information about him helped us to come to terms with his work. If this is so, then the fact that for different writers the creative process can involve different levels of consciousness of what they are trying to achieve obviously has some bearing on the extent to which biographical criticism is a helpful approach to their work. I do not want at this point to get involved in a discussion of psychoanalysis, about which I know little, but I would reiterate that it is probably more helpful to talk about different levels of consciousness in a more subtle manner than dualistic or triadic divisions of human consciousness usually allow. The writer can never be completely unconscious of some of the mediations with the external world that the art work has unless he writes whilst asleep; on the other hand, he can never be wholly conscious of all the contexts of which the art work may form a part. Any use of biographical information in a critical examination of a text must involve some consideration of the extent to which the author is conscious of the relationships which are being suggested. For example, the progression one can see from William Empson's critical perception of ambiguity of a largely unconscious type in poetry, through to his own poetic use of what Richard Eberhart has referred to as 'conscious ambiguity'[26] obviously involves a change in the significance of biographical information which seeks to explain and understand such ambiguity.

If we consider that commonly-described feeling of authors that one word is 'right' in a way that another is not, it is possible to see that no simple use of concepts of consciousness or unconsciousness is adequate to describe the process that is taking place. In one sense the writer is not conscious of why the word is right, it just 'feels' right. But in another sense one could argue that in this feeling there is the basis for an analysis leading to understanding of why the word is right. Very often the reader can move from a difficulty in reading a poem back to the author's feeling of 'rightness' through examination of textual alteration, and achieve a perception of the significance of the word which poring over the poem alone would not give him. The dialectical tacking moves from partly-comprehended poem, to the context of authorial alteration and 'feeling', back to better-comprehended poem. In an essay entitled 'Difficulty and Surface Value', Calvin S. Brown describes a similar process, distinguishing between the end-stopped movement involved in solving a puzzle, and the open-ended, creative process of building up a poem's identity:

> In the cryptogram, the puzzle disappears when the solution is reached, but in the difficult poem puzzle and solution coexist in the reader's mind. If the poem must be studied and puzzled out to begin with, a subsequent reading performs the operation rapidly and easily; the solution is now *inherent in the poem itself* and is consequently a part of its aesthetic impact.[27]

Brown's 'studying and puzzling' may involve more than just a poring over the poem: it may involve, as I have suggested, going out to other contexts than that of the poem itself so as to enrich the poem; building up the identity of the poem by consideration of its relationships. Brown's comments here are important because they show how study of a poem's relationships actually changes its identity.

A concern with unconscious elements in the literary process of comparatively recent date has bred a distinctive school of literary criticism— psychological criticism. Of course the growing awareness of the fact that writers and readers of literature are not always totally conscious of what is going on in a work of literature was not something that resulted from the development of psychology alone; William Empson has named Darwin, Marx and Frazer as well as Freud as those primarily responsible for a belief that the writer does not always know what he is doing.[28] It would be true to say, however, that of these four, it has been Freud who has most influenced the study of the unconscious in literature. I do not intend at this point to enter into an extended critique of psychological criticism; the subject is by no means so well-defined as to allow any brief treatment of it, and an extended treatment would not be immediately relevant to my present purpose. The extent to which psychological critics concentrate upon analysis of the unconscious of the reader or the writer, the extent to which they equate the two (in more archetypal critical theories), and the extent to which elements of the unconscious are seen to be unique, or shared within common social or personal situations, all these produce different forms of psychological criticism. What I would like to do is to examine some of the larger questions relevant to the general theme of this book raised by the unconscious, in the context of two examples of psychological criticism.

From the point of view of the basic critical division with which I started, psychological criticism would in general tend to be classed with Marxist criticism by many, in as much as it examines the relationships between the work and the writer or the reader, very often, it is claimed, at the expense of respect for the identity of the work of literature. The psychological critic has very often been suspected of using the work of literature as a means rather than an end, as a way into the mind of either reader or writer rather than as the end towards which all investigation should proceed and on which it should eventually rest. I feel that this has in some cases been a justified accusation, although if the critic is quite open about what he is doing then using the work as means rather than end seems to me to be a perfectly respectable operation, although obviously not a complete one. However, I feel that it is important that the critic should know what he is doing, and should realise that valid as certain of the methodological tools of modern psychology may be, if they are to be used by the literary critic they must be used in a manner which respects the identity of the work of literature. Perhaps I can make this point more clearly by referring to two essays written from what is basically a psychological approach: Geoffrey Gorer's 'The Myth in Jane Austen', and Norman N. Holland's 'The "Unconscious" of Literature: The Psychoanalytic Approach'. I choose these two examples because they seem to me to be examples of helpful and unhelpful uses of psychology and psychoanalytic theory in literary criticism, and this relates not to the validity of the particular theories used by them—which I am anyway not qualified to judge—but to the way in which these theories are used.

Geoffrey Gorer, in his 'The Myth in Jane Austen', isolates a particular 'myth' which he finds in all Jane Austen's novels except *Persuasion*. The myth involves the recurrent situation in most of the novels relating to the heroines' attitudes towards fathers and father-figures, and towards mothers. In *Persuasion*, instead of the heroine rejecting the 'Charming but Worthless' lover (who has of course become somewhat less worthless), she eventually marries him, and her attitude towards her father and mother is the reverse of what it was in the former novels. Gorer argues that the earlier myth had performed the function of asserting Jane Austen's belief in the rightness of her domestic situation, and that eventually, by reworking her fantasies,

. . . Jane Austen had finally uncovered for herself the hidden motive behind the too warm, too loving family relationships which circumscribed her life. Using symbols, she analyzed her own problems; *Persuasion* was her final solution. In this book she cried out against her starved life, and the selfishness of the fathers and sisters on whose account it had been starved . . .[29]

Gorer makes no larger claims for the significance of the pattern which he claims to have unearthed. He gives a feasible explanation for the recurrence of certain common situations in the novels, and for the apparent final rejection of this recurrent element in *Persuasion*. Although there is much reference to the author of the novels, we feel that Gorer is primarily interested in coming to terms with certain problems thrown up by a normal reading of the novels, rather than in investigating Jane Austen's private life because of the intrinsic interest of such an operation. More significantly, Gorer leaves almost untouched the question of the relationship between the aesthetic value of the novels and the result of his investigations. The reader would probably have preferred some indication of what Gorer thought this was, but at least he does not try to reduce the aesthetic value of the novels to their implied function of having provided Jane Austen with a means for psychological understanding and release. The reader is allowed to incorporate Gorer's insights—if he agrees with them—into his own response to the novels. I think that there is an important distinction to be made here between Gorer's approach and Bateson's comments on the Lucy poems, for whereas the unconscious elements in Wordsworth's creative mind are not directly connected with the aesthetic appeal of the Lucy poems, one's reading of Jane Austen's novels does throw up certain problems which can possibly be at least partially resolved by a reading of Gorer's essay. In other words, Gorer's essay seems to me to attempt to come to terms with certain problems which arise for the reader who respects the identity of Jane Austen's novels, whereas Bateson's comments on the Lucy poems seem to me to be—irrespective of their validity—almost entirely extrinsic to the aesthetic value of the poems, separate from their literary identity.

Norman N. Holland's essay seems to me to be an awful warning of what psychological criticism which does not start with a respect for the identity of the work can lead to. Holland's essay is concerned with Frost's poem 'Mending Wall', a poem which is itself concerned with the problem of relationships, and the extent to which defining an identity can paradoxically lead to a better relationship with another. In order to

facilitate reference I will quote the poem in full here, as Holland does in
his essay.

Mending Wall

Something there is that doesn't love a wall,
That sends the frozen-ground-swell under it
And spills the upper boulders in the sun,
And makes gaps even two can pass abreast.
The work of hunters is another thing:
I have come after them and made repair
Where they have left not one stone on a stone
To please the yelping dogs. The gaps I mean,
No one has seen them made or heard them made,
But at spring mending-time we find them there.
I let my neighbour know beyond the hill;
And on a day we meet to walk the line
And set the wall between us once again.
We keep the wall between us as we go.
To each the boulders that have fallen to each.
And some are loaves and some so nearly balls
We have to use a spell to make them balance:
'Stay where you are until our backs are turned!'
We wear our fingers rough with handling them.
Oh, just another kind of outdoor game,
One on a side. It comes to little more:
He is all pine and I am apple orchard.
My apple trees will never get across
And eat the cones under his pines, I tell him.
He only says, 'Good fences make good neighbors.'
Spring is the mischief in me, and I wonder
If I could put a notion in his head:
'*Why* do they make good neighbors? Isn't it
Where there are cows? But here there are no cows.
Before I built a wall I'd ask to know
What I was walling in or walling out,
And to whom I was like to give offense.
Something there is that doesn't love a wall,
That wants it down.' I could say 'Elves' to him,
But it's not elves exactly, and I'd rather
He said it for himself. I see him there,
Bringing a stone grasped firmly by the top
In each hand, like an old-stone savage armed.
He moves in darkness as it seems to me,
Not of woods only and the shade of trees.

He will not go beyond his father's saying,
And he likes having thought of it so well
He says again, 'Good fences make good neighbors.'

Holland never makes it quite clear whether he is concerned with the unconsciousness of the reader or the writer; he refers to '. . . what might be called the "unconscious content" of the work',[30] which fails to give a precise location to this unconscious element. His approach does however suggest that for all practical purposes he equates the two.

Holland's basic approach to a psychoanalytic understanding of the poem can be demonstrated by abstraction over a wide area of his essay. He writes

> When we explicate a literary work in the regular way, we proceed, I take it, in a series of three steps. First, we go through the text noticing particular words, images, phrasings, incidents, and the like.
> . . . .
> The second is to group these individual *aperçus* into themes.
> . . . .
> We can now take the third step, namely, using this knowledge of the oral stage to hypothesize a nucleus of fantasy that will bring together the separate themes and images of the poem with reference to the unconscious mind.[31]

I should, to be fair, point out that Holland distinguishes between two triadic explicatory processes—the 'regular' and the 'psychoanalytic'. However as both of them seem to be equally guilty of certain faults, and as the distinction between the two is not made clear in the course of his essay, this does not seem to affect my argument. Given the above statements of method, I think that the positive qualities of the New Critics stand out in sharp relief. In particular, the insistence of the latter on examining parts of the poem in the initial context of the poem can be contrasted with Holland's failure at any point in his essay to suggest that the poem is in some way a distinct 'whole' within which its parts assume a significance different from that which they have when abstracted from the poem. To suggest that the first step in explicating a poem is to go through the text 'noticing particular words, phrasings, incidents' and so on is to insist from the very outset that the critic should try not just to ignore the identity of the literary work, but actively to break it down, and construct as soon as possible a *new* and distinct context within which the words, phrases and so on can be understood. It is as if, in order to understand the role a brick played in the house of which it formed a part, the investigator had first to bulldoze down the house, stack the bricks in neat piles (according to a preconceived plan) and then set about seeing what the brick was doing.

I say 'preconceived' advisedly, for Holland has already decided that the poem must be an expression of one or another psychological fantasy stage—oral, anal, urethral, phallic and oedipal. A passing tear can be shed for the sad fate of our literary greatness, reduced to demonstrating various authors' fantasy involvements with their genitals, mouth or mother. Holland jumps to the conclusion that the poem is rooted in the oral stage, '. . . because of its references to speech and eating, both associated with the mouth.'[32] If we cast our eyes back to the poem for these references, we find that they consist of the narrator's talking to his neighbour, of the apple orchard and the cows, and of the fact that some of the stones are shaped like loaves. The fact that the poem might be more concerned with talking as communication rather than as an expression of oral eroticism, that the apple orchard and the cows have primarily a relevance related to the need for walls on farms, and that 'loaves' may have been the most accurate way to describe the shape of some stones, seems to have escaped Holland. He in fact confirms that the poem must refer to the oral stage, because it doesn't fall into any of the other 'familiar stages of childhood development'. Oh the delights of a self-enclosed, self-referential system! Personally, I would have thought that the phallic qualities of the pine trees, or the oedipal suggestions inherent in the cows (cow-milk-mother etc.) could have alternative psychoanalytic explanations for the devoted investigator. However, as if unwilling to leave any psychoanalytic stone unturned, Holland suggests in a note that recent psychoanalytic writings might lead us back to the poem,

> . . . and additional levels of fantasy, anal and phallic, in the boulders: as mess, as balls, 'handling them', and so on.[33]

And so on indeed. A vista of inexhaustible critical potentiality opens up before us. The palpable absurdity of the interpretations offered above, which ignore the possibility that the stones are meant to be considered as stones, that the poem is about mending walls made of stones, ignores the fact that there is no textual justification whatever for seeing them as either excrement or as testicles. And as the poet talks of wearing his fingers rough with handling them, the latter interpretation would appear to have certain mind-boggling ramifications.

I am insistently reminded at this point of the old joke about the psychiatrist giving a patient an ink-blot test. Each time the patient sees a blot, he tells the psychiatrist that he reminds him of sex. Eventually the psychiatrist explodes: 'You're obsessed with sex.' 'What about you,' replies the patient, 'showing me all those dirty pictures?' If the critic approaches a poem convinced that it will fall into one of a number of predetermined patterns, then the poem's identity will be destroyed in order to rebuild the image of the critic's obsession. But he will not have 'got anything out of' the poem, he will have used the poem as a means towards an end unconnected with the poem's identity as a work of literature. It is in view of all this ironic that the poem 'Mending Wall' is itself very much concerned with the whole question of preserving identity through respecting differences. Frost, using his unmentioned name as an incipient pun all the way through the poem, suggests that walls are of use only to prevent aggressive or destructive incursions into another's territory, but the poem works against this stated argument, suggesting (through the narrator's willing partaking of the rebuilding responsibility) that the more differences are defined, the better relationships are. The critic too must be aware of the need to respect walls, however much he may be tempted to see them as merely barriers to closer communion with the literary work, for when the walls which define the identity of the literary work are broken down, that identity changes.

Theories of the unconscious should therefore be used with great care in literary analysis, and should not lead the critic to believe that they give him a simple key to understanding the precise nature of the relationship between the literary work and its creator or its reader. We should however be conscious of the fact that a writer's consciousness of what he is writing, and the nature of this consciousness, varies from writer to writer and from age to age. In some cases the literary work can be seen as the intended result of a rational, conscious process of composition, in other cases it seems to be more like an emergent, connected in a far more subtle way with its creator. In his book on Kant, Lucien Goldmann suggests that the gravely sick individual is conscious only of his sickness, but that the healthy individual has his attention directed away from himself towards the external world, which he seeks to know and understand.[34] It is obvious that a writer in the former situation will tend to be less conscious of the significance of what he is writing, because for a start he is less conscious of the significance of his own life in a given situation. In addition the evidence would suggest that the writer has greater conscious control over his writing, more direct appreciation of its significance, in an ordered society of which he perceives himself to be an accepted part. One need only compare the general characteristics of eighteenth-century English literature with those of Romantic English literature to confirm this as a general rule. In the latter period, theories of the art work as emergent, as something 'new' and distinct from its creator, become far more prevalent, and it seems undeniable that the relationship between the conscious intentions, beliefs and attitudes of the writer, and the finished work, are more subtle and complex in the Romantic period than in the preceding one. It can be noted that there is an obvious relationship between this fact and the greater stress laid on the idea of the organic nature of the literary work.

Given such variation, a number of critics have argued strongly against *any* consideration of the author forming part of the process of literary criticism. Of these, Wimsatt and Beardsley in their article 'The Intentional Fallacy', and C. S. Lewis in his part of *The Personal Heresy* have argued most strongly against the critical relevance of the relationship between writer and work. The aim of the former writers is less all-inclusive than is that of C. S. Lewis, for they take care to distinguish between the use of biographical information in general, and the use of the 'intention' of the author as a basis for literary criticism. They note that biographical information may present us with knowledge as mundane but necessary as the meaning certain words normally had for a given author. Their argument is well summed up early on in the essay in the following manner:

> . . . to insist on the designing intellect as a *cause* of a poem is not to grant the design or intention as a *standard* by which the critic is to judge the worth of the poet's performance. . . . One must ask how a critic expects to get an answer to the question about intention. How is he to find out what the poet was trying to do? If the poet succeeded in doing it, then the poem itself showed what he was trying to do. And if the poet did not succeed, then the poem is not adequate evidence, and the critic must go outside the poem—for evidence of an intention that did not become effective in the poem.[35]

There seem to me to be a number of weaknesses in this initially convincing rejection of intentionalism, which it is worth considering now. For a start, I find that the argument presupposes a very simplistic idea of what is meant by the writer's intention, ignoring the possibility that an examination of intention can deal with more than a simple one-stage transference of idea from mind to paper. But more important is the suggestion that if the artist succeeds in what he is trying to do, then the poem will itself show what he was trying to do. The fact that a poet has been totally satisfied with his poem has never been sufficient to prevent disagreement about the poem, for the dimension of reader-response introduces a complicating factor which Wimsatt and Beardsley, concerned to see the poem as 'objective whole', cannot take into their considerations. There is in fact a confusion here between the poet's success in getting something into the poem he is writing, and getting the reader of the poem to appreciate the fact that he has succeeded here, a confusion which is related to the subsequent rejection of the 'Affective Fallacy' on the part of Wimsatt and Beardsley.

In fact some conception of authorial intention is absolutely necessary to adequate appreciation of a poem. It is difficult to find a firm principle on the basis of which one can reject intentionalism in general and accept the study of biographical information to determine the meaning of an author's words, or 'the dramatic character of his utterance', both of which are very intimately and subtly related to larger questions of aristic intention. It is true to say, as do Wimsatt and Beardsley, that the poem belongs to the public rather than to the critic or the poet, and thus cannot be reduced to the author's intention. But to say a poem cannot be *reduced* to the poet's intention is not the same as saying that a conception of the latter plays *no* part in an adequate response to the poem.

Beardsley has brought other arguments to bear against intentionalism in his book *Aesthetics* which are worth considering at this juncture. Part of his case seems to me to be assertion rather than argument, as in the following passage:

> If a quality can be seen in a statue *only* by someone who already believes that it was intended by the sculptor to be there, then that quality is not in the statue at all. For what can be seen only by one who expects and hopes to see it is what we would call illusory by ordinary standards . . .[36]

On the contrary, a good many things that are seen by many people are only seen because various social pressures lead them to look for and expect that which they eventually see. Beardsley's argument is a classic case of individualism, which ignores the fact that perception is not just an individual activity, but is conditioned by various social elements in the way we see the world. Expectation inevitably enters into our interpretation of what our senses bring before us as evidence; a mouthful of tea drunk when the recipient is expecting coffee has a peculiarly foul taste. But apart from this, it is just not possible to read a poem without having some conception of intention on the poet's part—unless a computer ignores Dr. Leavis's scepticism and manages to write a poem. This being so, we should be concerned not to avoid any consideration of the poet's intention, but to arrive at as accurate and helpful a knowledge of it as each reading seems to require. Beardsley offers another relevant argument in a different context, where he is talking about the truth-value of literary statements. He argues that

> . . . the sentence has truth-value quite independently of any intentions or wishes if the unique referent exists, and does not if it doesn't. And this is borne out by the practice of the courts, for it is possible for a person to libel another unintentionally.[37]

Thus, if a novelist writes about a certain character called Monroe Beardsley, even if he has never heard of the critic Beardsley, a court would uphold that the name 'referred' to the real Monroe Beardsley, and proceed accordingly. However, we should not allow ourselves, in this or any other area of discussion, to be too much influenced by court practice. There is an obvious difference here between literary response and legal responsibility which renders the analogy ineffective. In other areas of legal procedure establishing intention is of very great consequence, and there is no reason why this fact should not be equally relevant to literary response. An argument which depends on the peculiarities of the law of libel in some countries but not in others does not stand on a very firm basis.

Quite apart from legal analogies, it would seem to me to be clear that the truth-reference that literary statements have cannot be determined by recourse to any simple test, but must take into account all the components in the literary process at a given time—or as many as is feasible. Consider the example of a modern writer reading Ezra Pound's 'Hugh Selwyn Mauberley', and coming to the section entitled 'Mr. Nixon', which is a first-person description of how to make as much money from writing as possible. Now the poem contains no indication of to whom—if anyone—this makes particular reference. Our writer might read it for the first time, and imagine that it referred to no-one in particular, but was a literary amalgam of a number of unpleasant traits that Pound had noted in various writers. The truth reference would thus be to the characteristics of a 'type' of writer. But suddenly our reader realises that many of the things said by Mr. Nixon have been said by himself, and it dawns on him that the passage could very well refer to himself. In a state of some agitation he goes and visits a friend, and tells him this, and is told by the friend not to worry, as Pound wrote the passage using his knowledge of Arnold Bennett, to whom the passage 'really' refers.

Now it seems to me obvious that the intelligent reader, unlike Monroe Beardsley's law court, does not have to arbitrate between the respective claims of these three possible references and decide on one of them. In different circumstances and in different senses the passage in question 'refers' to all three possible things in the extra-poetic world, and it is part of the richness of literature that it does have this multiple reference. In some poems authorial intention is crucial in determining the meaning, in others it is not, just as in some poems a knowledge of a particular historical fact can be crucial, whereas it can be irrelevant to another. Our decision on such matters must always refer to as specific a reading situation as possible.

Wayne Booth argues against too mechanical an identification of author and work in his book *The Rhetoric of Fiction*, when he attacks the use of an implied 'sincerity' on the part of an author as a means of evaluating his work.

> A great work establishes the "sincerity" of its implied author, regardless of how grossly the man who created that author may belie in his *other* forms of conduct the values embodied in his work. For all we know, the only sincere moments of his life may have been lived as he wrote the novel.[38]

Even in such a situation as this, however, there has inevitably to be seen some relationship between 'implied author' and the man who created him, for as Booth demonstrates elsewhere in his book, the author cannot escape all responsibility by hiding behind his persona, for it is he who creates that persona in the first place. Of course over-mechanical attempts to relate the values lived in a man's life and the values contained in his work, or attempts to derive the latter from the former, need to be resisted; but this is again not to say that there is no connection between the two. The book does live a life separate from its author, but the author as human being will always exist within the book so long as it is considered as art rather than as a natural phenomenon, and so long as this is true a full literary response will want to consider the relationship between the author and his work. To say, as do Wimsatt and Beardsley, that the poem belongs to the public, is embodied in language, which is the peculiar possession of the public, and is about the human being—an object of public knowledge—is not effectively to demonstrate that it is unconnected with its creator. To continue Beardsley's legal analogies, one could point to the fact that an obscene slogan on a wall belongs to the public, is very often about the human being, and is embodied in language, but that this does not prevent a policeman from arresting the person who is suspected of having put it there, rather than those other people seen reading it and laughing at it. Wimsatt and Beardsley claim too that the poem is 'detached from the author at birth and goes about the world beyond his power to intend about it or control it',[39] but again this fact has no bearing on whether or not a perception of the author's intention forms part of an adequate reader response. A poem is a historical act as well as a free agent in the world, and can only be fully comprehended in the light of its genesis. Helen Gardner has shown how I. A. Richards's experiments with undated, anonymous poems proved only that 'divorced from their human and historical context, works were deprived of their power to speak to the heart and conscience'. A reading of the responses of Richards's students to such disembodied texts shows that one of the reasons for their eccentric readings was their insulation from evidence which would help them to determine authorial intention. T. S. Eliot is right to say that a poem cannot be reduced to what the poet experiences or wants to communicate,[40] but neither can the poem be totally detached from a conception of these factors. Otherwise we have no grounds for preferring our response to Swift's *A Modest Proposal* or Defoe's *The Shortest Way with Dissenters* to those of contemporary readers of Swift and Defoe who took the two works seriously and failed to perceive any element of satire in them.

I think that a practical example of the importance of some knowledge of authorial intention might make my argument a little less abstract at this moment, and I would like to look here at William Empson's poem, 'Note on Local Flora', which I feel offers much more to the reader with some understanding of what Empson's intentions were.

Note on Local Flora

There is a tree native in Turkestan,
Or further east towards the Tree of Heaven,
Whose hard cold cones, not being wards to time,
Will leave their mother only for good cause;
Will ripen only in a forest fire;
Wait, to be fathered as was Bacchus once,

Through men's long lives, that image of time's end.
I knew the Phoenix was a vegetable.
So Semele desired her deity
As this in Kew thirsts for the Red Dawn.

Empson has always implicitly admitted the need for his readers to be aware of his intentions, as he has always been very ready to offer notes and explanations to his poems, and to reveal intention in a more subtle way by actually reading the poems. (Julian Trevelyan, in his autobiography *Indigo Days*, describes Empson whilst still an undergraduate at Cambridge, reading his poems in a low drone, then accenting suddenly unexpected words to bring out some hidden cross meaning.)[41] In his 'Note on Notes' in the *Collected Poems*, Empson justifies his provision of notes as follows:

> It is impertinent to expect hard work from the reader merely because you have failed to show what you were comparing to what, and though to write notes on such a point is a confession of failure it seems an inoffensive one. . . . Also there is no longer a reasonably small field which may be taken as general knowledge. It is impertinent to suggest that the reader ought to possess already any odd bit of information one may have picked up in a field where one is oneself ignorant . . .[42]

As with so much that Empson says, this is so common-sensical that it seems difficult to imagine any possible objection to it; and of course in as much as the poet is allowed to give the reader information about facts, remembering my earlier comments on the subject-object dialectic, he is also giving him information about intentions. Now as far as the poem 'Note on Local Flora' is concerned, Empson does give us information which helps us to understand and respond to the poem. He points out that he picked up the information about the tree from 'a label affixed to it by the management' in Kew Gardens.[43] Knowing this the reader is able to read the poem secure in the knowledge that the tree referred to is not a metaphysical invention on Empson's part, but is a real tree which has an existence in the real world, and I think that this does make a difference to our understanding of the poem, for it means that the poem progresses from factual description through mythical reference to (I would claim) contemporary analogy, in a way that convinces us of the wide-reference, if not universality, of what Empson is talking about.

The reader of the poem who meets with it in Empson's *Collected*

Poems might also be misled by the fact that this volume has as its frontispiece a quotation from the Buddhist *Fire Sermon*, and might suspect that the poem was meant to refer to the religious ideas contained in the *Fire Sermon* referring to fire. Again, it is useful to be able to refer to Empson's comment on the significance of the mention of fire in his poetry:

> . . . when I mention fire in my verse I mean it to have the usual confused background of ideas, not . . . the specific and raging doctrine of the Fire Sermon.[44]

So the reader can now settle down to read the poem with a certain basic knowledge of the author's intention behind the poem of a very simple nature, which, as Empson himself says, it would really be impertinent to expect him to do without. However, intention can be a far more subtle thing than the rather crude pieces of information that I have proffered constitute. I have mentioned Empson's reading of his own poetry, and must say that my understanding of many of his poems has been considerably increased by listening to him read his own poems on record. As far as 'Note on Local Flora' is concerned, the crucial point that comes over when we hear Empson reading the poem is that it is meant to be humorous, at least in part. No-one who heard Empson read the line 'I knew the Phoenix was a vegetable', could ever find it anything but humorous—a deliberate anti-climax after the somewhat erudite mythical references earlier on.

What Empson seems to be doing here, as the quotation from his 'Note on Notes' suggests he often does, is comparing something to something else. The poem suggests that just as the tree, wrenched out of its normal context, is waiting for something which will not come, so too there are in contemporary society those who are similarly waiting, in a political and a religious sense. Empson's note to the poem compares the forest fire to the final burning of the world, and the capitalised 'Red Dawn' surely suggests a reference to political revolution. Thus the tree is humorously compared to the believer waiting for the second coming, and the revolutionary in an unrevolutionary society and situation, waiting for social upheaval. The effect of this yoking of themes together is to suggest a gentle and sympathetic humour at the expense of those, like the tree, who exist in an environment unsuited to their potentialities. The poem is not a tremendously profound one, but it does I think have a pleasing air of thoughtfulness and sympathy about it.

Now for the reader who attempts to approach the poem without

some information about the author's intentions, the poem offers certain
infuriating problems. Thom Gunn, reviewing the first edition of
Empson's *Collected Poems*, got himself into a number of tangles over
this particular poem which can be traced back to his having insufficient
information about the author's intention. His ignorance is partly excus-
able, although I feel not wholly so. Gunn starts from certain assumptions
about Empson taken from his critical writings, which he seems to
misinterpret anyway, but which he has no right to apply to Empson's
poetry.

> Empson is called a metaphysical, but, although Donne and Marvell
> are his chief inspirations, nothing could be more extravagantly
> romantic than to work on the notion that every word has endless
> layers of meaning . . . To the flabby vagueness of the modern
> romantics is opposed not rationality but an irrational use of the
> intellect.[45]

As one might suspect, with such an antagonistic (and inaccurate) conception of Empson's poetic intentions, Gunn makes heavy going of
'Note on Local Flora':

> . . . try as I can I am not able to see what the last line means. Is
> 'this' simply a tree in Kew Gardens? In that case, why does it thirst
> for a Red Dawn, which is surely meant politically? If it refers to a
> person being compared to a tree, what person is it? Not Empson
> himself, one assumes, since he appears to have been free from the
> more emotional side of the political enthusiasms of the 'thirties. If
> not Empson, who? And if a person is being compared to a tree in
> Kew Gardens, surely it would be simpler to omit Kew Gardens and
> compare the person directly to the tree of which the description
> starts in the first line. If, on the other hand, a tree in Kew is simply
> being compared to the tree in the first line, then the political con-
> notation of the Red Dawn is also a red herring, and extremely
> confusing.[46]

Confusion there certainly is, but it seems to me obvious that it is Gunn's
and not Empson's, and that it relates to Gunn's partly-wilful misunder-
standing of the intention behind the poem. Johnson's wonderment at
Donne's trepidity in comparing a man to a telescope is nothing to
Gunn's at Empson's comparison of a person to a tree, although if a
Johnsonian comparison is to be sought, perhaps his inability to ap-
preciate the double references to cat and nymph in Gray's 'Ode on the
Death of a Favourite Cat' would be a more appropriate one.

If, therefore, we treat the theories of Wimsatt and Beardsley with extreme caution, preferring to retain a belief in the not infrequent indispensability of some knowledge of authorial intention, how much more cautious must we be of C. S. Lewis's arguments in *The Personal Heresy*, where Lewis is led to claim that because

> Every work of art that lasts long in the world is continually taking on these new colours which the artist neither foresaw nor intended[47]

and because the value of the poem consists in what it does to its readers, 'all questions about the poet's own attitude to his utterance are irrelevant'.[48] A number of non-sequiturs here merit attention. Because the work of art is continually taking on new colours one cannot assume that readers' responses are entirely separate from a conception of authorial presence and intention in the poem. 'What the poem does to the readers' is arguably dependent to some extent upon what readers think of the author's relationship with his poem, even if they obtain such information, or grounds for speculation about it, from their reading of the poem alone.

Perhaps this is best demonstrated by trying to conceive of a situation where no conception of authorial presence in a literary work enters into a reader's aesthetic response to the work. One could argue, for example, that if a piece of Elizabethan prose ended up playing the role of demonstrating a particularly rare form of printing type-face, then no such conception of authorial presence or intention would enter into a response to the piece in question. It is apparent however that in such a case the piece of prose is not being treated as literature, and as soon as it is *read* rather than just looked at, the reader is forced to place it into a human context which includes its individual and social human genesis. The fact that such contexts often assume a similarity may lead the reader to suppose that they do not exist, but this is a supposition—as our example of Mr. A. the cutler showed—which should be resisted. In his book on Kant, Goldmann has shown how a dialectical investigation of a subject often involves positing an assumed constancy in one area of the subject investigated so that the dynamic element in other areas can be approached from a less shifting viewpoint. Such a 'freezing' process involves both sacrifices and gains, but is a normal part of the way in which we do understand the world. Goldmann notes that the treatise on politics, medicine or cookery can ignore the fact that the politician, doctor or cook may fall in love or die, although these facts could in certain cases affect the treatment of a patient or the cooking of a meal; from the particular viewpoint of the works in question they can be treated as constants, and ignored.[49] In like manner, the reader of literature has a more or less well-defined sense of various human contexts which act as constants, within which his reading of literature makes sense. Very often the reader will use terms such as 'human nature' to describe such contexts. The fact that we can treat large areas of human experience as constants for the purpose of examining other areas of experience should however always be seen as a temporary and working expedient, rather than as the result of the existence of genuinely constant and absolute elements in human experience. As far as our conception of an author is concerned, this is particularly true. Marxists should be prepared to admit that a reader can respond quite fully to several works of literature without having a detailed knowledge of the author's life and social situation. What it is necessary to stress to complement this statement, is firstly that such information will in many cases increase one's ability to respond to the work in question, and secondly that even without such knowledge, the reader is relying on an assumed context which includes some generalised picture of a human situation from which the work emanates.

It is above all necessary to stress the variations possible in the writer-work relationship, variations which render more or less significant biographical information as a part of literary criticism. As I tried to show in my chapter on dialectics, what a thing is is dependent upon where it is, and this has been stressed by a number of writers with regard to the dialectics of literary response. Lukács quotes from Marx's *Wage Labour and Capital* the section where Marx argues that although ? Negro is a Negro and a cotton-spinning jenny a machine for spinning cotton, they only become, respectively, a slave and capital, in certain precise circumstances.[50] Similarly, Bukharin makes the identical point with reference to matters intellectual:

> . . . when we import a new machine, we introduce it into a new complex of technical-economic organization, and the "meaning" of the machine thereby becomes different. Approximately the same thing happens in the realm of ideas—*mutatis mutandis*, of course.[51]

What follows from this is that a statement, opinion, attitude expressed by an author in the context of his day-to-day life is a different thing from the same statement, opinion or attitude expressed in a literary work. Aristotle makes essentially this point when he is talking about moral judgements on characters:

As for the question whether something said or done in a poem is morally right or not, in dealing with that one should consider not only the intrinsic quality of the actual word or deed, but also the person who says or does it, the time, the means, and the motives of the agent—whether he does it to obtain a greater good, or to avoid a greater evil.[52]

The same line of poetry appearing in two different poems is a different thing in each context—one can think of Eliot's use of quotation in *The Waste Land* for example. In like manner, attempts to criticise works of literature by means of comparisons between opinions expressed in the literary work, and outside the work by the author, are fraught with extreme danger unless this point is remembered. Marxists have in the past oscillated in a curious manner between an at times almost religious respect for certain classic texts of Marxism as the depositories of absolute truth, and an insistence on the dependence of their interpretation of these texts upon a correct assessment of authorial intention. Recent Soviet books and articles have renewed the attempts to show that Lenin's *Party Literature and Party Life* was intended to refer to the *belles-lettres* as well as to purely party literature, arguing from the basis of Lenin's intention rather than from the implications which can be drawn from the text—a rather unwise basis for argument, as there is a letter from Krupskaya extant which denies that this *was* Lenin's intention.[53] As Lenin wrote the text in conditions very different from those of a developed socialist society, his intention in an immediate sense would appear to be less important than the arguments which can be abstracted from the text bearing its genetic context in mind. The difference seems to me a crucial one, and one that has an important bearing on many questions of literary analysis.

The common-sense solution to many problems raised by questions regarding the relationship between a work of literature and its genetic context is given by Goldmann in *The Hidden God*:

> We must certainly not exclude the study of biographical details, since these often provide extremely useful information. However, it will always remain merely a partial and auxiliary method which must never be used as the final basis for any explanation.[54]

A sensible use of biographical information will normally be seen to be obviously relevant as far as the criticism of a particular piece of literature is concerned, because part of the context in which a literary work must exist if it is to have a developed identity is that of its authorial origin. Wayne Booth, working from a position very similar to our dialectical conception of identity, insists on precisely this fact:

> Without surrendering to relativism, one can recognise that our different interests and predispositions lead us to take different aspects of reality for different purposes. The same fact can be many different facts, depending on differences in our general orientation. Thus, every literary "fact"—even the most unadorned picture of some universal aspect of human experience—is highly charged by the meanings of the author, whatever his pretensions to objectivity.[55]

If we accept that this is the case—and I cannot see any alternative but to do so—then it must be admitted that to experience a literary work as fully as possible a reader should try to come as close to 'the meanings of the author', to be as sure as possible what these are, as he can. I wish to examine the respective claims of authorial intention on the one hand, and relevance to the reader's situation on the other in a later chapter, for it would be vain to suggest that practical criticism did not throw up cases where the two appeared to be in some sort of conflict. For the time being, however, I would rest my case that an adequate critical response to a literary text cannot ignore the complex relationship which exists between the author and his work.

I would like to conclude this chapter with a few brief comments on what has been called the 'problem of belief' in literary criticism, where the intrusion of certain beliefs of the author into a literary work has been held to make the reader's ability to respond to this work somewhat more difficult. The 'problem' only really arises for those who assume that there should ideally be an absolute, aesthetic response to any given piece of literature, from which the reader can somehow be distracted by an illegitimate intrusion into his work on the part of the author. But such a position is obviously riddled with inconsistencies. To say that our attitude towards a statement of political belief by an author should be different from our attitude to the same statement in the context of one of his works is not to say that our response to the latter should somehow be non-political and aesthetic. I. A. Richards makes this point whilst talking about Shelley, a favourite subject for such debates because, I suspect, his beliefs and opinions diverge from those of many of his bourgeois readers, rather than because of any isolable illegitimate intrusion into his poetry of such beliefs and opinions. Richards insists that our normal understanding of such questions must operate in our response to literature, even if our assessment of the significance of, say,

Shelley's political views in the context of his poetry, differs from our assessment of them in other contexts:

> We cannot e.g. read Shelley adequately while believing that all his views are moonshine—read *Prometheus Unbound* while holding that 'the perfectibility of man is an undesirable ideal' and that 'hangmen are excellent things'. To say that there is a purely aesthetic or poetic approach to, let us say, the *Sermon on the Mount*, by which no consideration of the intention or ultimate end of the poem enters, would appear to be merely mental timidity. . . .[56]

Thus for someone such as T. S. Eliot to find himself unable to read and enjoy some of Shelley's poems because they contain views that he not only dislikes but finds positively puerile[57] is not surprising, and really offers no desperately important problem. What else would we expect? Those who expect that we should all be able to reach an ideal and standard response to a work of art are in general those who insist on the 'objective' existence of the one work of art, to which all readers should, presumably, respond in one objective way.

The fact that a literary 'statement' is different from the same statement made in a different context should not lead us to argue that it is totally unconnected with the same statement in a different context. I wish to deal with the question of the truth-reference of literary statements later on, but at this point would merely stress that the reader should avoid the twin extremes either of thinking that knowledge of an author's ideas, beliefs and so on is totally irrelevant to a literary appreciation of his works, or of assuming that the two can be equated in any neat or mechanical way. Literary critics have suggested a number of ways whereby readers can come to terms with the distinct identity of literary works—one of the best known of these is Coleridge's 'suspension of disbelief'. The disbelief is only suspended, rather than abandoned, to allow the reader to experience a particular literary 'fact' within the context of his 'understanding' of it, but excluding the whole range of his value-judgements of it. This is one of the ways in which literature forces us to critically examine our beliefs and opinions, by vicariously experiencing forms of belief and understanding foreign to our normal habits of mind. Even in this situation one never completely escapes from one's 'normal' attitude to a set of beliefs, and different levels of suspension of disbelief very often involve the law of diminishing returns. It is one thing for a modern emancipated female reader to suspend her belief in the equality of the sexes when reading James's *The Bostonians*.

In another instance the reader may, to use the words of Graham Hough,

> . . . in the teeth of M. Sartre, decide that the work of Genet is tedious filth and refuse to go further with it. Every reader has the right to make such decisions, and probably at some time or another one must make them.[58]

Thus the fact that a work can never be separated from its creator, or its 'truth' be separated from his cognition of an attitude towards this truth, does not mean that the reader escapes from the responsibility of making judgements. The reader cannot feel that the process of responding to a literary work is ended when he has come to terms with the relationship between the writer and his work, for the reader has then to see the work in other contexts. But fuller discussion of the role of the reader merits at this point a chapter to itself. Perhaps the last word can be left to Laurence Sterne. Towards the end of *Tristram Shandy*, he comments:

> Let us leave, if possible, *myself*:—But 'tis impossible,—I must go along with you to the end of the work.

NOTES

[1] E. M. Forster, *Aspects of the Novel*, reprinted Harmondsworth 1970, p. 16.

[2] Graham Hough, *An Essay on Criticism*, London 1966, p. 164.

[3] Everett Knight, *A Theory of the Classical Novel*, London 1970, p. 44.

[4] E. M. W. Tillyard & C. S. Lewis, *The Personal Heresy*, reprinted London 1965, p. 25.

[5] Karl Marx, *Capital*, volume one, London n.d. (1967), p. 182.

[6] *What is Literature?*, p. 184.

[7] Graham Hough, *An Essay on Criticism*, London, 1966, p. 60.

[8] Lucien Goldmann, *The Hidden God*, London 1964, p. 48.

[9] *The Personal Heresy*, p. 35.

[10] *A Theory of the Classical Novel*, p. 50.

[11] T. S. Eliot, 'The Frontiers of Criticism', *On Poetry and Poets*, reprinted London 1969, p. 111.

[12] *On Poetry and Poets*, pp. 111–12.

[13] *The Socialist Register 1971*, p. 126.

[14] T. S. Eliot, 'Wordsworth and Coleridge', *The Use of Poetry and the Use of Criticism*, reprinted London 1968, p. 75.

[15] W. K. Wimsatt, 'Genesis: A Fallacy Revisited', *The Disciplines of Criticism*, p. 199.

[16] F. W. Bateson, *Wordsworth, A Reinterpretation*, reprinted London 1963, p. 163.

[17] William Empson, *Seven Types of Ambiguity*, third edition, reprinted Harmondsworth 1965, p. 215.

[18] 'The Strange Deaths of Sally, Ann, Lucy and others . . .', *Trivium*, vol VI, 1971, p. 70.

[19] *On Poetry and Poets*, p. 112.

[20] *On Poetry and Poets*, p. 111.

[21] *Critics and Criticism Ancient and Modern*, ed. R. S. Crane, reprinted London 1968, p. 8.

[22] Louis Althusser, 'On the Young Marx', *For Marx*, London 1969. I should point out that Althusser stresses that 'the developmental motor principle of a particular ideology cannot be found within itself but in what underlies it, 'its author as a concrete individual and the actual history reflected in this individual development according to the complex ties between the individual and this history' (p. 62). However, he then implies that this particular complex of relationships can only be understood in terms of itself, and that the later Marx cannot be used to understand the early Marx. This seems to me to deny the subject-object dialectic, and to categorise the investigator as contemplator.

[23] *The Socialist Register 1971*, p. 114.

[24] *Further Studies*, p. 230.

[25] There is an interesting development of Wittgenstein's rejection of the concept of the self-referential nature of mathematics in R. W. Beardsmore's book *Art and Morality*, where he draws conclusions from it which relate to art.

[26] Richard Eberhart, 'Empson's Poetry', reprinted in *Accent Anthology*, ed. Quinn & Shattuck, New York, 1946, p. 580.

[27] Calvin S. Brown, 'Difficulty and Surface Value', *The Disciplines of Criticism*, p. 48.

[28] William Empson, 'Rhythm and Imagery in English Poetry', 'British Journal of Aesthetics', January 1962, p. 36.

[29] Geoffrey Gorer, 'The Myth in Jane Austen', reprinted in *Five Approaches of Literary Criticism*, p. 98.

[30] Norman N. Holland, 'The "Unconscious" of Literature: The Psychoanalytic Approach', *Contemporary Criticism*, p. 131.

[31] *Contemporary Criticism*, pp. 133, 139.

[32] *Contemporary Criticism*, p. 136.

[33] *Contemporary Criticism*, p. 140(n).

[34] *Immanuel Kant*, p. 41.

[35] *The Verbal Icon*, p. 4.

[36] *Aesthetics*, p. 21.

[37] *Aesthetics*, p. 442.

[38] Wayne C. Booth, *The Rhetoric of Fiction*, reprinted London 1966, p. 75.

[39] *The Verbal Icon*, p. 5.

[40] T. S. Eliot, 'The Modern Mind', *The Use of Poetry and the Use of Criticism*, p. 130.

[41] Julian Trevelyan, *Indigo Days*, London 1957, p. 16.

[42] William Empson, *Collected Poems*, reprinted London 1962, p. 93.

[43] Note on sleeve of record *William Empson reading Selected Poems* by Empson, The Marvell Press, Hessle, Yorkshire.

[44] 'Mr. Empson and the Fire Sermon', 'Essays in Criticism', October 1956, p. 482.

[45] Thom Gunn, review of *Collected Poems* by William Empson, 'The London Magazine', February 1956, p. 71.

[46] op. cit. p. 74.

[47] *The Personal Heresy*, p. 16.

[48] *The Personal Heresy*, p. 119.

[49] *Immanuel Kant*, p. 140.

[50] *History and Class Consciousness*, p. 13.

[51] *Problems of Soviet Literature*, p. 208.

[52] *The Works of Aristotle Translated into English*, Oxford University Press, vol. 11, 1461a.

[53] Noted by Lukács in *The Meaning of Contemporary Realism*, p. 7.

[54] *The Hidden God*, p. 9.

[55] *The Rhetoric of Fiction*, p. 112.

[56] I. A. Richards, *Principles of Literary Criticism*, reprinted London 1961, p. 79.

[57] T. S. Eliot, 'Shelley and Keats', *The Use of Poetry and the Use of Criticism*, p. 91.

[58] Graham Hough, *An Essay on Criticism*, p. 80.

5. *The Reader and the Work*

A letter that ran in the "New York Times" earlier this season was anti-mystery and demanded answers. A theatre-goer who had seen "The Birthday Party" insisted that Pinter tell her (1) who were the two men? (2) where did Stanley come from? (3) were they all supposed to be normal? The theatregoer announced that she couldn't understand Pinter's play until he'd replied to her questions. Pinter replied that he couldn't understand her letter until she had answered three questions of his: (1) Who are you? (2) Where do you come from? (3) Are you supposed to be normal?[1]

WALTER KERR

Sartre has said that it is unthinkable that a great novel be written in praise of anti-semitism; except, one might add, for the anti-semite himself who may well find no greatness elsewhere.[2]

EVERETT KNIGHT

Just as Marx shows that price, which at first sight seems to be an objective property of a commodity, is in reality only a human and social valuation of it, so Kant shows that beauty, which at first sight seems to be an objective property of a beautiful object, is in reality a human valuation of it.[3]

LUCIEN GOLDMANN

One simple, and thus often-ignored, distinction between the writer and the reader of a work, is that the former is a man alone whilst the latter is one of many. Any attempt to consider the relationship between reader and work will be incomplete if it does not attempt to come to terms with some of the problems involved in the simple fact that a literary work is read by a large number of different people at different times and in different places, whose responses to the same work, although inevitably having elements in common, also have elements which are not necessarily shared by all. Certainly, an awareness of some of the initial implications of this fact can be seen to be behind the unwillingness to consider 'the reader' which many critics testify to. If the relationship between the work and the writer is swathed in mystery and ignorance, how much more confusion results from the fact that when the critic's gaze is turned from writer to reader, the uniqueness of the former is replaced by the theoretically potentially infinite diversity of the latter. How much more inviting it is to concentrate attention on 'the work itself', which exists as a unique and accessible focus of critical attention, possessed of neither the mystery of its writer nor the diversity of its readers!

Such an attitude is understandable, but misleading. As I have already attempted to show, 'the work itself' is a fiction, an imagined objective fact which disappears when removed from its life-giving complex of relationships, and of these relationships, one which cannot be neglected is that of the relationship between the reader and the work, separate from which the work ceases to exist. Given that this is so, the problem for aesthetics involves the fact that a literary response is both an individual and a social phenomenon, not only because any given individual response to a work of literature involves a whole complex of social attitudes, opinions, knowledge, but also in as much as it forms a part of a totality —the total social response to the work of literature. It is important at this point to insist, however, that the fact that literary response is both individual and social, both unique and shared, is only a problem if one starts off from the premiss that it should ideally be either one or the other, either totally private, a non-communicable shiver down the spine; or totally public, a quantifiable response to an objective 'out there' object. A new perception of external reality only becomes a problem if one tries to reconcile it with a previous, less accurate perception which it in fact replaces.

I would like at this point to make some comments about the fact that a response to a literary work is both unique and shared. It will be apparent that the analogy between the art work and the individual human being that I used previously is again relevant here, for the individual human being is both individual and unique, and a social, communicating being. Marxists have never denied that socially determined phenomena, whether art works or human beings, have individualistic, unique elements in their composition. But this must be seen in the context of a dynamic perception of identity; human individuality and uniqueness is constantly being broken down and socialised through the process of human practice, and is constantly reforming as the human individual finds himself in new situations. Individuality is not necessarily an asocial phenomenon. In 'Notes Towards a Supreme Fiction', Wallace Stevens shows how recurrent social phenomena—the return of the bees in Spring, falling in love—have both a repetitive and a unique characteristic. The individual who falls in love is doing something that many other individuals have done, something which can be perceived in a social sense; but his experience of falling in love is necessarily something unique and personal as well. Our experience of art and literature too partakes both of the social and the individual, and these different components of our response are neither fixed nor static, but are constantly growing and changing. As our individual experience alters, so does our individual response to a work of literature, and this in its turn can modify a social perception of the significance of an art work.

What is the theoretical basis for the claim made by Marxists that our cognition of the external world is both unique and social? Lucien Goldmann notes that the question of how two men can communicate about a third object, separate from both of them, is a problem for classical philosophy because it thought of theoretical man as contemplative, as a *spectator*. However, he continues,

> For us today it is a little clearer. In freeing the *a priori* from reification, in relating it to the real human community, we know that this community can only be based upon human activity, upon the common action of men. Now all action involves the transformation of the external world. It must relate to a common object. The function of theoretical knowledge is precisely to transform the unformed immediate given, which differs from one individual to another, into a common object.[4]

With certain modifications, this can be seen to be, in essence, the role of criticism—to transform the 'immediate given' of a personal response to a work of literature into a common object, made common through our joint *use* of it in transforming the world. I say 'with certain modifications' because the process is infinitely more complex than this, for the individual never starts off with a pure 'immediate given' in any perception, for any perception is only made possible by past experience of the world, by a socially-developed means of perception. If this is true of any object, it is true to a far greater and more complex extent of the work of art. The 'pure' 'immediate given' of a personal response to an art work is already saturated with socially-determined cognitive elements in terms of its component parts, although not necessarily in terms of its new totality, its artistic 'wholeness'.

Here, it behoves us to consider briefly the possibility that these initial elements of perception which are socially determined will differ from person to person in certain situations. Again, Goldmann puts his finger on the crucial point:

> So long as a higher form of knowledge, that is to say, a higher form of real human community, has not been achieved, the possibility of genuinely scientific knowledge will depend upon the anthropological and in the last instance fortuitous circumstance that in a given sphere social interests coincide. Elsewhere, particularly in the human sciences, scientific knowledge remains a problematic concept, a question which cannot easily be resolved. For present-day man, there is no criterion of truth which is both material and universal.[5]

In a note to the above comment, Goldmann adds that if one accepts that the only possible way to decide on truth is in action, practice, then in a society where the 'I' is the subject of action rather than the 'we', the community, the criterion of truth can only be individual, except in so far as limited groups constitute the subject of action, in which case

> . . . there arise class ideologies and national ideologies which may be true or false according to whether or not they have the whole of humanity as an end.[5]

The introduction of the 'end' of an ideology as a test of truth somewhat confuses Goldmann's point here, which is that if action is the sole way to decide on truth, then only with those with whom we share a common action to transform the world will we be able to perceive the external world from the basis of a shared value-system.

It is not difficult to see the implications which this, if accepted, has on our conception of aesthetics. Agreement about a work of art will be seen to be dependent *not* upon a common recognition that the same 'objective' object is being perceived, but upon recognition that a similar relationship to social action which is changing the world defines one's relationship to the art work in a common way. More precisely, the more the art work is itself 'used' to transform their knowledge of and control over the external world by a number of people, the more will these people be able to share a joint response to the art work. Further to this, and perhaps most important of all, the introduction of social practice as truth-criterion and as the creating force behind our ability to perceive the world at all involves a *dynamic* element in our perception of the external world. As far as our interest in artistic response is concerned, this involves of necessity a rejection of static, frozen concepts of artistic response, and their replacement by an understanding of the fact that our response to a work of literature is in motion rather than static, is constantly changing rather than fixed, is infinite in potentiality rather than limited to life within the edges of a fixed, 'objective' truth.

In the rest of this chapter I would like to examine the nature of the response to a literary work which takes place whilst the work is being read, or at least whilst the work is immediately in the forefront of one's attention; in the subsequent chapter I wish to follow this response further on in a temporal sense, to see what happens to it as it recedes further and further from the immediate reading experience. Like many other distinctions which we have had to make in order to break up the totality of the literary process into manageable parts, this one can be seen to be an arbitrary one. Graham Hough argues that one's first reading of a literary work is not a critical one,[6] and that criticism as such starts after the initial non-critical response has taken place. This seems to me to beg large questions, for there seems to me to be no qualitative difference between the nature of one's initial response to a work of literature and one's subsequent examination of this response apart from the fact that the former *is* an initial response and the latter a subsequent one. Even the most 'internal' individualistic responses to a lyric poem involve qualitatively the same sort of reference to social experience as does one's later consideration and development of these responses. However, for the purpose of convenience, one can refer back to our conception of the literary work's identity, and make a distinction between a response to the work where one's social experience is subsumed *into* the whole of the literary work, and one where one's initial response is subsumed into one's wider social experience, in the dialectical manner Rodway describes as 'tacking'. Thus with modifications, I would accept that the distinction Kenneth Burke makes between a treatment of the literary work in terms of its surrounding context which is a historical one, and a treatment of it in terms of its *being* which is, he argues, atemporal,[7] represents a real distinction in terms of the lesser or greater weight given to a work's identity and its relationships. I would argue that in both cases there has to be a reliance on the truth-criterion of social practice, but that in the former case this is more direct and immediate than in the latter. I hope that in the following pages, where I shall examine in more detail the account of reader-response which a Marxist aesthetics must take, it will be remembered that this distinction, although based on a genuine methodological pair of alternatives, does not even at an initial stage remove a literary response either from time or from social reality, nor does it refer to alternatives which are totally mutually exclusive.

I have suggested that the reason why many critics have argued for the consideration of an assumed atemporal, totally 'objective' work of literature, is that their recognition of the diversity of artistic response has led them to believe that any consideration of reader response to the work, like Hillis Miller's inventory of the ripples from the stone thrown in the pool, will lead to the critic's having to admit that his subject is too large for him to consider. The stone is more accessible than the multiplicity of ripples it produces. This, essentially, would seem to lie behind Wimsatt and Beardsley's attack on 'The Affective Fallacy'. Having anathematised the Intentional Fallacy on account of the unreliability or even undiscoverability of authorial intention, they likewise reject any affective study on the grounds that personal responses to literature are too diverse and unique to be studied in any rewarding way:

> The report of some readers, . . . that a poem or story induces in them vivid images, intense feelings, or heightened consciousness, is neither anything which can be refuted nor anything which it is possible for the objective critic to take into account. The purely affective report is either too physiological or it is too vague.[8]

The key weakness in this argument is its dependence upon the term 'purely affective'. Of course, if something were *purely* affective, then it would have no critical validity, for it would not be known about by anyone other than the person affected. But as soon as a reader describes the affects which a reading of a work has had on him, then these become more than 'pure affects', they become socially available items of knowledge. In addition to this, the statement implies that a distinction can be drawn between the images and feelings which a work of literature induces in an individual, and an individual's perception of certain 'objective' qualities resident in the work of literature. Wimsatt and Beardsley argue that the affects of a reading of a work of literature on the reader are not socially available, and that they cannot be refuted, suggesting that there is an alternative source of information which can be refuted and is thus more suitable for critical investigation. Unfortunately, this refutable evidence turns out to be, one presumes, comment upon the 'work itself', which is of course only to be perceived in terms

of its affects anyway. There are no real alternatives here, just two ways
of describing the same thing. As Louis Althusser puts it:

> . . . we can see that the play itself *is* the spectator's consciousness—
> for the essential reason that the spectator has no other consciousness
> than the content which unites him to the play in advance and the
> development of this content in the play itself: the new result which
> the play *produces* from the self-recognition whose image and
> presence it is.[9]

Wimsatt and Beardsley suggest exclusive and alternative processes,
one of which leads from the literary work to the reader, 'the affect',
and the other which goes from the reader to the objective work, which
is the critical scrutiny of that work. The one is seen to end in something
individual, unique, adventitious, whilst the other ends in something
socially-available, 'objective'. The one ends in the irrefutable and the
hidden, the other in the public and discussable. One is reminded of
unscientific concepts of sight involving eye beams reaching out and
touching objects, rather than light bouncing off these objects and hitting
the retina. The point is surely, that if both of these theories were to have
an equally respectable scientific support, it would make no difference
to our ability to talk about external objects of sight, for the process
would be the same whatever the explanation; we do not have the ability
to choose between being affected by a literary work and perceiving its
objective existence. This basic flaw runs through most of Wimsatt and
Beardsley's article, and it is worth looking at some of the ramifications
it has. They make much of the fact, for example, that affects are dynamic,
changing things, as if the critic can study only what is fixed and constant:

> . . . certain objects partly obscured in one age wax into apprecia-
> tion in another, and partly through the efforts of the poet. It is not
> true that they suddenly arrive out of nothing.[10]

The implication here is that a new element in the way a society sees
a work of literature comes from a more adequate perception of what is
'there' in the work, rather than being a case of artistic parthenogenesis.
This being so, it behoves the reader and critic not to be diverted by
what people say they have felt or thought as a result of reading a
particular work, but to concentrate on seeing the work itself as fully
and clearly as possible. Thus, the implication continues, if we rely on an
interpretation of affects to reach a critical judgement, we may be dealing
with that which is a historical accident rather than a genuine response

to the work. Had the eighteenth-century critic relied on contemporary readers' descriptions of the affects left by a reading of *King Lear*, they would have something very inferior to our own response to the same play. But if, instead, they had looked 'at the play', they would have surely had the same information, that is, the affects the play left in them which would have been conditioned to a large extent by the society they lived in and its attitude towards this play.

In the same way, the believer in the objectivity of the art work might assume that developments in artistic techniques—if genuinely progressive—were movements closer and closer to the objective reality which the artist is trying to capture. Certainly Virginia Woolf's comments on her novelistic methods would seem to suggest that this is the way in which she saw them. But there is another way of looking at such advances. One can argue that they constitute different ways of mediating between an external reality and a perceiving human being, which are induced by a number of factors, and which carry with them gains and losses. Everett Knight has made essentially this point about the artistic innovation of perspective, arguing that

> We must not imagine perspective to be a device the discovery of which enabled artists to picture things as they 'really are'; it was a new kind of perception, and one which would naturally accompany the change from the 'closed' aristotelian-christian world where all space was accounted for to the 'open' or infinite world of mathematics and geometry . . .[11]

It is not that we perceive more of the 'real' *King Lear* than did the eighteenth-century sentimentalist, but that our 'real' *King Lear* is different from a 'real', sentimental eighteenth-century *King Lear*.

If we cast our minds back to Lenin's description of Bukharin's approach to the definition of the mode of being of a tumbler, and his categorisation of this approach as an eclectic one, we can make a similar objection to Wimsatt and Beardsley's rejection of the fallacies of intentionalism and affectivism. Having proved that the poem cannot be reduced either to the author's intentions or the affects in the mind of the reader, one cannot then proceed to dismiss both of these aspects of the poem's mode of being as irrelevant. Because one cannot reduce a glass tumbler to the state of being just a glass cylinder or just a drinking vessel, it does not follow that these aspects of its mode of being can be ignored or rejected. Our policemen are far more dialectical in their approach to the definition of the mode of being of objects; in a given situation involving an alleged breach of the peace their all-transforming gaze can transform banners, ball-point pens and handbags into offensive weapons without the least feeling of philosophical unease. It is of no use to the poor demonstrator to show the magistrate that the object in question is a ball-point pen, as can be proven by writing with it. The latter, with that same incisive grasp of dialectical logic common to our judiciary will point out, in so many words, that part of the mode of being of a ball-point pen involves its becoming, in certain clearly defined circumstances, an offensive weapon. Whether or not he adduces the arguments of Lenin to confirm the demonstrator in his way of thinking does not affect the correctness of his dialectical perception at this juncture. The demonstrator may only console himself with the thought that a dialectical understanding of the mode of being of certain magistrates involves a conception of their identity also being radically changed given a different social context.

I have said that any given response to a literary work will to a certain extent be a unique thing, for it exists within and is defined by a context which includes the uniqueness of the reader's cognition of the work. But it is also true to say that no reader's response can ever be totally unique. When I was arguing against autonomist theories of art I noted that several critics had pointed out that the linguistic ties between writer, work and reader precluded any total autonomy of the literary work ever being achieved. Roger Fowler makes a similar case against seeing what is 'there' in the poem as cut off from the outside world, as the language the poem is written in ensures that it is linked with the outside world.[12] The importance of this link for us at this point is that it is an argument equally effective against theories of the autonomy of individual responses to works of literature; the person who responds to a work of literature does so in part because of the linguistic ability given to him by his society, and thus his response is inevitably in part a social one. If the literary work and any reader within a certain cultural-linguistic milieu are linked then it is surely true that the response of different readers in this milieu are also connected. This is not to imply that there is necessarily one 'correct' response to a given work of literature—even within a defined time and society—to which all readers should attempt to approach as near as possible. To say that we share common links with a work of literature does not mean that these common links will lead to identical responses, or that they should. Human beings all have certain sex drives in common, and within a given society these may manifest themselves in certain socially-determined ways, but in general we tend to fall in love with different people, and even when two men are in love with the same woman the nature of their love will tend to be different.

The ability to achieve a common perception of an object through social practice is never total, for an aspect of human cognition must inevitably remain individual and personal. Individual and personal elements may also be linked very closely with social aspects of a literary response, as I suggested when talking about the Lucy poems earlier; a common experience of love may allow a number of readers of these poems to respond to them in a common way, but the precise nature of the experience of each will vary, and so will their responses. It is still possible to communicate about an external object, and to achieve a shared cognition of it, without achieving an identical cognition of it. Helen Gardner has pointed out the fact that 'good taste' is not an absolute quality, and that there is no absolutely 'correct' response to a given work of literature, from a less-theoretical standpoint than that of Goldmann's:

> . . . certain writers and certain works mean more to some ages and to some persons than to others, and . . . our responses vary very greatly with our circumstances and our age.[13]

Does an acceptance of this lead to solipsism and the breakdown of critical discussion? Those who argue that it does imply that to discuss or argue about anything we must be discussing exactly the same thing, but it can be argued equally that if we did all respond in the same manner to a given work of literature there would be little need for critical discussion of the work in question. We learn to cope with differences in our cognition of the world because verbal contact is part of the way that man changes the world and learns to perceive it in a common way. Literary criticism is itself a method of breaking down individualistic elements in our response to literature, helping us to recognise them as such, and to perceive the literary work in a new way as a result of the social activity of discussing it and *using* it in the context of our lives. By modifying the relationships the work has with us, we change our cognition of what it is. The critic can perform the function of preparing the reader for a particular reading, modifying his expectations, his knowledge, so that when he actually starts to read it he responds in a more socially significant manner. In fact every reader prepares himself for any given reading of a literary work in various ways; we do not experience art accidentally, or if we do our state of mind resultant from

the accidental nature of the experience modifies our response whether
we want it to or not.

In his poem 'On Sitting Down to Read King Lear Once Again',
Keats describes the way in which the reader can predispose himself to a
fuller artistic experience:

> O golden tongued Romance, with serene lute!
> Fair plumed Syren, Queen of far-away!
>   Leave melodizing on this wintry day,
> Shut up thine olden pages, and be mute:
> Adieu! for, once again, the fierce dispute
>   Betwixt damnation and impassion'd clay
>   Must I burn through; once more humbly assay
> The bitter-sweet of this Shakespearian fruit:
> Chief Poet! and ye clouds of Albion,
>   Begetters of our deep eternal theme!
> When through the old oak forest I am gone,
>   Let me not wander in a barren dream,
> But, when I am consumed in the fire
> Give me new Phoenix wings to fly at my desire.

The poem is an interesting description of a number of ways in which
the individual can prepare himself for artistic experience, often unconsciously. Keats is rereading rather than reading the play, and so his
preparation for the experience is more well-defined than it might otherwise be, but nevertheless one can see from the poem very clearly, I
think, how the reader himself can modify the way in which he will
respond to a given literary work by preparing himself for the experience
of reading, by defining an initial relationship with the work which will
affect his further acquaintance with it. It is noteworthy that the poem
oscillates between words and phrases suggesting passivity on the part
of the reader who is to abandon himself to the literary experience, and
others suggesting that he himself has an active role to play in achieving
the final aesthetic response to the work. He must 'burn through' the
work and oppose his strength to the testing powers of the work, but
he must also 'humbly assay' its bitter-sweet; and open himself to what
the work has to give him. Again, the analogies of wandering through
the 'old oak forest', and being consumed phoenix-like in the fire of the
artistic experience, both consolidate this duality in his attitude to the
work, and can be compared with the dialectical alternation between
respect for the identity of the work, and movement away from this

to test and reform this identity by reference to social experience which I feel a successful reading of literature must involve.

The role of the reader as collaborator in reading a work of literature is well displayed here; Keats is aware that the way in which the reader approaches the work, the vantage point from which he attempts to make contact with the work, defines the response which the work produces in him. As W. J. Harvey says in his *Character and the Novel*, there is a relationship between the 'meaning' of a novel and the way in which we come to terms with this meaning; he argues that the process whereby we get to understand the meaning of the novel is itself part of this meaning, and concludes that 'how we travel determines our destination'.[14] In other words, there is no one destination which the reader of a literary work should aim for, no one optimum response which he should strive to reach. Nor is it possible that there should be a clear conception in the mind of the reader as to what the totality of his response will be before he starts to read; the reader is both free and unfree as Keats suggests, he must both determine the direction in which he proceeds as he reads a literary work, and also allow the work to influence his determination. By thus seeing a literary response as something to which both reader and work contribute, we can escape both from an unreal 'objectivity' resting on an assumed sameness of the work of literature which all must recognise, and a hopelessly subjective interiority which makes of a literary response something asocial and inaccessible.

Certain problems remain, however, if one accepts that any given literary response is of necessity in part unique to the individual reader. In 'The Study of Poetry', Matthew Arnold argues that one's 'real estimate' of poetry can be arrived at only by excluding the twin fallacies of the 'historic estimate' and the 'personal estimate'.[15] I wish to consider certain further problems relating to the question of the legitimacy of 'personal' responses to literature in the next chapter, but I would like to comment now on some of the initial problems which such a discussion raises. At the back of Arnold's argument lies a belief in an unchanging human nature (another topic to which I wish to recur) which offers him a theoretical basis for arguing that literary response can be purged of the adventitious until it approximates to an absolute standard of accuracy. One can sympathise with Arnold's motives here, for it seems obvious that what he is interested in achieving is a critical response to a given work of literature which is socially shared, and which has thus a greater power to forward human interests on a wide scale.

The problem is more complicated than at first appears however, and partly because of the fact that, as I have already argued, one cannot draw a neat distinction between 'personal' and 'social' elements in a given response. Johnson attacked Cowley for writing love poetry when he had only been in love once, without daring to declare his passion, and the implication behind such an attack is that Cowley's personal experience was inadequate to the task he set himself; but falling in love is not just a personal experience, it is something we do with the help of many socially induced linguistic and emotional tools, and the person who falls in love is not reacting in a purely individualistic, biologically-determined manner. This being so, to exclude the personal and the historical from one's literary response is, in a certain sense, to exclude everything. Even the response to those Arnoldian touchstones which I have already referred to would inevitably involve both personal and historic elements.

Arnold's intentions here would be better served by his recommending that the critic or reader should not try to impose purely individualistic aspects of his response on to the responses of other people. Just as the precise way in which Wordsworth came to an appreciation of those facts of human sexual love about which he writes in the Lucy poems is not of immediate interest to the reader of the poems, so too one reader of the Lucy poems should not assume that those personal recollections which the poems may trigger off in his own reading of them are of any wider social significance. There is an important distinction here between a response which is 'triggered' off by a literary work, and which by implication existed completely formed before reading of the work, and one which is to some extent *created* by interaction between reader and work. I will consider this distinction in more detail in my next chapter, but at this point it is necessary to point out that whatever the *social* significance of a particularly personal aspect of a reader's response to a literary work, it may have an important *personal* significance which is causally related to the reader's ability to progress towards a more social conception of the significance of his response. The precise nature of my experience of love is irrelevant to someone else with whom I am talking about the Lucy poems, but it is necessary for me to have had this experience before I can relate my literary response to his. One cannot relegate all personal aspects of literary response to the level of a 'Darling-they're-playing-our tune' reflex to a pop song. Arguments about the 'legitimacy' of a particular aspect of a reader's response to a literary work often seem to me to be misguided, for it is not the personal response itself that is legitimate or illegitimate, but what is done with it, and how the reader relates it to his wider social concerns through the critical act. Trotsky, in his *Literature and Revolution*, makes some perceptive comments about individuality which can be applied to those individual aspects of any given literary response. He notes that

> . . . even if individuality is unique, it does not mean that it cannot be analyzed. Individuality is a welding together of tribal, national, class, temporary and institutional elements and, in fact, it is in the uniqueness of this welding together, in the proportions of this psycho-chemical mixture, that individuality is expressed.[16]

Trotsky's comment here expresses well the impossibility of drawing a neat dividing line between personal and impersonal elements either in human character or in literary response; the terms relate to dialectically connected phenomena, not to completely separate aspects of human experience.

Thus there is no necessary contradiction involved in an aesthetic which sees that every literary response varies in some way or other from every other one, and which maintains at the same time that literary response is a social phenomenon which can be made socially accessible through criticism. Through the development of a critical sense the reader learns to relate his own personal response to a work of literature to those wider social responsibilities which he has as a member of a society. In all aspects of human experience we learn to distinguish between those elements which are of significance in a purely personal sense and those which have a wider relevance, and our attitude towards literary experience is no exception. One should be able to reach a position where one can say that a particular poem is important to one in a personal sense—as T. S. Eliot is not afraid of doing—but that one recognises the extent to which this importance is socially significant. The Czech structuralist Felix Vodička, writing about literary response, makes this point more accurately than does Matthew Arnold:

> Subjective elements of valuation, stemming from the momentary state of mind of the reader or his personal likes or dislikes, must in the historical criticism of sources be separated from the attitude of the times, because the object of our cognition are those features which have the character of historic generality.[17]

This recalls Goldmann's comments in *The Hidden God* on the difference between a personal vision which expresses some collective consciousness or aspiration, and one which is purely eccentric.[18] Trotsky's point, that the eccentricity is itself the product of social components, should not conceal the fact that this distinction between the personal as expression of the group, and as expression of an eccentric off-shoot of the group, is a real one. The reader cannot expunge personal, idiosyncratic, subjective elements from his literary response; but he must attempt to set them into a wider context, to see the general in the particular, and through the social use of literature to relate these elements to a common relation to the world on the part of humanity or of some section of it.

Vodička continues from the above statement to note that amongst all groups of 'perceivers of literary products' different strata will be found, and he mentions in particular those divisions related to class and to age. As Goldmann says, such differences will result in different literary responses on the part of those who are thus divided. Marxists have in general insisted upon the overriding importance of class distinctions in determining differences in consciousness, for such divisions strike most directly at the relationship the individual has with the external world through his control over it. But Vodička's mention of age reminds us that even in a classless society there will always be such divisions amongst human beings, and although membership of such a classless society will allow the development of a common relationship to the external world for its members, this will not result in an absolute uniformity of the way in which people are conscious of anything, let alone works of literature.

I think that it is important to insist that the way in which an individual responds to a given work of literature *is* modified by his consciousness of the external world which has been developed within the context of a particular group or groups, for membership of a dominant group in social or political terms often leads an individual to consider that he perceives the world in an absolutely objective way, that he is neutral in a way that those who belong to minority groups are not. Raymond Williams has commented on those right-wing critics who push orthodox (for them) politics into their writing and are not attacked for it, 'because orthodoxy can be said to be neutral'.[19] We are familiar with the accusation that left-wingers 'bring politics' into areas such as international sport and literary criticism, which before are alleged to have had a completely apolitical identity. We must conclude that literature may allow human beings to break down their individuality in various ways, but that it cannot iron out all those differences between human beings which mean that different people often respond very differently to the same work of literature. But criticism—and criticism, I would agree with Graham Hough, is a prolongation of normal intelligent reading—does help us to perceive these differences, and forces us to relate our personal experiences and responses to those of other people. Irving Babbitt, who is a critic with whom I do not in general have much in common, puts the matter well, I think, when he argues that the critic has taste only when, '. . . he refers the creative expression and his impression of it to some standard that is set above both', although I suspect that Babbitt's standard is not mine. He says that this standard must rest on a perception of what is 'normal and human',[20] and if this is to refer to some conception of social practice, and its ability to modify standards, then I would accept his point.

The fact that both the individual and the society of which he is a part are constantly changing implies, of course, that finality in critical judgement is a will-o'-the-wisp which can never be completely attained. Eliot has argued that it is the job of the critic to mediate between the literary work and the society to which the critic belongs, and again has reached the conclusion that because such mediation does not take place between static points it must constantly readjust to changed circumstances:

> No poetic reputation ever remains exactly in the same place: it is a stock market in constant fluctuation. There are the very great names which only fluctuate, so to speak, within a very narrow range of points: whether Milton is up to 104 today, and down to $97\frac{1}{4}$ to-morrow, does not matter.[21]

Reasons for such fluctuations in literary fortunes are complex, but in essence they point to the fact that the value a reader draws from a particular literary work is dependent not only upon the 'objective' characteristics of that work, but on himself as well, and his own situation will tend to change as the society of which he is a part changes. Eliot mentions Milton, and it is not surprising that 'Paradise Lost', a work intimately related to the Christian religion, should start to produce what would once have been considered highly eccentric critical reactions during a century when the role of the Christian religion in our society has changed so much. Perhaps Eliot's use of the stock market as an analogy is partly malicious, and the reference to the undisputed nature of Milton's greatness suggests that maybe a little coat-trailing in Dr. Leavis's direction is going on. But one does know of those in the academic world who treat the *Times Literary Supplement* as a business man might treat the *Financial Times*; looking for good investments and selling their outdated literary stock when its price seems to be on the decline.

Up to this point I have been talking in somewhat simplistic terms about literary response, suggesting perhaps at times that the latter is a simple, one-stage reaction to a given reading which can be isolated and examined within a given social context with complete confidence. We know by experience that this is not an accurate description, and that although we may think of our response to a given work in terms of the immediate effect of reading a poem or novel, our response starts long before we finish the work, and is constantly being modified whilst we read. We also know that unless criticism is an utterly vain pursuit, our response continues and changes after we have finished reading too. Our response to a work of literature is no more autonomous and fixed than is the work of literature itself, it is a complex, dynamic, multi-faceted process which can never be reduced to stasis, or hedged round with any absolutely fixed limits or boundaries. When we open a book for the first time—remembering, as I have already argued, that even at this point we are not starting from scratch—our response assumes all the characteristics of complexity and change that it will subsequently be distinguished by:

> About thirty years ago, Miss Maria Ward of Huntingdon, with only seven thousand pounds, had the good luck to captivate Sir Thomas Bertram, of Mansfield Park, in the county of Northampton, and to be thereby raised to the rank of a baronet's lady, with all the comforts and consequences of an handsome house and large income.

Those attuned to Miss Austen's characteristic mode will note without conscious effort the immediate marking-out of boundaries that this beautifully concentrated first sentence contains. The temporal, class, geographical and emotional areas of involvement of the novel are deftly and economically delineated for the reader, and the tensions which are to blossom as the novel develops are implied at once in the subtle contrasting of emotional abandonment and economic assessment implicit in the words 'captivate' and 'luck'. Our response to this sentence is not however a purely internal process, nor is it something totally 'contained', in embryo as it were, in the words on the page. We respond not by virtue of passively accepting what we are told, but by constant application of the critical faculty. The reader tacks between implications and ideas that the words suggest as alternatives, reaching conclusions both by reference to his own life and experience and also by attempting to come to terms with the 'internal' logic of what is being read. This to-ing and fro-ing involves a constant movement from hypotheses, selection, modification and assessment, with various half-rejected possibilities held in the mind for possible future reference. This can be seen in very simple terms in a reader's response to the first four words of the sentence; some assessment of the significance of the date and the reason for specifying it so precisely at the start of the novel has to be reached by the reader.

This one short sentence contains very explicit references to class, money, and marriage, and the reader's response to these are not contained ready-made in the words on the page; the words mediate between the writer and the reader and achieve their truth-reference or otherwise in so far as they are related to a shared connection with external reality. The reader has at his disposal a whole range of possible value-judgements to call into use in order fully to assess the significance of what is referred to in the sentence, and the way in which he uses these or 'suspends' them depends both on his experience of reading literature in general and Jane Austen's novels in particular, and also on his wider experience of reaching value-judgements in his normal life. In order to suspend his disbelief, or reject those interpretations of what he reads which are irrelevant to his literary experience, a reader must first of all refer to his beliefs and test their possible suitability for incorporation into his literary response. As Eliot says, it is only by going too far that we know how far we can go, and only by referring to possible reactions to the words on the page which are then judged to be not relevant to one's literary response can one define which reactions are relevant. In the course of reading a novel like *Mansfield Park* the reader has to make mental reference to innumerable possible reactions, beliefs, areas of knowledge and so on in order to build up what is considered to be a fruitful response to the words on the page. The final decision is not one which the reader can confidently arrive at merely by reference to the text; he must consult the range of his experience—literary and other. This surely must be seen to be in essence a critical activity, rather than something to be distinguished from a later, *post facto* operation of the critical spirit.

I have noted the faint but insistent conflict set up in the first paragraph of the novel between the words 'captivate' and 'luck'. Any reader approaching the novel for the first time has a range of possible ways to interpret the significance of this conflict, involving judgements on the extent to which irony is being used, and to which different value-judgements attach to the opposed concepts. Is the word 'luck' used innocently, without the darker suggestion that the captivation was anything but lucky that might be implied by later developments in the sentence? Or is it used with the intention to make the reader immediately aware of the ironic way in which the author considers such protestations of fortune? Does such irony, if it exists, reach out and engulf the word 'captivate', turning the latter word from a conventional metaphor suggesting emotional enslavement, to one with a force of ironic placing of the emotion within a more conscious area of feminine subtlety and guile? Such alternative reactions are, it is true, resolved to a large extent by the sentence immediately following.

> All Huntingdon exclaimed on the greatness of the match, and her
> uncle, the lawyer, himself, allowed her to be at least three thousand
> pounds short of any equitable claim to it.

The movement from the implied blind emotional abandon of 'captivate' is modified quickly and considerably by this swift movement to a discussion of the hard cash valuation of the attachment, and the irony involved in the mock respect accorded to the allegedly socially superior uncle—the lawyer—qualifies the earlier implications that the match was devoid of economic self-interest.

All this may appear to be very New Critical and formalistic, but it is important to note that such a close reading of the words on the page involves constant reference on the part of the reader to his own knowledge and experience, knowledge and experience existing before the work is read. One cannot simply say either that the work contains its own value-judgements, or that it informs the reader which of the value-judgements he already holds are relevant to it. The reader must bring his own values to a reading of a literary work, but must be prepared to see them modified and reformed; and out of this process new values will emerge. It is the continuity of the process of literary response which must be stressed; without something to start with, without a coherent understanding of his world, the reader could not start to respond to a work of literature, and once he has started to respond to it reverberations are set up which change his mental organization not just temporarily but permanently, as Keats suggests in his sonnet on re-reading *King Lear*. The reader's response is never a static, 'enclosed' thing; it involves a constant process of new relationships between its component parts, seeing, for example, a scene in a novel in the changing circumstance both of the reader's own life, and also in the changing circumstance of his knowledge of the author's work and society. A reader's response to a great novel such as *Mansfield Park* can never reach a final equilibrium. The reader's attitude to those finely balanced interlocking considerations of class, money, love and moral duty never reaches a final stasis, for the novel mirrors the external world in as much as experience of both involves a constant process of self-modification. In his note to his poem 'Bacchus', William Empson claims that '. . . life involves maintaining oneself between contradictions that can't be solved by analysis . . .'.[22] The only way they can be solved is by practice, by actually living in one way or another, and as life involves change, so too the way in which these contradictions are reconciled also has to change. Much the same must be said about our relationship with a work of literature, which is both a part of life and also a reflection of it. We can never solve the contradictory impulses raised in us by a reading of *Mansfield Park* merely by literary analysis; we must constantly relate our response to this novel to the wider process of social living, and build up a living and changing relationship with what the novel has to offer us. Just as there is no final solution to the contradictory demands of social duty and private advantage in our lives (although as Brecht implies in *The Good Woman of Setzuan*, a more equitable society allows a better compromise to be reached), so too we can never reach a final aesthetic equilibrium in terms of our response to the respective claims of these contradictory pressures in Jane Austen's novels. Our response to her treatment of this problem must involve compromise and adaptation, and no simple hermetically-sealed 'placing' of our response to these questions in her novels is possible when in the course of social life our own solutions to comparable problems are constantly being modified.

I stressed the importance of recognising the continuity of literary response earlier, and it is particularly in the field of novel criticism that an awareness of this fact has been most apparent of late. Ian Gregor stresses this fact within the temporal limits of actually reading a novel when he notes that

> . . . novel reading is a response to a process, a process which has critical implications insufficiently grasped by those intent on conveying the significance of the completed work.[23]

To this needs to be added the comment that the response to this process is itself a process, a fact which in its turn also has very important critical implications. It is not surprising that it should be in the realm of novel criticism that this recognition of the fact that literary response is a process rather than a one-stage reaction should be most marked, for the near-impossibility of reading a substantial novel at one sitting is a forcible reminder to reader and critic that even in temporal terms literary response is not a self-enclosed entity. The person who reads a couple of chapters of a novel and then engages himself in some other activity will inevitably restart the novel from a vantage point different from that which he would have had had he read straight on without a pause. Poe's comments on the necessity of poems being short if they are to retain their poetic qualities, although confused, makes an important point, for the length of time taken to read a literary work does affect one's total response. It affects it because it modifies the way in which the literary response is related to other aspects of one's consciousness, as to be unable to read a literary work in one sitting means that one's reference out to one's external life can be more complex. Sitting reading a novel, one inevitably has to refer to one's wider experience of life to understand what is written, as I have already argued, but there is a difference between this more intellectual reference out, and the reference out involved in breaking off a novel and thinking about what has been read—perhaps discussing it with others—whilst engaged in a non-literary activity. In like manner, there is an important distinction in terms of the nature of one's response to be made between seeing a one-act play in total silence, and seeing a three-act play and discussing it with others during lengthy intervals.

There is an excellent discussion of this and related questions in W. J. Harvey's *Character and the Novel*, where Harvey examines response to novel reading as process rather than as one-stage reaction. I have already referred to his comment that how one travels determines one's destination in terms of literary response, for the travelling *is* the destination in an important sense. This leads up to important questions relating to the difference between first and subsequent readings of literary works, which again have been most fully discussed within the context of novel criticism. John Preston's chapters on *Tom Jones* in *The Created Self* consider the way in which Fielding's novel actually seems to create the reader adequate for the novel, a reader who develops in a manner calculated to increase his aesthetic response to *Tom Jones* each time that he reads it.[24] Of course, the literary work can make a reader change in certain ways which the author intends, but this will never be reducible to a completely common reader-modification precisely because each reader starts off from a more or less varied position anyway. Preston's discussion of the way the novel changes and assumes a more complex identity for the reader on each reading, reminds us of Goldmann's description of his dialectical method, whereby the 'work itself' is constantly being modified as the contexts in which it is placed become better defined. Obviously in a second reading of a novel, one such improved context is that of one's knowledge of the 'whole' of the work even when one is only reading the early part of the novel. Tom Jones's expulsion by Mr. Allworthy is a different event when seen in the context of a knowledge of his eventual reacceptance by Allworthy from its significance in the context of a first reading, when his eventual fate is unknown.

W. J. Harvey points out that one's inability to read a long novel in one sitting means that one's response to it is inevitably intermeshed with 'extra-literary' elements in a more complex way:

> Let us suppose . . . that a massive novel enforces a prolonged and probably interrupted reading. To this extent the reader is himself much less a fixity and much more a variable; the variety of his responses to the novel, therefore, will be much greater. The act of reading, after all, is not a special event, nor time out of our lives, but runs concurrent with our everyday existence. Thus with a prolonged reading our lives will, so to speak, run alongside our imaginative response and the fact of our changing, multiple viewpoints in actuality may confer a greater density and reality on the world of fiction.[25]

To talk about the literary experience running 'concurrent' with our everyday existence, and our lives running 'alongside our imaginative response' does not fully convey the extent to which these are dialectically related and influence and define one another, although clearly Harvey means to imply that this is so. The issue is complicated by the fact that the variability of the reader is partly but not wholly a result of his reading, so that the connection between literary experience and extra-literary experience is that of an infinitely complex interrelationship. The implications for critical practice that such facts have are enormous, and seem to be as yet little developed, probably largely as a result of the hitherto powerful influence of theories of the autonomy and fixity of the art work and our response to it. It is, on the face of it, extraordinary that Wayne Booth, writing as recently as 1966, can ask whether anyone has ever formulated a law of first and second readings that will tell us just how many of our pleasures on reading page one should

depend on our knowledge of what happens on page the last. It is no
exaggeration to say that such a question could hardly be imagined by
the critic who accepted *in toto* the assumption that the art work is a
hypostatised whole which produces an autonomous response when read.
Booth notes that

> We quite properly ask that books we call great be able to stand up
> under repeated readings, but we need not ask that they yield identical
> pleasures on each reading.[26]

Yet this is precisely what many critics have assumed when discussing
not only novels but even poems which the serious reader will probably
read not two or three times, but scores of times in the course of study.
Most literary criticism written within the Anglo-American academic
traditions of the past century has assumed that discussion of the literary
work or of a response to it need not be qualified by any reference to the
dynamic nature of response, or the extent to which response is altered
by the situation of the reader.

I have already suggested that I feel that Graham Hough's distinction
between an initial, non-critical literary response, and a subsequent
critical consideration of this response, misrepresents the way in which
literary response develops. Malcolm Bradbury makes a very similar
distinction in his introduction to the *Contemporary Criticism* anthology
referred to earlier:

> . . . criticism is always and necessarily a *post facto* activity—one not
> only dependent on the existence of creative work, but having its
> standard of relevance determined by it . . .[27]

Acceptance of such a view would undoubtedly lead the critic to share
the misgivings expressed by George Steiner about the critic's role, when
he talks of the critic writing about books 'in an eternity of second
hand'.[28] There is an alternative way of looking at criticism, however,
which Hough also suggests in his *An Essay on Criticism*, and to which I
have already referred, that criticism can be seen as a prolongation of
normal reading. I think that this distinction is an important one, and
not just a playing with words, for to limit criticism to a *post facto*
activity implies that it deals with a well-formed and final response
which it can examine at great length *but which it cannot change*. Of course,
for the sake of convenience, we may generalise about the reading
process in the case of a particular work, assuming it, or parts of it, to be
constant in the way that Goldmann says is a necessary part of a dialectical method. But as I have argued before, such assumptions should

always be temporary, and should be recognised so to be. For the sake of convenience again it may prove useful to distinguish between the critical activity that takes place during a reading, and that which takes place after a reading is finished, but unless the critic realises that the latter is dependent upon and formed by the former, and is in fact an extension of it, he will inevitably misrepresent the nature of literary response.

The central mistake made by the formalistic critic, as we saw in chapter three, was to confuse the real necessity of seeing a literary statement in the context of the work in which it appears, with the assumption that this context is totally autonomous and is not connected with the particular situation of the reader, the writer, or their societies. I. A. Richards, in *The Principles of Literary Criticism*, in spite of his insistence that the critic must study the affects of a work in the mind of the reader and not 'the work itself', also tends to exclude the reader from the context which defines the meaning of a literary statement. Taking the word 'night', he notes that this word has the power to raise as many thoughts and feelings as there are persons to hear it, if, that is, it is presented to them apart from a discernible linguistic context.

> But put it into a sentence and the variation is narrowed; put it into the context of a whole passage, and it is still further fixed; and let it occur in such an intricate whole as a poem and the responses of competent readers may have a similarity which only its occurrence in such a whole can secure.[29]

What Richards says here is basically true; obviously the more well-defined the linguistic context in which a word is presented, the more clear its meaning will be—its identity will become better defined the more its relationships are clarified. But apart from a gesture implied in the word 'competent', Richards does not move on from this point to note that the reading itself exists in a particular spatio-temporal context, part of which is the particular situation of the reader in question.

It is this failure, I feel, that leads Richards to move towards a familiar formalistic fallacy, that the emotional use of language appropriate to poetry (distinguished by Richards from the scientific use) has no reference to the real world. He accepts the fallacy—now fortunately having no serious defender—that science deals with the objective and the quantifiable in a way that emotional language does not, and he comes very close to Elder Olson's position described earlier, that statements made in literary works have no reference to the real, external world. Richards is correct to argue that the literary value of *Robinson Crusoe* does not depend on any approximation to the actual experiences of Alexander Selkirk, but this does not mean that its literary value is totally unconnected to the real world, a fact that would be more apparent if the creative role of the reader were given greater stress. Unless the reader is in some way or other able to relate his literary experience to his extra-literary experience, then his response will be sterile, in fact it is doubtful if it could exist at all. As W. J. Harvey says

> (the reader) . . . begins, as he probably does in life, by assimilating what is familiar to him; this he then uses as a base to explore the unknown.[30]

But the reader does not just *begin* from the basis of the known. He must continually refer to his experience of an extra-literary world as his reading continues if he is to understand what he is reading. Wayne Booth comments that Prufrock's description of the evening sky as etherised patient is no longer fact or description if what the reader wants is knowledge about the real weather. However, unless the reader has some knowledge and experience of evening skies and etherised patients, the lines will mean little or nothing to him. It seems to me apparent that a consideration of the role of the reader in the literary process is the most effective way of demonstrating the practical unworkability of formalistic theory, for without some conception of the way in which the reader and the work come into contact the critic has no basis for evaluating the respective merits of alternative possible responses to a work.

Richards' comments about the non-referential nature of poetic language have had a considerable influence on criticism, and have, I feel, caused a lot of needless confusion. To state the obvious somewhat crudely, it is just not true, as Olson claims, that the poet can make anything happen in the poem, that we accept as true within the poem anything that the poet tells us. We may be prepared to suspend or modify many of our 'normal' responses to words and phrases if the work appears to require this, but unless we can hold on to some familiar element we are not able to do this beyond a certain point. There is an interesting development of what is in essence Richards's position by J. M. Cameron in his *Poetry and Dialectic*, where he argues that

> A distinction between the poetic and other kinds of discourse is that some of the entailments that belong to other kinds of discourse are, in poetic discourse, cut.[31]

Cameron suggests that poetry is unique in this respect, but surely what he says of poetic discourse is true of any specialised discourse. I am given to understand that the normal discourse encountered in the changing rooms of rugby clubs also habitually cuts many of the entailments of other kinds of discourse, and this is surely true of all kinds of discourse. As Roger Fowler puts it, 'natural languages develop thousands of varieties specialised to the needs of topic, function, situation, etc.'[32] It may well be true that the sort of entailment-cutting we find in poetic language has certain common features not found elsewhere—although I doubt if this be true—but this does not make poetry or poetic language in any way a qualitatively unique linguistic form of utterance. Surely it is more important to insist that different literary works cut linguistic entailments in different ways, which makes Cameron's large generalisations about poetic discourse seem rather shaky. Both Richards and Cameron imply a sort of combination-lock view of the mind's function with the mind clicking round all possible meanings of a word until 'snap!' the poetic meaning opens up. Now this description of the way we select meanings which are relevant in a given context may, so far as it goes, be a reasonably accurate one. What it misses out is any theory of the basis on which the mind makes these selections, and this really is crucial. From my own position of ignorance about linguistics I am not competent to suggest a full explanation here, other than to note that unless such a theory includes some account of the way in which social practice modifies our attitude to language it will be incomplete.

Cameron sees that the reader must have some experience of an extra-poetic world, but tries to limit this experience to playing a very minor, initiating role in the total literary process.

> It is truistic that poetry of some merit can be written only by men who have contemplated the natural and social worlds in a more or less perceptive way, and equally truistic that a minimum of experience has to be had before we are capable of responding to what they write; but no particular poem is related to a particular state of affairs as a map is to a piece of country mapped, or a narrative of events to the events themselves.[33]

Cameron chooses a bad analogy with his mention of maps, for the map has itself a symbolic rather than an exact representational value—maps being flat and the world being round. Cameron's view of the artist as *contemplator* of the world rather than *changer* of it is a classic example of the way in which a view of the 'objective' reality of the external world which is unchanged by contemplation and which ignores the subject-object dialectic leads logically to a view of the art work as similarly objective and self-referential, although he does allow that it exists only in as much as it is related in some way with the real world through writer and reader. Surely it is true that in order fully to respond to a great work of literature a good deal more than just 'a minimum of experience' is necessary, which is why we are justly suspicious of the literary responses of the very young or the very immature. Is 'a minimum of experience' really an adequate basis for responding to the plays of Shakespeare? Does not a book like Jan Kott's *Shakespeare our Contemporary*, whatever its particular faults and weaknesses, demonstrate that our ability to respond to Shakespeare's plays is related intimately and fundamentally to our lived experience? Does not Kott's own experience of brutality during the Nazi occupation of Poland allow him to respond more fully to Shakespeare's treatment of political brutality in his plays? Of course, those of us who have not had firsthand experience of such brutality can have our ability to respond more fully to Shakespeare increased by reading a book such as Kott's, but again, unless we have some firm basis of lived experience to use as a basis for understanding Kott's book, then it will bring us no new richness in our response to Shakespeare. When Cameron moves to talking of a 'world of poetic fictions where the remarks of Dr Johnson and Miss Elizabeth Bennet are equally at home',[34] he reduces literature to a representation of certain unchanging truths about an abstract human nature which a 'minimum of experience' can inform us about. The picture is no more appealing than E. M. Forster's picture of the novelists of history all sitting in the reading-room of the British Museum.

Perhaps my case that a literary response is a continuously changing complex of interrelated processes which, although determined in part by the context of the work's identity also involves constant reference out to other complexes of knowledge and experience, can be better illustrated by discussion of a specific poem. I have chosen 'September Song' by Geoffrey Hill,[35] because I feel that it demonstrates well that to respond adequately to it the reader obviously needs to refer to his knowledge and experience of the world far more than is implied by Cameron's phrase 'a minimum of experience'.

September Song
born 19.6.32—deported 24.9.42

Undesirable you may have been, untouchable
you were not. Not forgotten
or passed over at the proper time.

As estimated, you died. Things marched,
sufficient, to that end.
Just so much Zyklon and leather, patented
terror, so many routine cries.

(I have made
an elegy for myself it
is true)

September fattens on vines. Roses
flake from the wall. The smoke
of harmless fires drifts to my eyes.

This is plenty. This is more than enough.

One's immediate response to this poem, I think, rests on a perception of
the ironical contrast between the words of the popular song 'September
Song', which state that it's a long time from May to December, and
that the days grow short when you reach September, and the fact that
the life-span of an individual victim of the Nazis is cut short in this
month. All the way through the poem the song hovers as a cruel ironic
comment in the background, perhaps more ironically than I have
suggested because of the fact that the music for it was composed by
Kurt Weill. However, the force of the poem seems to me to stem from
the way this ironic contrast is associated with the appearance and the
reality of Nazi brutality. The neat way in which the dates at the head
of the poem reduce the complex life of an individual to a book-keeper's
order mirrors the way in which the worst excesses of brutality and
horror are given the appearance of normality and control by being
made to conform to certain regularised forms. The contrast between
the way in which the individual is seen as undesirable, to be excluded
from one system of approval, but not untouchable, and incorporated
into another system of extermination, is not merely a poetic statement
internal to the poem, but has to be related by the reader to his knowledge
of the particular reality being described.

In an interview given just before he died, Franz Stangl, commandant
of Treblinka, described his horror at the lack of order apparent when he
arrived to take up his duties at the camp:

When I got out of the car on the *Sortierungsplatz* I stepped kneedeep
in money: I didn't know which way to turn, where to go. I waded
in papernotes, currency, precious stones, jewellery and clothes. They
were everywhere, strewn all over the square. The smell was in-
describable: the hundreds, no, the thousands of bodies everywhere,
putrefying, decomposing.[36]

The horror of this account is that his horror was at the disorder rather than at the human suffering, and he soon set about ordering what had to be done in the camp according to his well-disciplined police mind. '. . . the only way I could live was to compartmentalise my thinking . . .', he told the interviewer, and described how the 'correct' procedure in everything was gone through, including applying for ration-cards for the camp inmates who up to that time had not had them. When he described the way in which the inmates were driven to their death, his interviewer asked him if he could not have modified its horror. 'No, no, no', he replied. 'This was the system. Wirth had invented it. It worked. And because it worked it was irreversible.'

I have referred to this interview because I think that it demonstrates that the reader's response to the poem in question depends on an understanding of the peculiar nature of the horror with which the poem is concerned, which is not the horror of naked brutality and violence, but the horror of a brutality somehow made acceptable and orderly by being confined within certain rules. Thus the actual violence is rendered more horrific by being seen in the context of its being made to appear 'normal'. The lines

> Just so much Zyklon and leather, patented
> terror, so many routine cries

obviously gather much of their impact from the juxtaposition of 'leather' and 'patented', suggesting 'patent leather'. But the reason why this is effective has to be sought in the whole theme of the poem, the way in which brutality is made acceptable to those who perpetrate the atrocities by being nicely wrapped up, controlled by men in smart uniforms and polished shoes. Stangl, in the same interview, continually makes reference to the fact that his instructions always came from impeccable authority, not from gangsters or criminals—in his understanding of these terms. Again, a phrase like 'so many routine cries' brings out, in its contrast of the personal horror involved in 'cries' and the uninvolved ordering of these in the word 'routine', the same horrific ability to 'legitimise' suffering. Phrases like 'Just so much' and 'so many' hover between being emotionless book-keeping estimates of the quantities involved in the slaughter, and expressions of an intellectual inability to come to terms with the infinity of human suffering that they represent, and the same ambiguity is present in the final line of the poem. The sudden switch in the third part of the poem to self-scrutiny on the part of the poet appears to suggest a horror at the possibility of his own ability to distance himself from what he describes, and thus the last line relates both to the poet and to what is being written about. At this point the poem leads the reader towards the necessity of coming to some sort of realisation of the way in which the gap between subjective experience and objective knowledge can have a tragic significance in the life of men, a realisation which forces him more and more into an examination of his own relationship to the situation described in the poem.

At no point then can it be said that the reader's own knowledge and experience of the external world are irrelevant to the way in which he will respond to a given literary work, and as this knowledge and experience grows and changes, so too will his literary response. Perhaps I can best conclude this chapter by quoting from Sartre's account of the reading process in *What is Literature?*

> In reading, one foresees; one waits. One foresees the end of the sentence, the following sentence, the next page. One waits for them to confirm or disappoint one's foresights. The reading is composed of a host of hypotheses, of dreams followed by awakenings, of hopes and deceptions.
>
> Reading seems, in fact, to be the synthesis of perception and creation. It supposes the essentiality of both the subject and the object.[37]

NOTES

[1] Walter Kerr, 'The Theater of Say It! Show It!', *Dialogue*, 11.3, 1969, p. 84.
[2] *A Theory of the Classical Novel*, p. 133.
[3] *Immanuel Kant*, p. 184 (n).
[4] *Immanuel Kant*, p. 155.
[5] *Immanuel Kant*, p. 158.
[6] *An Essay on Criticism*, p. 5.
[7] Kenneth Burke, 'The Problem of the Intrinsic etc.', p. 123.
[8] *The Verbal Icon*, p. 32.
[9] Louis Althusser, 'The "Piccolo Teatro": Bertolazzi and Brecht', *For Marx*, p. 150.
[10] *The Verbal Icon*, p. 38.
[11] *The Objective Society*, p. 13.
[12] Roger Fowler, 'The Structure of Criticism and the Languages of Poetry', *Contemporary Criticism*, p. 184.
[13] *The Business of Criticism*, p. 7.
[14] *Character and the Novel*, p. 72.
[15] Matthew Arnold, 'The Study of Poetry', *Essays in Criticism (Second Series)*.
[16] Leon Trotsky, *Literature and Revolution*, reprinted Michigan, 1960, p. 59.
[17] Felix Vodička, 'The History of the Echo of Literary Works', *A Prague School Reader etc.*, p. 71.
[18] *The Hidden God*, pp. 19, 20 etc.
[19] Raymond Williams, 'On and from any shore', *Stand*, vol. 12, no. 2, p. 36.

[20] Irving Babbitt, 'Genius and Taste', reprinted in *Five Approaches of Literary Criticism*, p. 38.

[21] T. S. Eliot, 'What is Minor Poetry?', *To Criticize the Critic*, London, 1965, p. 48.

[22] *Collected Poems*, p. 104.

[23] Ian Gregor, 'Criticism as an Individual Activity: The Approach Through Reading', *Contemporary Criticism*, p. 200.

[24] John Preston, *The Created Self*, London, 1970.

[25] *Character and the Novel*, p. 110.

[26] *The Rhetoric of Fiction*, p. 256.

[27] *Contemporary Criticism*, p. 24.

[28] George Steiner, *Language and Silence*, London, 1967, p. 249.

[29] *Principles of Literary Criticism*, p. 9.

[30] *Character and the Novel*, p. 71.

[31] J. M. Cameron, *Poetry and Dialectic*, Leeds 1961, p. 16.

[32] Roger Fowler, *The Languages of Literature*, London 1971, p. 67.

[33] *Poetry and Dialectic*, p. 23.

[34] *Poetry and Dialectic*, p. 7.

[35] Geoffrey Hill, *King Log*, London 1968, p. 19.

[36] 'Colloquy with a Conscience', Franz Stangl interviewed by Gitta Sereny, *The Daily Telegraph Magazine*, October 8 1971, p. 59.

[37] *What is Literature?*, pp. 28, 30.

6. The Dynamics of Literary Response

> I look back, and I am suddenly and irresistibly assailed by
> *the* question: are not these few pages, in their maladroit and
> groping way, simply that unfamiliar play *El Nost Milan*,
> performed on a June evening, pursuing in me its incomplete
> meaning, searching in me, despite myself, now that all the
> actors and sets have been cleared away, for the *advent* of
> its silent discourse?
>
> LOUIS ALTHUSSER[1]

> Read it . . . and you'll never be quite the same again.
>
> Blurb on paperback *Catch 22*.

It is on the face of it curious that so many critics should have ignored or
failed to notice the significance of the fact that one's response to a work
of literature changes after the reading has been finished, because if the
critic intends to achieve anything, it is surely to alter and enrich the way
in which the reader responds to literary works. In spite of this fact, many
critics write as if response were fixed and complete at birth, capable of
being further understood but not expanded. The critic in such a pre-
sumed situation fulfils a role similar to that of the doctor, explaining to
the patient what the cause of the pain is but not affecting, at least
initially, the nature or intensity of the pain. In contrast to such views, a
number of recent critics who have concentrated their attention on the
role of the reader have pointed out that such a view of literary response
will not square with the reader's actual experience of the literary work,
and have insisted upon seeing his response in a more subtle, developing
manner.

David Lodge, in his *The Language of Fiction*, has a definition of the
reading experience which can provide us with a useful starting point
for our investigations. Lodge tends to be somewhat unnecessarily
defensive about his 'New Critical' approach, for this does not lead him
into a view of the literary response as a static thing as it does with a
number of those earlier critics who adopted such an approach. He
defines the 'reading experience' as

. . . the sustained effort of critical understanding focussed on a particular text, which usually continues after we have 'finished' it. Even after this process is concluded, or abandoned, a book does not, of course, cease to affect us. But its affects will mingle with and be modified by the affects of all the other books we have read and of other kinds of experience; and our assent to the beliefs of the implied author, if it survives at all, will be less complete than when we were reading him.[2]

Lodge's definition here recalls the analogy of Hillis Miller's of the stone cast in water which W. K. Wimsatt referred to, but it differs from it in seeing some focus to the infinite ramifications that the literary work has in terms of its affects. This focus is that of the life of the reader, whose literary response is moulded by 'the affects of all the other books we have read and of other kinds of experience'. In other words, the total response to a work of literature that a reader experiences does not take place in isolation, as the stone in water analogy of Hillis Miller's suggests, but its very nature is formed and modified by the life led by the reader. This being the case, a Marxist interpretation of literary response should be concerned to detail the way in which a Marxist understanding of the way social experience generates consciousness can be applied to our understanding of the literary process.

One implication contained in Lodge's comment which may worry some readers is that the 'affects of a book' (the choice of phrase has un-fortunate connotations of reader passivity) gradually lose their force, like a bullet shot into a resistant material, until finally the response dies away and is completely absorbed by the other aspects of the reader's consciousness, as static items of knowledge. Lodge, to be fair, doesn't actually say this, but his remark about the response—'if it survives at all'—unless it is to refer to the reader completely forgetting everything connected with his reading of a particular work, must be taken to mean that the response has faded from consciousness without having left any trace in the mind of the reader. Whether it is possible for this to happen may well be doubted, as even the most minor modifica-tion of our experience or knowledge sets up a chain of other changes which in their turn, even if they do not survive, will survive in their offspring. Whether these can legitimately be seen as part of a response to the original work of literature is perhaps a rather academic question, like that which asks whether the bicycle which has all its parts replaced is the same essential bicycle. Whatever linguistic decision one makes here in terms of nomenclature is, I suspect, an arbitrary one which still leaves one with the problem of coming to terms with understanding the significance of the way in which a literary work affects us.

Certainly we do accept in practice that there is an important difference between an immediate, fresh response to a work of literature, and those distant modifications to our consciousnesses caused, originally, by a reading of a specific work. Lecturers who attempt to hold tutorials on works of literature not read for many years soon discover this fact (or at least their students do), however fundamental the difference made to their lives by reading the work in question. There are, however, two ways of explaining this fact which presuppose entirely different interpretations of what the literary response consists of. One can either see the literary response as entire and perfect soon after the work is finished, but fading from the memory (although not changing) as time passes, or one can see response as a dynamic process which, in as much as it lives at all, like all living things is constantly being modified. Although I incline to an acceptance of the latter rather than of the former interpretation, I feel that there is a certain validity in both ways of looking at literary response. To a certain extent a work of literature does live in us through our memory of certain relatively fixed elements of the literary work—of events in a novel, or images in a poem for example. But as my comments on identity imply, these fixed elements —what Goldmann refers to as 'constants'—are themselves defined and created by the context in which they exist, and so even here we cannot posit the existence of an unchanging response. As Goldmann says, the fiction of certain 'constants' is a necessary part of our investigation of dynamic elements in any given whole, and should not be seen as in any way undialectical, so long as the fictional and temporary nature of this methodology is remembered.[3] It is certainly true that the practical problems encountered in discussing a work of literature can on occasions be lessened by assuming that we are talking about fixed events or images in a particular literary work.

To hold a past response to a literary work in suspension, as it were, in the memory, is then only a part of a total literary response, and I am inclined to think that it is an unimportant part. More significant, I think, is that dynamic vision of the literary response flowing on through one's life and experience, being modified by other literary and non-literary aspects of one's consciousness, and modifying them in turn, which Lodge's description suggests. Reading a novel like *Wuthering Heights* means that one's potentialities with regard to human relationships are increased, for as Arnold Kettle says in his book on the novel, no one who reads it is ever quite the same again. But this, it seems to me, is only part of the story, for the more rich and widespread one's experience of other people in the real world, the more richly one is capable of responding to *Wuthering Heights*. This is why one needs time to arrive at even an ill-formed judgement of a work of literature; one's response to it if it is to have any value must involve both a bringing of past experience to bear on one's reading, and a bringing to bear of one's reading on one's immediate, practical social life. Immediately the last page of *Wuthering Heights* has been read, the reader is in no position to arrive at an articulate and coherent description of his response to the novel, because in an important sense his response does not yet exist. Just as Keats shows how one must prepare for a reading of a work of literature if it is to be rich and rewarding, so too it is important to insist that one must take time and effort to reach an adequate response to the work even after the actual reading of it has finished. After finishing the last page of *Wuthering Heights* the reader has not so much a unified response to the work as a number of diverse responses, reactions, impressions, which must be brought into contact both with one another and also with one's memory and one's present experience in order to create a response which has any value. If a literary work still lives in us, then it cannot live in a static way, unchanging and un-developing; our changing life and consciousness will, because of the dialectical nature of the subject-object relationship, change it willy nilly.

To respond to *Wuthering Heights* it is of course not necessary to have been in love with a woman who for primarily social and economic reasons marries someone else with whom she is not in love. Human imagination is capable of rising to the creation of a sense of what this experience would be like—although its success in the operation will be greater or less depending on the extent of the existence of some experi-ence of love, disappointment, class-consciousness and so on possessed by the reader. But if the reader adds to his experience, say, of un-returned love *after* having finished the novel, this too will inevitably affect his response to the novel, allowing him to recall elements of his response to the novel and compare them with his lived experience—to substitute felt for imagined emotions in his response to the work. The process is obviously neither a neat one-way one, nor a slightly less neat two-way one. Literary and lived experience must constantly inter-mingle and modify one another in a variety of ways.

Lodge also mentions that subsequent literary experience can also interact with an earlier literary response, and there are certain examples of this which seem to me to be indisputable. I cannot, for example, believe that anyone can maintain quite the same response to *Jane Eyre* after having read Jean Rhys's *Wide Sargasso Sea*, which is written from the viewpoint of the first Mrs. Rochester. The latter novel presents a new way of responding to certain aspects of the former novel, which it is unlikely that any reader of *Jane Eyre* could achieve totally satisfactorily without having read *Wide Sargasso Sea*; nor can any reader of *Wide Sargasso Sea* ever escape from the influence of this novel when subsequently reading—or even thinking about—*Jane Eyre*. No doubt the formalist would say that such an extending of one's response to *Jane Eyre* is 'illegitimate' or 'extrinsic', as the identity of this novel is obviously something which predates the writing of *Wide Sargasso Sea*. One can only respond with T. S. Eliot, that what a work of literature 'means' is as much what it means to others as what it means to the author—as W. K. Wimsatt has argued whilst attacking intentionalism. In fact this particular example is an interesting one, because deeper investigation reveals how very complex and unamenable to simplification the literary process is. In a sense, *Wide Sargasso Sea* can be seen as an element of Jean Rhys's own response to *Jane Eyre*, a response which was obviously unusual because the fact that the first Mrs. Rochester is supposed to come from the West Indies obviously had a greater significance to Jean Rhys, who was brought up in the West Indies, than it would have had to a reader brought up in the British Isles. So the British reader who finds that his response to *Jane Eyre* has been changed by reading *Wide Sargasso Sea* has had his response widened both by contact with other literary experience, and also by other social experience, that is, Jean Rhys's experience of life in the West Indies. One sees in this complex net of interrelationships the way in which the richness of any given literary response derives from its contact with social life both in a direct, practical sense, and also in a far more indirect, 'literary' or academic sense.

A similar example which also raises comparable questions about the nature of literary response is the relationship between *Hamlet*, and Tom Stoppard's *Rosencrantz and Guildenstern are Dead*, where lines spoken by the two baffled characters in the former play are repeated in a different context in the latter play. The fact that the same lines assume a different significance in the two plays proves the point that the identity of a literary statement is defined by its context, but other interesting points can be made about this same example. Although seeing

Stoppard's play must modify our response to *Hamlet* in a certain sense—giving us, for example, a greater sympathy for the two courtiers as we gained a greater sympathy for the first Mrs. Rochester—it would obviously be ridiculous to imagine as we watched *Hamlet* that the other play was going on backstage. For one thing, it need only be pointed out that an infinite number of other plays based on the same lines abstracted by Stoppard from *Hamlet* could be written, and there is thus no justification whatsoever for assuming that elements in his play should have the same artistic status as elements in *Hamlet* itself for a spectator of the latter play. Nevertheless, having said this, one needs to add that to experience Stoppard's play is to modify all future experiences of Shakespeare's play that one has—however little the modification may be—for one will listen to the lines of Rosencrantz and Guildernstern in the context of a knowledge of their use in the other play. *Rosencrantz and Guildenstern are Dead* modifies and widens our response to *Hamlet* in the same way that Shakespearian criticism does; it suggests a range of possible reactions to the play of which a reader or member of an audience must take account. Jan Kott has said that we are separated from the text of *Hamlet* by the independent life of that play in our culture,[4] and if this is true then it must be remembered that part of that culture is the existence of Stoppard's play. In an interesting section of *Shakespeare our Contemporary*, Kott compares Hamlet the dramatic character with the Mona Lisa, noting wryly that the latter's smile

> . . . contains not only what Leonardo expressed in it but also everything that has been written about it.[5]

There is a very similar comment to this made by Caudwell in his *Further Studies in a Dying Culture*, where he again talks about the smile of an artistic character:

> The smile of a Polycletan Hermes has qualities, not only in me, but in the Hellas which produced it, and all that has happened since and before to man. It is not, however, merely resident in society considered as a group of men. It stretches into all parts of the Universe because society, as active subject, is related to all other reality as object.[6]

Caudwell expresses well the sense in which any aspect of the identity of a work of art is connected with everything else that forms part of the totality of man's universe, and implies that as the latter is constantly changing so too the former cannot be seen as in any real sense static. Kott merely mentions that which has been written about the Mona

Lisa's smile, but this is only the visible part of the iceberg, for any great work of art such as the Mona Lisa sets up innumerable reverberations in a culture which cannot be separated from the work of art itself. The work of art becomes what it does to the culture to which it belongs. In fact Kott speaks as if Hamlet the literary character were somehow atypical in this respect of having an identity separate 'from the text', but surely what he says of Hamlet and the Mona Lisa applies to a greater or a lesser extent to any work of art or any literary character. We cannot escape from what our culture has seen in the smile of the Mona Lisa, but neither can we escape from our response to a poem read yesterday and reread today; yesterday's response is now part of 'our' poem. Once again the Father in *Six Characters in Search of an Author* expresses the matter concisely and perceptively:

> . . . authors usually hide the details of their work of creation. Once the characters are alive. . . . Once they are standing truly alive before their author. . . . He does nothing but follow the words and gestures that they suggest to him. . . . And he must want them to be what they themselves want to be. For woe betide him if he doesn't do what they wish him to do! When a character is born he immediately acquires such an independence. . . . Even of his own author. . . . That everyone can imagine him in a whole host of situations in which his author never thought of placing him. . . . They can even imagine his acquiring, sometimes, a significance that the author never dreamt of giving him.[7]

What the Father says here is really central to the significance of Pirandello's play, that the author's creation—as the word 'creation' implies—is to a certain extent separate from him, belonging to those who read about him or see him on the stage as much as to the author; acquiring, in other words, a social rather than a purely personal identity. The bourgeois artist and critic, convinced as he usually is of the central importance of possession, has usually contented himself with the thought that though his work may move away from him, it moves away unchanged, fixed in its hard, gemlike autonomy. Pirandello's characters understand that this is not the case. Pirandello cleverly uses the observable distance between the author's conception of a character and the actor's conception of the same character to point to the inevitable difference between the author's relationship with his work and the reader-spectator's relationship with the same work. The infinite possibilities inherent potentially in an actor's interpretation of a dramatic role are analogous to the possible multiplicity of response to any work of art, with the proviso that the form of any given society imposes certain limits on the consciousness of its members.

Our ability to respond to a single work of literature must be lost if a strictly formalistic approach to its identity is taken. The formalist is committed to seeing the work as a work as a work, just as a rose is a rose is a rose, and whether the rose is seen growing in a garden or is stuck in one's eye is considered to be irrelevant. It seems obvious to me that an ideal reading of a work of literature would include a conception of the wider context of the writer's total literary production, not necessarily in a dogmatic or mechanistic manner, reducing all the poems written by a given poet to the status of one long poem, but seeing the individual poem as part of an extended attempt on the part of the writer to come to terms with certain problems. Of course, there is a sense in which reviewers of books can fall back on a somewhat simplistic use of such terms as 'promising' or 'disappointing', which places a given work in a hypothetical developing totality in a rather unhelpful way, but a more subtle and complex view of the work as part of a developing process can help the reader to respond more fully to it.

Felix Vodička describes well the way in which a given artistic response must, because of the changing nature of its component parts and their relationships, be a dynamic rather than a static thing:

> In the perception of any artistic work with thematic elements there always enters the relationship between the reality of life and the values of daily living on the one hand, and the reality as communicated by artistic means, on the other, so that the evaluation is the result of a complex process conditioned by the total structure of the life and values of the period . . .[8]

As the life and values of a period change and develop, it follows that our evaluation of a literary work must do the same—and so too must one's literary response. Important in Vodička's description is the implied dialectical tacking which must take place between the various 'wholes' mentioned by him: 'the reality of life', 'the values of daily living', and the 'reality as communicated by artistic means'.

In this context perhaps a personal description of the way in which 'the reality of life' may affect one's literary response will help to make Vodička's point less abstract. The first time that I read Joseph Heller's *Catch 22* I found it difficult to take the abrupt transition from a more or less realistic, if heightened, description of the American air-base, to the surrealistic chapters where Milo Minderbender contracts with the

Germans to bomb his own airfield, and makes a handsome profit on the deal. Since then, however, the spectacle of American planes bombing their 'own' men in the ultimate pursuit of profit has been forced upon our consciousness in the unfortunately non-literary context of Vietnam. Rereading *Catch 22*, the 'abrupt transition' that I noted before no longer seems so abrupt, and the surrealism of Milo Minderbender's obsessive pursuit of profit is perhaps not so surrealistic as I originally thought. My perception of *Catch 22* has been changed by the experience of normal life—if what is happening in Vietnam can be dignified by the word 'normal'.

There again, the reader has a certain amount of control over the relationship which he has with the work of literature, and can, to a certain extent, define the identity that the work has for him. He cannot do *anything* with the work, which in the last resort is one thing and not another, nor can he bring *any* consciousness or context to see the work in terms of. But he can decide to increase his practical knowledge of a particular area of life, or to increase his knowledge of a writer's life and personality, or to study the significance that a given work has within his own or another culture. For this reason I cannot agree with the argument presented in an article by Lowry Nelson, that each work of literature presupposes an 'optimum reader', as this seems to me to deny the essential fact that literary response is a dynamic process. If each work of literature does demand such an optimum reader, then the formalist can happily accept that the reader to a certain extent defines the response, with the proviso that the reader is defined and created by the work itself. The creative function of the reader does not then interfere with the assumed autonomy of the literary work. Nelson's argument is worth quoting in detail:

> . . . I should like to stress the role of the reader as accomplice (literally after the fact) whose responses are written into the literary work itself which then becomes normative for any individual performance. Each work requires in its integrity what I would call by way of emphasis an *optimum* reader, initially well-disposed, fully competent in "historical semantics" in the sense Leo Spitzer gave the phrase, and free from irrelevant associations of the sort I. A. Richards exposed and analyzed. . . . His role is as ambivalent as that of a dramatic actor in being both performer aware of his real self and collaborator within the fiction.[9]

I find Nelson's analogy between reader and actor more satisfying than his notion of the optimum reader, for the former does contain the implication of a dialectical relationship between the consciousness of the reader and the identity of the literary work. The actor, as Jan Kott says, '. . . always enters a ready part, written not only for him', but he hopes to be able to put something of himself into the part, as the characters in Pirandello's play realise with horror. Pirandello's characters know that they must submit to wills other than their own if their story is to become art. Actors are traditionally supposed to want to play Hamlet not only because of what is in the play, but also because of what is in them—what they will *put into* the role. It is in this sense that one hears of actors who have *made* certain roles. In like manner the reader must in some sense 'make' the work which he reads; his response must be directed and expanded as he plans, although I repeat that he can only plan this to a limited extent.

Theories similar to that of the optimum reader have been suggested in order to grant the reader a creative role, but one controlled by the literary work. Just as Wayne Booth in *The Rhetoric of Fiction* splits the writer into real and implied authors, so W. K. Wimsatt, in his introduction to *The Verbal Icon*, attempts to perform the same surgery on the reader:

> The actual reader of the poem is something like a reader over another reader's shoulder; he reads through the dramatic reader, the person to whom the full tone of the poem is addressed in the fictional situation.[10]

Although one can recognise a certain truth in what Wimsatt says here—especially if we think of the way in which a novel like *Tristram Shandy* can create a strong sense of a reader who is almost a character in the novel—I feel that such formulations as Wimsatt's are perhaps a little too stratified. We read over not one but over many shoulders, and often, as in the case of *Tristram Shandy*, the shoulders merge into the work itself, or their owners turn round and start looking at us.

Such a view of literary response—changing, developing as the reader's literary and non-literary knowledge and experience affect it, obviously carries with it certain problems for the critic, which I shall now go on to look at. The questions of relevance and value, so central to the critical activity, must now be considered.

NOTES

[1] *For Marx*, p. 151.
[2] David Lodge, *The Language of Fiction*, reprinted London 1967, p. 69 (n).
[3] *Immanuel Kant*, p. 140 (n).

[4] Jan Kott, *Shakespeare our Contemporary*, revised edition, London 1967, p. 52.
[5] *Shakespeare our Contemporary*, p. 47.
[6] *Further Studies*, p. 88.
[7] *Six Characters in Search of an Author*, p. 88.
[8] *A Prague School Reader etc.*, p. 75.
[9] Lowry Nelson, Jr., 'The Fictive Reader and Literary Self-Reflexiveness', *The Disciplines of Criticism*, p. 175.
[10] *The Verbal Icon*, p. xv.

7. *Validity and Value*

Literary criticism should be completed by criticism from a
definite ethical and theological standpoint. . . . The 'greatness' of literature cannot be determined solely by literary
standards; though we must remember that whether it is
literature or not can be determined only by literary standards.[1]

T. S. ELIOT

The difference, then, between the literary critic and the
critic who has passed beyond the frontiers of literary
criticism, is not that the literary critic is 'purely' literary. A
critic who was interested in nothing but literature would
have very little to say to us, for his literature would be a
pure abstraction.[2]

T. S. ELIOT

We can therefore ask, about any writing which is offered
to us as literary criticism, is it aimed towards understanding
and enjoyment? If it is not it may still be a legitimate and
useful activity; but it is to be judged as a contribution to
psychology, or sociology, or logic, or pedagogy, or some
other pursuit—and is to be judged by specialists, not by men
of letters.[2]

T. S. ELIOT

Lee Lemon, in his *The Partial Critics*, remarks ironically that Eliot has
argued much and forcefully that the judgement of the poem does
require something beyond the poem—and that it does not.[3] Eliot is not
however guilty of simple self-contradiction and inconsistency, but is
constantly grappling with one of the most baffling and difficult of
critical problems. Stated briefly, this concerns the existence or non-
existence of boundaries, frontiers, over which the critic may either not
cross, or at least may not cross whilst still calling himself a literary critic.
Can we resolve the paradox contained in the three quotations above,
that there is a difference between the literary and the non-literary, but
that the former must contain the latter? These questions are vital,

because any attempt to define whether a reader's response to a work is valid, or has value, has sooner or later to answer them. To use our by now familiar terminology; can we reconcile the fact that a literary work has an identity which is distinct and one thing not another, with the fact that this identity is defined by, created by, its relationships with that which is outside it? It will be noted that the strict distinction between the literary and the non-literary which Eliot makes is related to the distinction which the formalist makes between the 'objective' work of art, which is itself and not anything else, and that which is outside it, extrinsic to it. Eliot is too honest a critic to be satisfied by such a rigidity as this however, and has to admit that into a full and rich definition of what is 'literary' must come some appreciation of the fact that the 'literary' is composed of the 'non-literary'.

Just as the formalist can argue that a particular response or critical approach of which he disapproves is not concerned 'with the work qua work', so the critic wedded to a belief in a fixed distinction between the 'literary' and the 'non-literary' can, as Eliot does in the third quotation, distinguish between 'literary criticism' and other disciplines which may be concerned with literature, but not in a 'literary critical' way. If, as I have done, this strict distinction is rejected, is there any firm basis for evaluating the 'legitimacy' or value of a particular critical interpretation of or response to a work of literature? Is the formalist right in suggesting that just as critical discussion is made impossible if there is not general agreement that the same 'objective' work of literature is being discussed, so too a failure to distinguish between 'literary' and 'non-literary' criticism of a literary work leads to critical anarchy, with no basis remaining for assessing the relevance or value of a particular piece of criticism?

These and other problems relating to evaluation can be solved, or at least can be seen to be less insuperable than they may at first appear, if we once again insist on the necessity to reject absolutist interpretations of the terms with which we are dealing. To give terms like 'literary' and 'non-literary' absolute and 'objective' meanings, which remain unchanged irrespective of situation, is to render the problems mentioned insoluble right from the start. Eliot in fact oscillates between relative and absolute definitions of these terms. He gives the terms a relative significance when he says that 'literary' must include 'non-literary', but suggests an absolute distinction between the two when he starts talking of frontiers between the two, in a manner that implies a fixed and unchanging separation between the two terms. It is on the basis of this essentially dualistic approach that his criticism wanders into so many theoretical paradoxes and confusions.

I would suggest that we try to leave behind such unhelpful metaphors as 'frontiers' and 'boundaries' when talking about the distinction between different ways of responding to or criticising literary works. As I suggested in my first chapter, one cannot make any *absolute* distinction between approaching *Absalom and Achitophel* as historical evidence and as literature; any concern with it will include elements of both, albeit in varying proportions. To take Eliot's distinction between literary criticism and psychology; can it be said that Ernest Jones's classic psychoanalysis of Hamlet's character does not help us to 'understand and enjoy', as Eliot puts it, *Hamlet* more? Is it in fact possible to imagine any psychological, sociological, logical or pedagogical treatment of a work of literature which is intellectually respectable within its own discipline which does not allow us to 'understand and enjoy' the work in question just a little bit more?

If we dispose of our fixed frontiers, guarded by armed and uniformed defenders of literary critical purity, and think rather of shifting relationships between the peoples of different lands, rather than the fixed delineation of national boundaries, the metaphor comes closer to our aesthetic problems. To fail to do this seems to me to be disastrous. Eliot's criticism achieves greatness because when his theories do not fit the experience he has of a work of literature he is prepared to drop them, or at least modify them. If we consider a group of critics such as the 'Chicago' critics, who really do try to impose a pure 'literary' criticism on to literature, the result is at times quite horrific. All through the massive and often torpid collection of essays *Critics and Criticism*, one feels that life has escaped, that the antiseptics administered to kill 'foreign bodies' and preserve a pure literary criticism, have merely succeeded in killing off the patient—literature itself. Summing up the approach of the group, R. S. Crane offers ample confirmation of Eliot's point that 'A critic who was interested in nothing but literature would have very little to say to us, for his literature would be a pure abstraction':

> What is held as constant in this criticism is the whole complex of accidental causes of variation in poetry that depend on the talents, characters, educations, and intentions of individual authors, the opinions and tastes of the audiences they address, the state of the language in their time, and all the other external factors which affect their choice of materials and conventions in particular works. The

provisional exclusion of these is necessary if the analysis is to be concentrated upon the internal causes which account for the peculiar construction and effect of any poem qua artistic whole.[4]

We may have our hopes raised by Crane's mention of merely a provisional exclusion, which recalls Goldmann's suggestion that a dialectical method must examine the dynamic of one aspect of the subject being studied in the light of an assumed and provisionally accepted stasis on the part of other aspects. But Crane's exclusion turns out to be provisional in much the same way that the introduction of income-tax in Britain was a temporary expedient. Whereas Goldmann, having examined the dynamic in one component of the literary process, will achieve a new assumed 'constant' as a result of his investigation and will then proceed to examine the dynamic in another component, the Chicago critics never seem to move from their initial constant at all. It strikes me as a terrible irony that Marxists are accused of reducing the diversity and richness of life to a grey conformity; they have certainly never gone so far as to suggest the exclusion of all the variables which Crane enumerates—variables which are, in the last resort, life itself. To try to reach a pure literary criticism in this way, one which has value because it is concerned with literature qua literature and not something else, and which is thus 'legitimate', is like trying to discover a person's morals by examining him independently from anything said, done or thought by him—all accidental elements in his makeup determined not by his inner core of moral being but by accidental pressures from outside himself. We must accept, I think, that literature, and the value of literature, is not what is left when Crane's 'accidental causes of variation' are removed, but is to be found only in the context of these 'accidental causes'.

It can further be pointed out that those who have argued that the value and relevance of literature and literary criticism can be distinguished in an absolute way from other areas of value and relevance, have succeeded in expressing this only in terms of tautology. Cleanth Brooks—like Eliot, a critic good enough to rise above his own theories at times—gives us a typical example of this:

> One can, to be sure, treat *Antony and Cleopatra* sociologically, historically, morally, etc., but the play is, after all, a work of art, and if we consider it to be a work of art we shall find ourselves talking about it in terms appropriate to aesthetic structure . . .[5]

Unfortunately, the terms appropriate to a work as aesthetic structure are also very often appropriate to or derived from sociology, history, moral discourse, and so on. We cannot assess the value or relevance of a critical comment on a literary work just by asking if it is treating the work 'as literature', or 'as aesthetic structure', if we are then going to define literature or aesthetic structure merely in the tautological way expressed above.

This is not, I insist, to deny certain simple facts, such as the fact that the critic has a choice of ways he can approach a way of literature, a choice of comments he can make about the work within a single approach, that some approaches are to be preferred to others, and that some statements about works of literature are invalid or irrelevant. But what I am saying is that we can find no secure basis for making judgements of the respective merits of different approaches, or for preferring one statement about or response to a literary work to another, so long as we rest on the bedrock of a formalistic 'objective' work, or a concealed formalism expressed in an absolutist distinction between 'literary' and 'non-literary' qualities. I would now like to suggest what I think such a secure basis could be.

In the same essay from which the above quotation comes, 'Literary Criticism: Poet, Poem, and Reader', Cleanth Brooks gives us more productive food for thought in a comment on the respective values of different sorts of literary responses—an example analogous to the problem of assessing the respective values of different critical comments on a literary work. Unlike Elder Olson, Brooks does not deny the reader any creativity in the literary process, but he tries to distinguish between a creative response and a 'triggered' response:

> . . . if we may . . . enhance a poem at will by importing into it all sorts of associations and meaning, then we can theoretically turn an obscure poem into a clear poem—and a poor poem into a good poem. Even the verse from the newspaper agony column beginning "It is now a year and a day/Since little Willy went away" might move us deeply if we actually knew little Willy and his sorrowing mother. But only the unwary would take the triggering of such an emotional response as proof of the goodness of the poem.[6]

Brooks admits that it is difficult to distinguish between 'legitimate parts of a poem' and 'merely adventitious associations', but that although no hard and fast boundary can be drawn there is nonetheless a real difference between these two sorts of response.

Brooks distinguishes between the 'poem as poem', and the 'poem as personal document' to explain the origin of the difference between a creative and a triggered response, a distinction with which I am not totally happy, as I have already tried to show that a personal response to a poem also partakes of the social, and that there is no hard and fast distinction to be made between the two. Monroe Beardsley makes a similar, rather over-rigid distinction when he argues that it is easy to mistake other experience for aesthetic experience, and to confuse, for example, one's agreement with the social message of a novel with an aesthetic response to it.[7] He does not appear to consider the possibility that one's aesthetic response to a novel may have as one component one's agreement with the novel's social message. Like Brooks and Eliot he implies that there is an absolute boundary between the aesthetic (or the literary) and the non-aesthetic (or the non-literary).

If we wish to use terms such as legitimate and illegitimate—and I think that there is a good case for discarding their use—we must, at least, specify to what the alleged legitimacy refers. It is no good saying 'legitimate to the poem'. We must at some point escape from this circularity. Little Willy's mother's response to the verses quoted by Brooks is not illegitimate, but it is of limited value and relevance to other people. She has a perfect right to respond as she does, and it would be a curious form of morality which tried to prevent her from so doing, but her response is, as I say, not to be treated as having a value or relevance equal to certain other sorts of literary response. Her response has only very indirect social implications, and is of little value except from within the narrow context of her own emotional unhappiness. Now whilst all individuality has *some* social significance, this latter can be very minor indeed, and this is certainly true of little Willy's mother's response. In addition to this we can, I think, profitably seize on Brooks's word 'triggered', and note that her response is not a creative one, but exists in embryo, as it were, prior to her reading of the lines in question. It cannot really be said that the relationship between little Willy's mother and the lines she reads is one from which anything fundamentally new will emerge; we have a quantitative change in her (her grief finds a new form of expression) rather than a qualitative one (her grief developing towards a solution through the aesthetic experience of art). Of course a preformed response can form a valuable part of any literary response, and in a certain sense all responses to literature are preformed. But the great work of literature modifies these components of our response that are preformed, whereas the triggered response does not. I think that Pound is getting at something similar when he talks of

literature as news that STAYS news; for on each reading it gives us
something new, whereas we very quickly get bored with third-rate
literature, for we get only the same triggered response each time; as
Pound says, the only reason for rereading a detective novel is that we
have forgotten it. As Keats makes clear in his sonnet on rereading *King
Lear*, he reads it because he remembers it, and because he wants to
produce something new from his relationship with it, not the same old
response already experienced.

It is for this reason that we respect the evidence that a literary work
has been admired by a large number of people, over a long period of
time, for if this is the case its effect on its readers is unlikely to be either
a primarily personal one, or a repetitive 'triggered' one. But how do we
reach a judgement about the greater or lesser value of a particular way
of criticising or responding to a work of literature? Firstly, I think, as
Allan Rodway suggests, by 'tacking out', by moving between alternative ways of responding to a work of literature so that they mutually
enrich one another. But we decide which of the possibilities between
which we tack is the most fruitful, in the last resort, by reference to
our concrete situation, to social practice. As Goldmann puts it in his
essay 'Criticism and Dogmatism in Literature':

> One of the most important ideas in dialectical philosophy is that
> thought is always an attempt to discover a meaning in life under
> certain concrete conditions and to establish a praxis which will tend
> to change reality in the direction of the hopes of human groups. . . .[8]

In as much as a work of literature allows human beings better to come to
terms with their environment, and to develop themselves and their
environment in a way that is of benefit to humanity, then it will be of
value. Now seen from this point of view, perhaps little Willy's mother's
response has some value; it perhaps prevents her going mad, or commit-
ting suicide. It does not however allow society at large to 'discover a
meaning in life under certain concrete conditions', or to 'establish a
praxis which will tend to change reality in the direction of the hopes of
human *groups*'. It thus may have an individual value, but its social value
is utterly negligible. Goldmann's discussion of value in the same essay
has the virtue too of insisting that there is no such thing as an absolute
value. He argues that 'global structurations of categories' (and one
could argue that the same was true of a particular literary response or
critical approach)

. . . have only temporary value. They are generally valid for certain specific social groups in a certain concrete historical situation, but to the extent to which—through the very action of men who use them as jumping off points, or through external influences—the world is transformed and situations change, mental categories cease to be efficacious, lose their rationality and must transform themselves in turn.[9]

Some responses to literature are more valuable than others not because they are faithful to the objective work, or because they are literary responses rather than sociological, logical or psychological investigations, but because in a given concrete historical situation they contribute to the needs of humanity by allowing understanding and forward movement. Maurice Cornforth (to whose writing and conversation my understanding of this problem owes much), expresses this point well:

> It is not merely that feelings may be expressed in language, but that human feelings are not felt by animals lacking the use of language, since without language they lack imagination and could not enter into human relationships. (This example provides a clue, incidentally, to the role which literature plays in developing human relations; the expression it gives to them and the image it makes of them are factors in making and changing them.)[10]

If I may be allowed to refer back to my comments on Keats's sonnet on rereading *King Lear*, I think that the stress laid by Goldmann and Cornforth on the way in which literature *changes* reality, and is to be valued to the extent that it does this in a way beneficial to humanity, explains why it is that Keats wishes to be both active and passive in his reading. He wishes to bring into creative contact his past experience of the play, his subsequent experience, and his new reading of it. He thus uses the play to change himself, as well as using his own experience to 'change' the play.

R. M. Hare has noted that we only talk of 'good' things when the question of making a choice arises, that is, when different ways of changing our reality are possible. He notes that

> . . . it must not be thought that 'good egg' is exclusively descriptive, or 'good poem' exclusively evaluative. If, as the Chinese are alleged to do, we chose to eat eggs that are decomposed, we should call that kind of egg good, . . . And if I said that a poem was good, and was not a very eccentric person, my hearer would be justified in assuming that the poem was not 'Happy birthday to you!'[11]

Whether intentionally or not, Hare demonstrates that our evaluation of things is not a seeking after an absolute, objective 'quality' of goodness or value in them, but is an assessment of the value and potentiality contained within them for us in a specific, concrete situation. If this value and potentiality is either socially or temporally limited—if it only exists for one person, or for one age, or for people at a particular time (such as on their birthday)—then its contribution to humanity is so much the lesser. There is a good example of this in Sartre's *What is Literature?*, where he notes that a work called *The Silence of the Sea*, concerned with the situation in occupied France, was received with some hostility by émigré anti-fascists, because it portrayed the occupying German soldiers as, in general, normal human beings, but was understood by those in occupied France who understood by experience that every German soldier was not a beast or an ogre.[12] However, Sartre goes on to note that although the work was well received early on during the occupation, when it helped people to come to terms with their experience of the occupying Germans, once they had succeeded in so doing the work lost its appeal, and by the end of 1942 Sartre notes that Frenchmen no longer wished to know whether those who tortured their friends were victims or accomplices of fascism; the war was starting again and demanded a new attitude towards and understanding of the occupiers. The work had been left behind by events and no longer had anything of importance to offer French readers. Its value was limited in a temporal sense, and thus inferior to the value of a book not so limited.

Goldmann talks of discovering 'a meaning in life under certain concrete conditions', and establishing 'a praxis which will tend to change reality in the direction of the hopes of human groups', and it is this simultaneous explanation of life and contribution to progress that Everett Knight, in a different context, captures in his comment that, '. . . identity *reconciles explanation and value*'.[13] As Cornforth also suggests, to give words to a thing is to change the relationship between the namer and the named, and is to make the named more amenable to being changed. In an infinitely more complex way this is how literature modifies our reality. Monroe Beardsley, also rejecting the idea that the value of a word is an absolute or objective quality that it possesses, comments:

> How could anything have value except in relation, direct or indirect, to the needs and desires of human beings? . . . If value is not a quality of perceptual objects, like their redness or grandeur, *then it*

must be a relation, and consist in someone's taking a certain attitude towards the object. (My emphasis, J. M. H.)[14]

As the 'needs and desires' of human beings change as they are satisfied, or modified, as Goldmann says, by external circumstances, then so too must the value of the object change.

Goldmann makes the point that to insist on the importance of the practice rendered possible by literary experience is, of necessity, to take up a social rather than an individualistic attitude to value. After having pointed out that the distinction between theory and practice is one that *appears* with social life, he shows how experience—within which one can subsume literary experience—plays a different role in the life of a social being from that which it plays in the life of an asocial being:

> Social life implies common action and the division of labour; it presupposes the possibility of communication. Now the given, matter without form, changes with each individual; there are no two identical perceptions. If two people are in a room, each sees the same table in a different way . . .

But being social beings, who can communicate, and who can join together to change their environment, their cognition can, through practice, become a social rather than an individual one.

> Communication, however, presupposes at least that each (person) transform his own immediate given, his own matter, in such a way that the other understands what is communicated to him and can relate it to his own given, to the matter of his own immediate apprehension; but it also implies that each should be able to understand the matter of his own acquaintance as a special case of knowledge held in common and his own knowledge as dependent upon that of other men. *Experience* is the name given to the result of this transformation of matter which, it must be stressed, leads at least to the possibility of mutual communication . . .[15]

When we read a work of literature then, we are given socially perceived means for transforming the world, as well having to go to the world, engage in practice, to assess and evaluate *our* response to the work. The process tacks between the personal and the social. It is through this tacking movement that a response is arrived at which is both socially accessible and individually convincing; which relates to the experience of the individual, and allows him to go back to the domain of practice regenerated and with increased potentiality. Graham Hough, in his *An Essay on Criticism*, expresses a similar viewpoint:

(the) interaction between moral and formal considerations is a dialectical process; and it is this process and this alone that allows us to see the work as a totality. The synthesis between moral and formal criticism must be dynamic—always in motion, back and forth, from one pole to another.[16]

If this back and forth motion is extended to include motion between literary response and social practice, then we reach a position similar to that suggested by Goldmann.

Thus the truly great critic is great not because he achieves and communicates a final and complete insight into the work of literature, seeing it completely objectively, excluding all extra-literary considerations, but because he tacks dialectically between the different components of the literary process and relates the experience and insight thus gained to the human situation at a particular time and place, thus revealing *new* relevance, *added* significance in the work of literature. This is what Marx, in the *Theses on Feuerbach*, calls the revolutionary, 'practical-critical' activity, insisting that it is *in practice* and not in contemplation that man must prove the truth. This, as many have pointed out, is why the final thesis appeals to philosophers to change the world and not merely to interpret it, because it is only in changing it that its reality can be revealed. In the past the critic, all too often, has sought to interpret the work of art; the point, however, is to change it by allowing it to help us change ourselves and our reality.

Very often, however, the critic is faced with a range of choices in approaching a work of literature which it is not always easy to decide between. Kenneth Burke, in his essay 'The Problem of the Intrinsic', gives a useful simple example of this:

> Consider as an illustration the fourteen stations of the Cross: The concern for them in the totality of their progression would be dramatic. But the pause at any one of them, and the contemplation and deepening appreciation of its poignancy, in itself, would be lyric.[17]

I cannot agree that one can ever see one of the stations of the cross as 'poignant' if it is abstracted from the sequence, and the narrative context, of which it forms a part. However Burke is right that the critic—and the reader—often has the choice of concentrating more on the identity of the work and less on its relationships, or vice versa. As Graham Hough suggests, however, the good critic tacks between the two, and the precise direction of his route must be determined by, to repeat Goldmann once more, the need to

. . . discover a meaning in life under certain concrete conditions and to establish a praxis which will tend to change reality in the direction of the hopes of human groups . . .

Thus many critical disagreements about method, for example, assume that there is a 'right' way, a correct 'literary-critical' way, to approach a given work of literature, irrespective of time and place. Consider the argument between the followers of Bradley and L. C. Knights about the 'legitimacy' or otherwise of abstracting a literary character (or situation), from the fixed context of the work in which he or she appears. Rather than saying that it is always wrong (or right) to do this, it is far more fruitful to argue that there is no hard and fast rule in the abstract about such procedures, but that they must always be assessed in a particular concrete situation. Certainly it would seem that some works of literature encourage such extension more than others, as do certain reader-situations, and certain historical contexts. The way in which a novel ends, for example can have a direct effect on the desirability or otherwise of such abstraction and extension; the neat, all-explaining end of a detective novel or the comforting 'they lived happily ever after', do not encourage the sort of searching extension that, say, the end of *The Portrait of a Lady* does. John Bayley, reacting against L. C. Knights's critical position as the latter reacted against Bradley's, argues that

> . . . it is as relevant to ask ourselves what was the nature of Othello's and Desdemona's love, and what were their chances of happiness, as it is to wonder whether Isabel, in *The Portrait of a Lady*, would ever have left her husband, or how Elizabeth and D'Arcy would have got on after marriage. These queries are relevant because the resonance of such situations can never be stilled.[18]

In other words, there is no absolute border between the intrinsic and the extrinsic treatment of a literary work, and judgements about the relative virtues of different approaches must appeal to *all* the components of the literary process at a particular time and place, and not just one, the work itself. We cannot freeze the relationship between Isabel and her husband, for as Bayley says, the resonance of such situations cannot be stilled, pointing to the essentially *dynamic* nature of literary response, a dynamism which is no respecter of frontiers.

To quote Henry James once again—'such relations end nowhere', and though he goes on to say that the novelist must give the impression that they do, the reader's life and experience will continually remind him that they do not.

Perhaps I can summarise the position I have now reached as follows. Any artistic response involves a dialectical interrelationship between writer, reader, and work. The consciousnesses of both writer and reader are likewise related to the totality of their worlds, including the 'congealed experience' of the past. Thus the search for any static core around which the literary process can be woven and in the light of which it can be explained, and responses to it evaluated, is the modern equivalent of the search for the philosopher's stone. No unchanging work of art, unchanging human nature, 'legitimate' or 'literary' response can, when investigated, maintain its immutability. In any given complex of time, place, reader and work, the reader and the critic have to make anew the decisions that were made by readers and critics in preceding generations, but in the light of these decisions. In the last resort, the process of living distinguishes good works from bad, and fruitful responses to them from unfruitful ones. Questions of 'legitimacy' only confuse the issue. Using a Chippendale chair to batter down a door in a fire is not an 'illegitimate' use of it, but it is not a use which develops and utilises all the rich potentialities which the chair has, in the long term, for humanity. Similarly, productions of Brecht's plays which attempt to demonstrate that the activities of the Nazis Brecht was concerned to attack can be equated with the actions of Communists in the world today, cannot be very fruitfully attacked simply on the grounds that this is not what Brecht intended. Brecht would obviously not have 'intended' many of the positive results that his plays may have had, and what a deceased person would approve or disapprove of in changed circumstances after his death is one that spiritualists can be left to investigate and answer. What one can say is that such performances, in a specific context, do not either help people to understand the world, or to change it in a positive way.

Around 1968, for example, there was a production of *The Resistable Rise of Arturo Ui*, which tried to link the final warning of the play with the Soviet intervention in Czechoslovakia. Whatever one thinks of the latter, it would seem obvious that this attempt to draw a parallel with a contemporary event and the content of a literary work is at best confusing, for there are just no lessons to be learned from the play in question which could be profitably applied to the situation in Czechoslovakia in 1968—and this would remain true if Brecht came back from the dead and told us that he thoroughly approved of the point made by the production—an unlikely event in more ways than one.

NOTES

[1] T. S. Eliot, 'Religion and Literature', reprinted in *Selected Essays*, revised edition, reprinted London 1969, p. 388.

[2] *On Poetry and Poets*, p. 116.

[3] Lee T. Lemon, *The Partial Critics*, London, 1965, p. 52.

[4] *Critics and Criticism*, p. 20.

[5] Cleanth Brooks, 'Literary Criticism: Poet, Poem, and Reader', reprinted in *Perspectives in Contemporary Criticism*, ed. Grebstein, London 1968, p. 100.

[6] *Perspectives in Contemporary Criticism*, p. 102.

[7] *Aesthetics*, p. 534.

[8] *The Dialectics of Liberation*, p. 140.

[9] *The Dialectics of Liberation*, p. 139.

[10] Maurice Cornforth, *Communism and Human Values*, London 1972, p. 11. (This book consists of slightly modified versions of the later chapters of the same author's *Marxism and the Linguistic Philosophy*, second edition, London 1967.)

[11] R. M. Hare, *The Language of Morals*, Oxford 1952, p. 122.

[12] *What is Literature?*, p. 52 et seq.

[13] *A Theory of the Classical Novel*, p. 66.

[14] *Aesthetics*, p. 123.

[15] *Immanuel Kant*, p. 123.

[16] *An Essay on Criticism*, p. 39.

[17] Kenneth Burke, 'The Problem of the Intrinsic etc.,' p. 133.

[18] John Bayley, *The Characters of Love*, reprinted London 1968, p. 139.

8. The Social and Temporal Context of Literary Response

> Understanding the social necessity that has produced a given style is something quite different from evaluating the aesthetic results of the style.[1]
>
> György Lukács

> . . . what the sentence means depends not on the whim of the individual, and his mental vagaries, but upon public conventions of usage that are tied up with habit patterns in the whole speaking community.[2]
>
> Monroe C. Beardsley

The best-known contribution to aesthetics made by Marxism has been the insistence that there is a causal relationship between a writer's consciousness and the society of which he is a part, which society can be fully understood only in terms of its basic economic structure. Marxist critics have always stressed the necessity of examining a work of literature in the context of the society out of which it emerged, and to understand the economic forces operative in the society as well as their forms of manifestation in the superstructure of the society. Of course, critics have for many years stressed that the social milieu of the artist must be understood if his art is to be properly comprehended, but Marxist criticism has in general gone further than this and has seen a much closer link between the aesthetic qualities of the art work and its socio-economic origins, rather than seeing the latter as a temporary barrier to achieving full understanding of the timeless qualities of the former. Now I do not intend in this chapter to argue for the necessity of approaching literature from the vantage point of a full knowledge of its social origins. There is no shortage of Marxist polemic on this question. What I would like to do is to examine some of the unresolved problems which such a basic commitment throws up. I assume that it will be understood both that I feel that the basic premises of Marxist criticism are correct on this question, and also that I feel that they have on occasions been misapplied in an over-mechanical manner. I find an approach such as that shown in Caudwell's *Illusion and Reality*, where there are neat tables equating 'period', 'general characteristics', and 'technical characteristics',[3] to hover on the boundary between essential information and misinformation. Any reader of literature should be aware of the sort of basic correlation between literature and society given by Caudwell, but he should also be very much aware of its partial nature, and of the dangers of over-simplification contained in such a schematisation. I take it that it will also be accepted without much dispute that certain practical problems may arise from a basic Marxist approach here which do not raise any significant theoretical difficulties. For example, the extent to which and the way in which a writer's consciousness is conditioned by his society may vary from writer to writer in the same society, and details both about the society and about the writer's consciousness may be difficult to discover.

The problems I shall consider in this chapter relate to the fact that literary works exist in several different contexts, social and temporal, which complicates their aesthetic identity—as one would expect. Time and space—historical and social dimensions of literary identity—render aesthetic questions complex, and this complexity cannot be ordered by the use of simplistic, one-stage causal relationships in critical method. Any Marxist literary criticism which is content merely to approach a work like *King Lear* by attempting to place it, once and for all, in a static social context, must end up in dogmatism and tedium. Such an approach ignores the subject-object dialectic, the indirectness of the base-superstructure relationship insisted upon by Marx and Engels, and ends up with an absolutist rather than a dialectical result; a fixed, immutable, Marxist 'placing' of a work of literature in the context of its own fixed, immutable society; a result that is as un-Marxist as the fixity of the formalist's art work or the bourgeois critic's unchanging aesthetic effect. The one thing that must be seen to be basic to any Marxist aesthetic is the rejection of any theory of the finality of any judgement, or the fixity of any component in the artistic process. As Goldmann puts it in an as-yet untranslated article:

> . . . chaque fois que la pensée scientifique fait un progrès décisif, elle modifie par cela même et la praxis et la manière de percevoir et de coordonner les données; elle est donc amenée à restructurer son objet. (Whenever there is a decisive advance in scientific thought, it modifies, by the very fact of advance, both praxis and the manner of perceiving and relating the data; it is thus led to the restructuring of its object.)[4]

An interesting early critical discussion of the problems involved in reconciling a historical and an aesthetic view of the literary work occurs in W. C. Brownell's pioneer work *Criticism*, first published in 1914. Brownell recognised the contribution made by what he referred to as the 'historic' method to criticism, but he insisted upon the fact that certain unsolved problems still remained once this contribution had been admitted:

> In fine, the historic method, great as have been its services to criticism and truly constructive as it is, has two erroneous tendencies. It tends generally to impose its historical theory on the literary and aesthetic facts, to discern their historical rather than their essential character; and, as inelastically applied, at all events, it tends specifically to accept its 'documents' as final rather than as the very *subjects* of its concern.[5]

Brownell's distinction between the 'historical' and the 'essential' character of works of art is not happily expressed, and suggests that the two can be seen as totally separate—which would make historical examination of works of art somewhat of a waste of time. What is more interesting in his comments here is his objection to using works of art as fixities to explain history, rather than seeing them as dynamic, as having a changing significance and identity. The work of art is considered, to use Goldmann's terminology, as a constant to investigate its historical context, but there is no dialectical tacking back to using the new understanding of the context as a constant in the light of which the work can be more fully understood. The identity of the art work is seen as a given which does not change, rather than as an identity which is modified as its context is changed or more fully perceived. Brownell dismisses the suggestion that the historical examination of art can be discredited by proving that similar influences in the same period produced both Tintoretto and the ordinary Venetian gondolier, noting that, 'One might as well hold that immunity in some cases is not the result of the vaccine that fails to take in others . . .', an argument for which Marxists should be grateful, and should have learned from. However, his criticism of the historic method is one which needs to be taken seriously, for it has been repeated by many critics since. Helen Gardner, for example, in *The Business of Criticism*, argues that the historical approach can take us towards the meaning of a literary work, but cannot explain its value, which is connected with its extra-historical life, as she calls it. She writes that:

> The total meaning of a work of art cannot be analysed or treated historically, though I believe we cannot approach it except through

history as we ourselves meet it in history. It is extra-historical, I believe, because it is the expression and creation of a human mind and personality and so is ultimately irreducible into anything but itself.[6]

The statement is confused, and the final claim is a non-sequitur, but nevertheless there is a genuine problem contained in the statement relating to the way in which historical and aesthetic approaches to literature are connected which must be examined. My own feeling is that so long as the Marxist critic sees his job merely to be that of discovering the connection between the work of art and the society which produced it, and not that of also considering the dialectical relationship between his own socially-formed consciousness and the work, then such problems will persist. Gramsci points out that it is not enough to know the *ensemble* of relations as they exist at any given time as a given system. He insists that they must be known genetically in the movement of their formation, and adds that

. . . each individual is the synthesis not only of existing relations, but of the history of these relations. He is a précis of all the past.[7]

In like manner, Everett Knight points out that in the last analysis, 'structure' is something that men have done, and is 'congealed praxis'.[8] From our point of view the important thing to stress is that this applies equally to reader and to writer, and that the socio-temporal forces that form both, *and their dialectical relationship*, must be understood if the critic is to escape from a dogmatic and essentially a metaphysical position.

From all that I have said it would appear that a dialectical approach to literary criticism should, and must, commit itself to a view of literary evaluation as a temporary act, which becomes dated and irrelevant when the consciousness of a particular society or group changes. It has been a constant puzzle to those who have approached literature from what can be broadly defined as a sociological position that this does not seem to be the case in practice. In fact one of the most consistent grounds for attacks on Marxist literary criticism has been that of the lasting aesthetic value of literature and art. Such attacks have pointed to the fact that although Marxists deny the existence of absolute, unchanging human values—which would imply an extra-social area of human consciousness or experience—they are unable satisfactorily to explain why it is that the great art of the past has the power to elicit a consistently admiring response from readers in successive and very different societies.

The non-Marxist has his own relatively simple explanation for this phenomenon. He admits that as history progresses man changes, but insists that this change is only in externals, leaving unchanged an inner core of unchanging 'human nature' to which art appeals and on which its immortality rests. A classic expression of this theoretical standpoint can be found in the writings of eighteenth-century literary and aesthetic theorists, by whom it was assumed that to achieve a desired 'generality' was to escape from the temporary and adventitious, and to make contact with what Johnson, in his *Life of Cowley*, describes as those 'great thoughts', which he claims are always general, and which

> . . . consist in positions not limited by exceptions, and in descriptions not descending to minuteness.

The *Discourses* of Sir Joshua Reynolds are full of very similar comments, and in them frequent use is made of that analogy beloved of the time, between the unchanging human body and the changing human dress on the one hand, and the unchanging human nature and changing human customs on the other. Thus Reynolds can regret that

> Art is not yet in so high estimation with us, as to obtain so great a sacrifice as the ancients made, especially the Grecians, who suffered themselves to be represented naked, whether they were generals, law-givers or kings.[9]

The conflict between artistic integrity and delicacy has not always been responsible for such nice crises of conscience as faced the eighteenth-century gentleman. In essence, Reynolds's arguments are representative both of his age and also of a recurrent trend in aesthetic theory. Two centuries later, defining the ways in which his principles differ from those of Marxist critics, F. R. Leavis can appeal to what is, essentially, the same basic theory:

> The ways in which (my way of thinking) is at odds with Marxist theories of culture are obvious. It stresses, not economic and material determinants, but intellectual and spiritual, so implying a different conception from the Marxist of the relation between the present of society and the past, and a different conception of society. It assumes that, enormously—no one will deny it—as material conditions count, there is a certain measure of spiritual autonomy in human affairs, and that human intelligence, choice and will do really and effectively operate, expressing an inherent human nature.[10]

Although a Marxist will feel that there is a certain amount of Aunt Sallyism going on here—have Marxists, warts and all, ever totally rejected human intelligence, choice and will?—the statement of disagreement is clear and represents a real distinction. For both Reynolds and Leavis, material conditions count, but they are extrinsic to that unchanging core of human nature, the constancy and continuity of which allows the reader to draw the same value from his reading of a literary work as was drawn by a reader of the same work two centuries earlier. The bourgeois critic, as I have argued before, must have his hard gemlike autonomous element somewhere in the literary process, and if it is not to be the autonomy of the work of art, it is, as Leavis puts it, the autonomy of the spirit in human affairs. Only with something autonomous and unchanging to hold on to can he feel that his values are 'real', and refer to something tangible. The relative is not real for the bourgeois; he must have his God or his fixed cash value if he is to feel that he is in contact with a real world in which the reality of human relationships has been denied him.

In spite of his insistence that the critic must have a developed historical sense, and his comparable insistence on the conditional nature of literary critical judgement, T. S. Eliot too provides us with a classic example of the same theoretical stance, demonstrating, I think, the way in which he continually searches for ways to reconcile an intrinsic and an extrinsic critical approach which his theoretical presuppositions prevent him from reaching. In 'The Frontiers of Criticism', he argues that

> What matters most, let us say, in reading an ode of Sappho, is not that I should imagine myself to be an island Greek of 2,500 years ago; what matters is the experience which is the same for all human beings of different centuries and languages capable of enjoying poetry, the spark which can leap across those 2,500 years.[11]

However much Marxists may modify their literary critical theory and practice so as to make it less mechanical and more dialectical, there is no possibility of reconciling a theory such as Eliot's statement rests upon, and any approach which rejects such absolutes as that of an unchanging human nature. If there is any one concept which is totally at odds with Marxism, it is surely that of the unchanging human nature which all human beings of any time or place are supposed to be possessed of. Gramsci, in *The Modern Prince*, insists upon this point:

> The basic innovation introduced by the philosophy of praxis into the science of politics and of history is the demonstration that there

is no abstract "human nature", fixed and immutable (a concept which certainly derives from religious and transcendentalist thought), but that human nature is the totality of historically determined social relations, hence a historical fact which can, within certain limits, be ascertained with the methods of philology and criticism.[12]

Central to dialectical materialism is not only the belief that human nature changes, but the conviction that it can be changed in a particular way by man's conscious efforts—in particular, by changing the society which forms and directs the way in which human nature develops. But how then do Marxists explain what Eliot refers to as the 'spark that can leap across those 2,500 years'? The explanation is, I would suggest, more complex than that offered by the doctrine of an unchanging human nature.

It is significant that the most interesting piece of writing on aesthetics by Marx himself attempts to answer this problem. In what has become known as the 'Introduction' to his *Critique of Political Economy*, which was not published in Marx's lifetime and was replaced by the published 'Preface' when the latter work was published in 1859, Marx presents the basic problems in terms of admirable clarity.[13] Starting from the observation that some of the peaks of artistic achievement 'by no means correspond to the general development of society', or to the 'material substructure', he draws the conclusion that social progress does not guarantee the production of great art—a conclusion which Zhdanov and his ilk could have studied with profit. From this Marx concludes that

> . . . certain important creations within the compass of art are only possible at an early stage in the development of art. If this is the case with regard to different branches of art within the sphere of art itself, it is not so remarkable that this should also be the case with regard to the whole sphere of art and its relation to the general development of society.[14]

Marx does not however consider this to represent a really crucial difficulty, as he does not feel that there should be a direct and mechanical relationship between the economic base of a society and its intellectual and artistic superstructure. He suggests one way in which this problem can be set into a clearer perspective when he makes the point that if art is a means whereby man gains imaginative control over nature, then when he gains a real control over nature such art is neither necessary nor useful. Essentially, however, this is not seen to be a major problem by

Marx. He shows that it is not difficult to demonstrate convincingly that any given work of art owes its existence to the particular society which produced it, and could not have been produced by another society. What for Marx *is* the crucial problem is not how or why this art emerged when and how it did, but how and why it manages to maintain an aesthetic value in societies totally different from that which produced it, and which would be incapable of producing a similar work.

> The difficulty we are confronted with is not, however, that of understanding how Greek art and epic poetry are associated with certain forms of social development. The difficulty is that they still give us aesthetic pleasure and are in certain respects regarded as a standard and unattainable ideal.[15]

Marx's attempts to explain away this difficulty are less satisfactory than his clear presentation of the problem—which may perhaps be one reason why he never published the 'Introduction'. He suggests that the aesthetic appeal of the great art of the past may be seen to be analogous to the endearing qualities children have for adults, which the latter can admire but cannot, and do not want, to emulate.

> . . . does the naivete of the child not give (the adult) pleasure, and does not he himself endeavour to reproduce the child's veracity at a higher level?
> . . . .
> The Greeks were normal children. The charm their art has for us does not conflict with the immature stage of the society in which it originated. On the contrary its charm is inseparably linked with the fact that the immature social conditions which gave rise, and which alone could give rise, to this art cannot recur.[15]

Many non-Marxist critics have noted that there appears to be a difference of tone between this argument, in which Marx's 'constant' in Goldmann's terminology seems to be his awareness of the great aesthetic appeal of the art of the past, and the argument of the later, published 'Preface', in which the 'constant' appears to be the belief in the primacy of socio-economic determination of the superstructure, including art:

> The mode of production of material life conditions the general process of social, political and intellectual life. It is not the consciousness of men that determines their existence, but their social existence that determines their consciousness.[16]

Peter Demetz, for example, in his book *Marx, Engels and the Poets* contrasts the above 'dogmatic formulation' with the more sympathetic (to literature) tone of the 'Introduction', where 'Marx, the friend of literature, finds himself . . . in open revolt against Marx, the theoretician'.[17] This seems to me to be pitching it a little high, for, even in the 'Preface' Marx does not argue that there is an immediate and mechanical relationship between economic basis and superstructure, noting that the former affects the latter 'sooner or later', or 'more or less' as some translations have it.

However, even allowing for the fact that the divergence between the 'Introduction' and the 'Preface' has been overstressed it must be admitted that Marx's explanation for the discrepancy between the socially determined production of art, and its seemingly atemporal aesthetic qualities, is not altogether satisfactory. In *The Necessity of Art* Ernst Fischer raises one important query regarding the analogy between Greek art and children, in which Marx categorised the Greeks as 'normal children'.

> Today we may doubt whether, compared to other nations, the ancient Greeks were 'normal children'. Indeed, in another connexion Marx and Engels themselves drew attention to the problematic aspects of the Greek world with its contempt for work, its degradation of women, its eroticism reserved solely for courtesans and boys.[18]

What seems to me to represent a far greater objection is that between Marx's reference to the 'charm' of Greek art, and his description of its representing a 'standard and unattainable ideal', there is an enormous, even insuperable gulf. If the great art of the past had only a 'charm' for us, then the Marxist would not feel that there was much problem in explaining this—perhaps even along the lines of Marx's own analogy with the attractive qualities of children for adults. But 'charm', which implies a somewhat untesting and patronising pleasure for the beholder, is a different thing from a 'standard and unattainable ideal'. Men do not tell women that they are charming if they are trying to declare their undying love. The analogy between the art of the past and children is unsatisfactory in other ways. The adult and the child normally belong to the same society and would presumably share various common aspects if consciousness is seen to be socially conditioned, whereas the same cannot be said of Ancient Greek writers and modern readers. Marx's theory in the 'Introduction' can, I think, be categorised as an 'inclusion' theory; primitive society contains in embryo much that remains, albeit in an altered and developed form, in later societies. Thus our admiration for Greek art relates to the fact that we have in our society, and thus in our socially determined consciousnesses, elements analogous to elements in Ancient Greek society. It will perhaps be noted that this comes dangerously close to accepting the concept of an unchanging human nature by the back door.

In a short article entitled 'What is Revolutionary Art?' Herbert Read discussed Marx's 'Introduction', and suggested that

> Marx's hesitation, and indeed faltering over this problem should at least have deterred his followers from a superficial treatment of one of the most complex categories of history that still await dialectical analysis.[19]

It is indeed a dialectical approach to this problem which is required, and I am afraid that I cannot say that an 'inclusion' theory seems to me to be a dialectical one. In fact most Marxist critics who have attempted to come to terms with this problem have oscillated between acceptance of such an inclusion theory and acceptance of what is in essence the bourgeois theory of the unchanging human nature, and neither of these approaches can, I feel, help us to satisfactorily solve our problem, as they both rest on an essentially undialectical assertion of an unchanging element in man. Christopher Caudwell, in *Studies in a Dying Culture*, adopts a position which seems to suffer from such a shortcoming, among others.

> All art is produced by this tension between changing social relations and outmoded consciousness. The very reason why new art is created, why the old art does not satisfy either artist or appreciator, is because it seems somehow out of gear with the present. Old art always has a meaning for us, because the instincts, the source of the affects, do not change, because a new system of social relations does not exclude but includes the old, and because new art too includes the traditions of the art that has gone before.[20]

I suggested that there were a number of weaknesses here. One which is immediately apparent is that slight but crucial distinction between 'satisfaction' and 'having meaning'. Old art, according to Caudwell, lacks the former (although perhaps he means only for the creator of new art), but it possesses the latter. One is reminded of the distinction between Marx's 'charm' and 'standard and unattainable ideal'. Must the Marxist critic forever suffer this split personality when he talks about art? Again, non-Marxist critics such as Demetz have, it would seem, a strong point when they argue that Marxist critics cannot have their cake and eat it too, maintaining that on the one hand being determines consciousness, and that, on the other hand, present consciousness includes past consciousness irrespective of the fact that the economic base of the society has changed. Caudwell's mention of 'unchanging instincts' would also seem to be closer to Desmond Morris than to Marx, and is probably an ill-considered importation from then-current psychological theory which later revision might have removed or amended. It would be difficult to define exactly how 'unchanging instincts' and 'unchanging human nature' differ from one another.

Attempts by other Marxist writers to give a satisfactory answer to this question have also, in my opinion, been limited by a like failure to recognise the dialectical nature of the literary process. Ernst Fischer also espouses the inclusion theory, arguing that 'Ancient, apparently long-forgotten things are preserved within us, continue to work upon us—often without our realising it . . .',[21] which recalls nothing more clearly than the archetypal or mythopaeic variant of psychological criticism. Neither Caudwell nor Fischer can adequately explain why it is that a changed society with a changed superstructure and base *produces* different art but *appreciates* the art which it is no longer capable of producing. In addition one can doubt whether Caudwell's assertion that new art 'includes the traditions of the old' is true over more than a very limited period of time—if then. In what sense does modern drama include the traditions of Ancient Greek drama?

Attempting to deal with the same nagging problem of reconciling the lasting aesthetic qualities of works of art with their socio-temporal genesis and identity, Lucien Goldmann appears to me to stray from that consistently dialectical approach which characterises most of his work. In *The Hidden God* he argues that

A philosophy or work of art can keep its value outside the time or place where it first appeared only if, by expressing a particular human situation, it transposes this on to the plane of the great human problems created by man's relationships with his fellows and with the universe. Now since the number of coherent replies that can be given to these problems is limited by the very structure of the human personality, each of the replies given may correspond to different or even contradictory historical situations.[22]

The weaknesses in this argument can perhaps best be seen by noting how very little separates it from F. R. Leavis's statement of the way in which his approach differed from a Marxist one. Goldmann's mention of 'the great human problems' and of the (implicitly eternal) human personality are surely just alternative ways of describing Leavis's 'inherent human nature'. Elsewhere in *The Hidden God* Goldmann distinguishes between the many accidental factors which may for a limited period of time ensure a book's success, and the one lasting factor, which, he claims, is

> . . . the fact that, in certain works of the past, men rediscover what they themselves think and feel in a confused and obscure manner today.[23]

This of course is a description of a phenomenon rather than an explanation of it, but it also implies that same old core of unchanging human nature to which we keep recurring.

A dialectical attempt to solve this problem must start with an awareness of the totality of the problem, seeing all the components involved in our appreciation of the great art of the past. If it is accepted that one such component is the subject-object dialectic between our socio-temporally conditioned consciousnesses and the work of literature which is in its turn similarly conditioned, then we must accept that our response is in some ways unique. In other words, to say that a work of art constitutes a source of aesthetic value for two societies is not to say that it constitutes the same aesthetic value in both cases. If this were the case then the ideal, absolute response to a given work of art would be a desirable end for the reader or critic to aim at. I hope that I have demonstrated that this is not so in previous chapters of this book. Treating a piece of literature as something totally encapsulated in its own time and place, so that the ideal response is that of the 'first night audience', as it were, is as partial and misleading an aesthetic ideal as treating it as a piece of writing contemporary with the reader. If Dr. Leavis is right that we read Donne as we read the living, and along with Helen Gardner I do not think that this is so, then at any rate it can be said that we misread him. Neither of these two absolutes are particularly helpful if we wish to understand what literary response involves and how and why it lasts, and yet both have, at various times, been insisted upon with a rare fervour. The following two quotations are pretty representative:

> What the critic is concerned with is the sentence's cultural significance in the continuum of English literature *from the viewpoint of the present*—not because the twentieth century can see more, or more

clearly, than earlier centuries (losses have to be balanced against gains), but because an Englishman who happens to live in the twentieth century is committed to it willy-nilly. To become accessible to us critically, the literature of the past must in fact be translatable into the present tense. When confronted therefore with obsolete words or forms in it our only concern *as critics* is to know what they mean in modern English.[24]

To read later emotions here and there into a poem is a tedious error in criticism . . . The original meaning of a word in a great poem is the only one worth attending to. However delightful the meaning arising out of new verbal connotations, such meaning is irrelevant to the author's poem.[25]

Both quotations, in spite of the final qualification about 'the author's poem' in the second one, are surely absurd. Anyone's practical experience of responding to literature must surely reveal that both a knowledge of the genetic origins of the poem and its 'first night' meaning as well as its contemporary significance enter into a full and rich response. It may be true that we are committed to the twentieth century, but this does not mean that we are debarred from an understanding of and sympathy for previous centuries and their literary works. Otherwise no background knowledge of the social and political state of a particular society, the literary conventions of an age, or the personal situation of a writer could help us better to understand a literary work, and we surely know from experience that this is just not so. What happens if the word is not just obsolete but has *no* modern meaning? In that case not much possibility can be held out for our understanding Anglo-Saxon literature. As Caudwell says when talking about love,

The natural human failing is to suppose nothing changes, that ideas are eternal, and that what is denoted by a word is as changeless and invariant as the word.[26]

In passing, I would point out that this is an analogous mistake to that which assumes that literary response is a term which refers, in the case of a given work, to something unchanging. There is also a difference between saying that the literature of the past must be translatable into the present tense, and saying that the words in the work in question must have only their modern meanings. We translate French into English by first of all recognising that it is French and not English. An adequate reading of and response to a work of literature involves both an awareness of its historical genesis and context, and also an appreciation of its modern significance. To quote Caudwell again, 'History cannot seize hold of the past by a divine ingestion; it can only seize hold of the present in the past'.[27] This, it need hardly be added, is not to pretend that the past *is* the present.

One can, as I implied, agree that new verbal connotations are irrelevant to 'the author's poem', whatever that is. They are certainly not irrelevant to the reader's poem, although the precise extent of their relevance is not constant from poem to poem or connotation to connotation; the social significance of such connotations, and the extent to which these are linked with elements in the poem perceived as historical object, are factors which the reader must bear in mind in reaching a decision here. The reader's poem, as I have tried to demonstrate in previous chapters, involves a conception of authorial intent and historical genesis, context and significance, but it is not limited to these. Our response to a great literary work of the past is neither a wholly modern nor a wholly historical one; it involves both an awareness of the modern significance of the work and a historical perception of its mode of being, for as W. J. Harvey has observed, great works are Janus-faced, and we must recognise their pastness even if it is their apparently being eternally present that seems to make them great for us.[28]

The pastness and the presentness of a work cannot be quantitatively defined in theory or in practice; there is no ideal mixture of the two that can be laid down, partly because the two to some extent include one another. We cannot, as Caudwell says, think of the past except through the present, but then neither can we think of the present except with the consciousnesses handed down to us, in part, from the past. The mixture must change from work to work and from time to time. No doubt at some future date critics may object as much to Jan Kott's assumption that Shakespeare is his contemporary as modern critics object to the similar assumption made by Nahum Tate whilst revising *King Lear*—that Shakespeare would have been better off if he had been his contemporary. Wellek and Warren are right when they say that we cannot stop being men of the twentieth century, but neither can Shakespeare really become our contemporary in a total sense. The work of literature in fact mediates between the writer's age and our own, as we tack between our knowledge of its historical identity and its present significance. As Helen Gardner says of our response to *Hamlet*

> That the answers we find are conditioned by our own circumstances does not destroy their value. *Hamlet* is not a problem to which a final

solution exists. It is a work of art about which questions can always be asked. Each generation asks its own questions and finds its own answers.[29]

I think that, albeit in a somewhat roundabout manner, we have begun to see how the lasting aesthetic attraction of art can be squared with a historical perspective which insists that consciousness is determined by being. Because Greek drama has a lasting aesthetic appeal it does not follow that it has an unchanging aesthetic appeal, and a close consideration of our aesthetic perception of a Greek tragedy will reveal that it must differ from the aesthetic perception of such a tragedy experienced by an Ancient Greek, because it contains elements not available to the latter. The fact that we can still find aesthetic value in the plays of Aeschylus shows not that human nature is unchanging, but rather that in a changed social context men can find new significance in the art of the past because they are looking at it from a new vantage point, and thus at a different thing. If human nature did not in fact change it is difficult to see what the point of reading literature would be, for it would only tell us what we already know. Nor would there be much point in producing new literature, as the old would be perfectly adequate in performing the task of revealing this unchanging human nature. Literature, not to mention life, would be a bore.

At this point I would like to backtrack a little and examine anew the question I have dealt with somewhat summarily regarding absolute elements in the aesthetic appeal of great art. I am sure that in general Marxists have been correct in categorising a belief in absolute elements in literary response as undialectical, and dependent upon a religious or metaphysical outlook. Paradoxically, however, if one insists that there are no absolutes, no unchanging things in the world, if 'motion is the mode of existence of matter', then a paradoxical reappearance of an absolute—motion—becomes apparent. The *Fundamentals of Marxism-Leninism* express the matter as follows:

> There are no permanently fixed, ossified things in the world, only things undergoing change, processes. This means that nowhere is there absolute rest, a state that would preclude motion. There is only relative rest.
>
> . . . .
>
> Only motion is absolute, without exceptions.[30]

The classic formulation of this point is made by Lenin in his *Philosophical Notebooks*, where he writes as follows:

The unity (coincidence, identity, equal action) of opposites is conditional, temporary, transitory, relative. The struggle of mutually
exclusive opposites is absolute, just as development and motion are
absolute.
NB. The distinction between subjectivism (scepticism, sophistry,
etc.) and dialectics, incidentally, is that in (objective) dialectics the
difference between the relative and the absolute is itself relative. For
objective dialectics there *is* an absolute *within* the relative. For
subjectivism and sophistry the relative is only relative and excludes
the absolute.[31]

Lukács also insists on the relationship between the absolute and the
relative as a cornerstone of dialectical method:

> The essence of the dialectical method lies in its encompassing the
> indivisible unity of the absolute and the relative: absolute truth has
> its *relative* elements (depending on place, time and circumstances);
> relative truth, on the other hand, so far as it is really truth, so far as it
> reflects reality in a faithful approximation, has an *absolute* validity.[32]

Thus not only does dialectical materialism accept that certain statements about the world are absolutely true, that even within the mutability of matter there is an absolute immutable truth contained, but it
also has certain conceptions of the way in which these absolutes manifest
themselves, which is what the study of dialectics involves an examination of. It is therefore possible for a work of literature to reflect or
enact these absolutes in one way or another. Jack Lindsay, in his wartime
pamphlet *Perspective for Poetry*, makes the point in the context of
artistic response:

> True art is that which embodies an image of life in movement.
> Though it may deal with social conditions long passed away, and
> foreign to everything we are accustomed to, yet it will evoke our
> response if its pattern is true, if it really mirrors change and develop-
> ment. Through all the conditioning and relative factors there bursts
> a living element which remains perpetually significant. We respond
> because our experience of process has a similar basic pattern, however
> differently related.[33]

Lindsay's approach to this question seems to me to be one of the few
Marxist attempts to explain why it is that art outlives its origins without
having recourse to bourgeois conceptions of either an unchanging
human nature or an unchanging work of art. Lindsay sees, as Lenin
puts it, that there is an absolute within the relative, and that it is the
universal fact of movement, of process, and the fact that this is

manifested in similar ways from age to age, that allows each society to respond both in its own way and in a common way to a great work of art which mirrors change and development. It is now easier to understand that 'spark' that jumps across 2,500 years. Just as we do not need to know the precise way in which Wordsworth came to an awareness of and understanding about certain aspects of the relationship between men and women to be able to appreciate his insight in the Lucy poems, so too it is unnecessary for us to know the specific experience which brings a poet or dramatist of the past to an appreciation of the fact that life is movement, and that nothing in life is fixed, absolute. His experience will be foreign to us—just as Wordsworth's relationship(s) will mean little in emotional terms to us. But from both, through 'all the conditioning and relative factors' as Lindsay puts it, 'there bursts a living element', which is our recognition of the same pattern in different experiences.

Ernst Fischer is perhaps trying to make a similar point when he says that '. . . constant features of mankind are captured even in time-conditioned art',[34] but his expression and its place in his larger argument do not entirely remove the suspicion that he has in mind something nearer to an unchanging human nature than to the laws governing the physical world which manifest themselves in different ways in different societies. Fischer links these constant features with a humanist perception of constancy in human endeavour and experience in a manner which seems to me to hover on the boundary between allegiance to an unchanging human nature and recognition of a more scientific view of the constant features which emerge in different forms in great art.

Perhaps I can bring my argument nearer to the flesh and blood of actual literary response by looking at two poems. The first I would like to examine is the 'Bright Star!' sonnet by John Keats.

> Bright star! would I were stedfast as thou art—
>   Not in lone splendour hung aloft the night
> And watching, with eternal lids apart,
>   Like nature's patient, sleepless Eremite,
> The moving waters at their priestlike task
>   Of pure ablution round earth's human shores,
> Or gazing on the new soft-fallen mask
>   Of snow upon the mountains and the moors—
> No—yet still stedfast, still unchangeable,
>   Pillow'd upon my fair love's ripening breast,
> To feel for ever its soft fall and swell,

> Awake for ever in a sweet unrest,
> Still, still to hear her tender-taken breath,
> And so live ever—or else swoon to death.

Now we cannot read this poem adequately without fitting it into the context of our own experience of life, as well as our knowledge of the situation in which this was written. I do not wish to labour the former point, as I have already presented my arguments in my chapter on Marxism and formalism, but in this particular case some interesting points concerning the importance of our knowledge of the context in which it was written can be made. In his *Marxism and Poetry*, George Thomson discusses this poem under the mistaken impression that it was written by Keats on board ship for Italy, where he was to die of the tuberculosis already affecting him.[35] In fact it has now been convincingly demonstrated that Keats only rewrote the poem at this time, and that in fact it dates from some time earlier. Now although this is not a momentous piece of knowledge, it does, I think, change our response to the poem in a number of subtle ways. If we read the poem thinking that Keats wrote it on board ship in the situation he must have found himself in at that time, then not only does the poem have a generally more pessimistic sense, but the significance of a number of seemingly small details is altered. For example, the star itself, instead of being seen as I think it ought to be seen in an adequate reading of the poem, as something foreign and inhuman, if immortal, becomes a star to guide the ship by, something which does have a human use and importance. Similarly the seas lose some of that same inhumanity which is I think important to the full effect of the argument in the poem.

In the sonnet Keats contrasts the transience of human life and experience with the eternity of the star, very much as he does elsewhere. The wish to fuse the eternal qualities of the star and the living qualities of himself and his love is presented in a way that does not just tell us something about Keats's emotional state when writing the poem. Nor does it just allow us to luxuriate in emotions similar to those which Keats describes. In an important sense the poem, as well as having perhaps part of its value contained in these two elements, describes and enacts aspects of the nature of the material world which are absolutely true. The very nature of his description of the star and of the loved one reveals their incompatibility and separation. The star is described in terms of immutability it is true, but also in terms of isolation and lifelessness; it is significant that the only two human associations it has are those of the hermit and the priest, both suggesting social isolation and sterility. Its 'lone splendour' is presented in association with life-denying images—the night, the moving waters (also stressing mutability), and the snow. It is at this point useful to know that Keats recurrently uses cold images to suggest death—which is why the final description of the Grecian Urn as a 'cold pastoral' is particularly significant as a qualifying element in the ode. In the 'Bright Star!' sonnet it is not just that the star is associated with cold ideas, but that every aspect of its description stresses its incompatibility with life, so that as Keats describes his longing for immortality he also describes its impossibility. The star 'watches', but with 'eternal lids apart', an unpleasant image which makes the reader recoil—blink in distaste. The reference to the sleeplessness of the Eremite reinforces this feeling that the star and its associations are antipathetic to human life. The star watches the sea, which is associated with the implied chastity of the priest—later to be contrasted with the sexuality of the loved one—and its purity is stressed by 'pure ablution' round, significantly, 'earth's *human* shores'. The shoreline is used effectively here as the boundary between the human and the non-human to reinforce this picture of the star as apart from humanity and life. The sea, the mountains, and the moors are all places antipathetic to human life, and the 'mask' of snow suggests not only a lifeless lack of emotional expression but also a death-mask.

As Keats looks at the star then, and describes his wish to share its immortality, he has to describe it in terms which reveal its essential and unbridgeable distance from human life, and in doing so he describes the impossibility of man's ever achieving an immortality which would imply a fixity incompatible with that process which is life. In like manner, when he turns to describe his loved one and describes his wish for his relationship with her to achieve immortality, he has to describe her in terms of movement, of process, which again torpedoes the ostensible argument of the poem. He wants to be stedfast and unchangeable, but pillow'd upon his fair love's *ripening* breast. Thus when, at the end of the poem, he turns to death, it is not a suicidal, defeatist movement, but a recognition of the implications of what has gone before. If one is to live and experience life, then one must accept change, and, logically, death. Keats's acceptance of death in this poem is paradoxically an acceptance of life, for the 'immortality' offered by the star is a lifeless one even if it is a deathless one too. It is better, Keats implies, to live and to die, than to do neither, and there is no third alternative. At this point I think that we can see the absolute in the relative, the living element bursting out of the poem for all men. Our response to the poem is to a large extent personal. We must call upon our own experience of fear of death, of regret at the passing of sexual love, of regret at the passing of everything human. But in this personal element there is an absolute element. It is absolutely true that if life is movement then to live in an immortal fixity is a contradiction, an impossibility. The poem's greatness—the spark that jumps in this case a century and a half —contains different components. It involves our knowledge of Keats's life and other poetry, our knowledge of the significance of the Romantic revolution. It also contains our own experience and knowledge of the world, our recognition of its relevance in our own social context. But it also contains a core of absolute truth—the absolute truth that life is process, and cannot be otherwise.

Because these different components do exist in our response to literature, a changed social context does affect our response to a poem even if within that poem certain absolute truths may reside. Reading a poet such as Yeats in the context of the nineteen-thirties must have involved particular problems for the progressive reader with a knowledge of his political sympathies. There is no purely 'poetic' response to lines like

> The best lack all conviction, while the worst
> Are full of passionate intensity.

The lines make a statement which cannot be limited to the 'internal world' of the poem, but must be applied to the outside world, and this being so the reader's knowledge that Yeats has a different and irreconcilable scale of values from his own will inevitably affect his reading of the poem. However, our situation today is different from the reader of the twenties or thirties, and our response to Yeats's poetry, although perhaps containing the same elements of disagreement, contains them in a different total context. Because we read from the vantage point of our own time where the negative aspects of Yeats's poetry no longer have the immediately sinister significance that they once had, we are in a better position to suspend our disapproval of these aspects and to concern ourselves more with what can now be seen as positive aspects of the poetry. Let me give an extreme analogy. If a progressive political grouping were today to stage an exhibition of fascist propaganda, books and films these would have a different significance from their original significance in, say, Nazi Germany. They would in fact play a progressive rather than a reactionary role, for in the context that they would now be perceived in they would be different things—exposing the reality of fascism rather than propagandising for it. One can see Nazi anti-semitic propaganda in the Museum of German History in East Berlin. It would be a foolish person who concluded from this that the East Germans were in fact anti-semitic, for it is precisely because in East Germany it is assumed that anti-semitism is an evil thing that the material has a positive, anti-fascist significance. (One would, from my experience, have reservations about the progressive quality of a similar exhibition in West Germany.)

Our response to art is of course more subtle than our response to propaganda, but similar factors operate. If, moving back to Yeats, we consider a poem such as 'Easter 1916', I would argue that the political shortcomings in it are of less immediate importance now than they may have been at various times in the past, and that we are in a better position to appreciate that which, because of the uniqueness of our present social and political situation, has a peculiar relevance for us. I believe that, like the 'Bright Star!' sonnet of Keats, this poem reaches out to a perception of certain facts about the world which are in an important sense universally true—notably the omnipresence of change, and the dialectical form which it takes. In his earlier poetry Yeats tends to see change in a rather clichéd, self-regarding manner as the great thief of experience. His later experience of the revolutionary days in Ireland leads him to perceive its creative, life-giving qualities as well. From an initial impression of the ordinary, unprepossessing nature and appearance of the people who are to be swept up in the social upheaval he moves to the perception that 'A terrible beauty is born', that the emergence of the new from the familiar and the old demonstrates that the latter was in movement, was not the static and lifeless mass that he previously thought. At this moment of perception he moves from his purely personal, aristocratic suspicion of the particular social forces involved to a recognition of the principle of creation contained in what he sees—a recognition of the absolute in the relative. From this point he can look at the world with new eyes, and see that movement that he had denied in one area in other areas:

> Hearts with one purpose alone
> Through Summer and Winter seem
> Enchanted to a stone
> To trouble the living stream.
> The horse that comes from the road,
> The rider, the birds that range
> From cloud to tumbling cloud;

> Minute by minute they change;
> A shadow of cloud on the stream
> Changes minute by minute;
> A horse-hoof slides on the brim,
> And a horse plashes within it;
> The long-legged moor-hens dive,
> And hens to moor-hens call;
> Minute by minute they live:
> The stone's in the midst of all.

The sheer beauty of this vision is not to be simply explained. However, it is certainly associated with Yeats's dialectical understanding of change and emergence, an understanding of the universality of which allows him to move from a perception of change and its nature in society to the same perception in the context of nature.

Perhaps particularly relevant to a present-day reader is Yeats's perception that in order to change society, the revolutionary has, paradoxically, himself to be inflexible; just as the hard stone makes the most impact in the stream, so too the hard heart makes the most impact in a social context. At this point he asks questions no doubt more disturbing for us today than for most of his progressive readers thirty or forty years ago:

> Too long a sacrifice
> Can make a stone of the heart.
> O when may it suffice?
> That is Heaven's part, our part
> To murmur name upon name,
> As a mother names her child . . .

The unsatisfactory nature of Yeats's response to the question he has raised should not blind us to the particular, present-day relevance that it has. The lasting value of the poem resides partly in its concern with certain facts about the world which will always be true, and partly in the particular relevance to us of certain problems these facts seem to Yeats to raise.

Thus I would argue that there is no necessary contradiction involved in a Marxist insistence upon the importance of perceiving the social and temporal context of a work of literature (and a reader), whilst at the same time maintaining that a literary work can have a lasting value which contains 'absolute' elements. It is only when the personal and the social, the temporal and the universal, the absolute and the relative are seen as dialectically connected opposites rather than as mutually exclusive opposites, that this problem can be seen to be no problem. For the non-Marxist there is no solution to this problem for, as Caudwell puts it,

> Although the bourgeois is always trying to reduce the literary process to simple opposites of this nature, he is perpetually defeated by the dialectic nature of art.[36]

NOTES

[1] *Writer and Critic*, London 1970, p. 120.

[2] *Aesthetics*, p. 25.

[3] *Illusion and Reality*, p. 117.

[4] Lucien Goldmann, interview with Brigitte Devismes, p. 35.

[5] *Criticism*, p. 75.

[6] *The Business of Criticism*, p. 20.

[7] *Prison Notebooks*, p. 353.

[8] *A Theory of the Classical Novel*, p. 15.

[9] Sir Joshua Reynolds, Seventh *Discourse*.

[10] F. R. Leavis, 'Literature and Society', *The Common Pursuit*, reprinted Harmondsworth 1966, p. 184.

[11] *On Poetry and Poets*, p. 117.

[12] *Prison Notebooks*, p. 133.

[13] See the account of the publishing history given in *Marx, Engels and the Poets*, by Peter Demetz (London 1967), which is helpful. Demetz uses the term 'Foreword' to refer to what has been traditionally known as the 'Preface' in English.

[14] Karl Marx, *A Contribution to the Critique of Political Economy*, London 1971, p. 216.

[15] *Critique*, p. 217.

[16] *Critique*, p. 20.

[17] *Marx, Engels and the Poets*, p. 71.

[18] Ernst Fischer, *The Necessity of Art*, Harmondsworth 1963, p. 11.

[19] Herbert Read, 'What is Revolutionary Art?', *Five on Revolutionary Art*, ed. Rea, London 1935, p. 11.

[20] *Studies in a Dying Culture*, p. 54.

[21] *The Necessity of Art*, p. 12.

[22] *The Hidden God*, p. 20.

[23] *The Hidden God*, p. 315.

[24] F. W. Bateson, 'Linguistics and Literary Criticism', *The Disciplines of Criticism*, p. 7. (I should say that my abstraction of this comment from its original context tends to make it appear more extreme than in fact it is; Mr. Bateson's position with regard to historical scholarship is far more reasonable than might be suggested here.)

[25] Geoffrey Tillotson, *Essays in Criticism and Research*, Cambridge 1942. Quoted by Graham Hough in *An Essay on Criticism*, p. 68.

[26] *Studies in a Dying Culture*, p. 129.

[27] *Further Studies*, p. 146.

[28] *Character and the Novel*, p. 18.

[29] *The Business of Criticism*, p. 51.

[30] *Fundamentals of Marxism-Leninism*, Moscow n.d., p. 35.

[31] V. I. Lenin, *Collected Works*, vol. 38, London 1961, p. 360.

[32] György Lukács, *Writer and Critic*, p. 62.

[33] Jack Lindsay, *Perspective for Poetry*, London 1944, p. 10.

[34] *The Necessity of Art*, p. 12.

[35] George Thomson, *Marxism and Poetry*, New York 1946, p. 15.

[36] Christoper Caudwell, *Romance and Realism*, Princeton 1970, p. 33.

9. *Conclusion*

Although I would not like it to be thought that I had written a sort of literary-critical *Rasselas*, ending with a conclusion in which nothing is concluded, I do feel that I should restrain the impulse to end up with a neat series of conclusions which follow on from what I have said before. If there is one thing that seems to me to be apparent regarding our relationship with literature it is that it never reaches any final conclusion, but is continually changing and being regenerated. We would quite rightly treat with considerable contempt the person who announced that he had finally discovered the key to Shakespeare, and had at last understood what the latter's writings were all about. What I hope will be implied by what I have written is that any attempt to limit or fix the significance of literary experience is unwise and unrewarding. An appreciation of the fact that the identity of a literary work is dependent upon its relationships with the person who writes it and those who read it should lead us to see the reading of literature as a part of the experience of living, rather than an isolable and special sort of experience which has its own rules and laws, and which can be reduced to the status of an 'objective' science.

I would, however, like to conclude with a few comments on the way in which the study of literature is treated within our educational system, partly because of my involvement in education, and partly because it is at school or college that most people in our society are introduced to literature, and develop habits of dealing with it. My own opinion is that if there is one fundamental accusation which can be levelled against the way in which our educational system introduces people to literature, it is that it obscures the relationships between literature and life which give to literature that identity which makes it a thing of such value. I have frequently been quite appalled by the way in which what should have been the liberating effect of reading great literature has been somehow transformed into an arid procedure for amassing a number of 'facts' which can be churned out at the convenient time when examinations are sat. Interviewing a candidate for admission to university some time ago, a colleague and I asked him what it was that he liked about Chaucer's *Franklin's Tale*, which he had claimed was his favourite work. 'Now let me see', he replied, 'there are three things to remember about this tale, aren't there?' As I have in the past marked Advanced Level scripts containing answers on this particular piece of literature, I know that this is not an isolated case of insensitivity, but relates to something more fundamentally wrong than a merely individual lack of imagination and enthusiasm.

There is, I suppose, little doubt that this poor schoolboy must have received some less than adequate teaching, but it is not sufficient to explain away his reaction by recourse to such a 'reason'. The whole system of Eng. Lit., with its heavy concentration on a totally discredited system of assessment leads almost inevitably—as so many other writers have pointed out—to a reliance on memory which of necessity reduces the dynamic of literary experience to stasis. As someone with an interest in literary theory, I am often amazed at the way in which examination questions are set by those unaware of the sort of theoretical problems which many of them raise, and with which the poor examinee has to contend (whilst remembering in some detail the work in question) in a matter of thirty or so minutes. There is a grotesque irony in the fact that the teacher or lecturer who can go through *Hard Times* with a class or a tutorial group showing how Dickens demonstrates that a scientistic reduction of life to hard facts denies the human significance of life, can then proceed to set examination questions which would bring joy to the heart of a Gradgrind, who would undoubtedly be capable of getting a splendid result in the examinations in which they appear. As my chapter on value demonstrates, perhaps the most difficult aspect of any critical theory is that connected with value, and yet educationalists feel no difficulty in evaluating students' relationships with and responses to literature in a matter of minutes rather than hours. When tackled about this, most of them will say that assessment is something forced on to schools and universities by the government, who want to have some objective record of attainment, and that they would happily dispense with the necessity of assessment if they could.

In a sense they are right in this assertion. It seems to me that the reduction of the richness and diversity of our response to literature to a single mark or class can only be understood if it is seen as yet another manifestation of alienation or reification, a reduction of a complex relationship full of human significance to an 'objective' fact. The trouble is that those who disclaim any belief in the possibility of assessing literary response are often those who put greatest store by examination results—perhaps partly because they themselves have succeeded within the system. I do not think that reform is possible in this area; it seems to me that either one accepts that our relationships with a literary work are infinitely complex and cannot be reduced to stasis, or one does not. If one does, then I cannot see that any assessment system which aims to end up with a neat grading or mark can possibly be seen as an adequate reflection of the fact that it is allegedly reflecting. Even from within many of the false assumptions of examining there are innumerable contradictions. If a student gets a first-class mark on one Finals paper, but does badly in others, he will end up with a second or a third-class degree. And yet surely his attainment of that one mark suggests that he is, in some sense, of 'first' quality. And if he wishes to proceed to research in the subject on which he wrote his first-class answer, why should he not be preferred to someone who has achieved eight first-class answers and yet has obtained a second-class standard on, again, the one subject on which he wishes to proceed to do research?

But one could multiply such contradictions indefinitely, for an absurd system will never produce a shortage of specific absurdities. F. W. Bateson has pointed out many more such absurdities,[1] but it seems to me that in suggesting that the Finals system be replaced by assessment on essay performance he is not striking at the root of the problem, which is that any method which attempts to reify the complexities of an individual's relationships with literature into one fixed, unchanging grading out of a possible half dozen, is attempting the absurd and the impossible. Our society must decide whether it has the courage to say that the study of literature is important because it involves a complex enrichment of human experience and potentiality which by its very nature cannot be assessed in any simple manner, or whether it wants its teachers and lecturers to go on telling it lies to order every June.

Such reification as I have mentioned above is encouraged throughout the study of literature in our society. The research student who can reduce the extraordinary complexity of our relationship to Shakespeare to a collection of arid lists of irrelevant information, though he might object to being told so, is really on the same level as the interviewee capable of reducing the *Franklin's Tale* to three points. Now I am very much aware that very often it is difficult to relate any research to fully-conscious values which are socially acceptable; and there is obviously a very common sort of philistinism which seeks to 'measure' everything according to known values. Were I not to admit this I would myself be falling into the camp of the Gradgrinds. I know too that when attacking certain manifestations of psychoanalytic criticism I argued that the reader must not go to a work of literature with fully formed pre-conceptions of what he is to find there. But I see as equally disastrous the attitude that one should have *no* attitude towards what one is investigating and should attempt to discover the 'objective' truth about it, assuming that there is equal significance in all truth which can be isolated, just as there are great statues hidden in all blocks of stone. This attitude of total impartiality, to which Marxists have I think correctly countered the needs of a partisan approach to art and life, whatever exaggerations may have accompanied such arguments, seems again to be connected with scientism. Certainly one keeps meeting as a defence of motiveless research that 'spin-off' argument used by the Americans to justify the enormous amounts of money spent on space-research, that in the course of such research all sorts of accidental contributions to human knowledge would be made. (We have had the first instalment —non-stick frying pans, and are eagerly awaiting the next.) Now of course there is a legitimate argument for saying that space-research is a justified area for the expenditure of human energy and resources, and it is significant that the Americans (more concerned with beating the Soviets, as Kennedy's correspondence showed, and spin-off of a military nature) are incapable of formulating what it is. They cannot formulate such value because it is not to be expressed in the neat, reified terms of the cash-nexus.

Similarly, the justifications that one comes across for the study of literature exhibit a similar failure of nerve, having no coherent system of living values to appeal to. Much defence of academic research rests on the arguments mythically attributed to the Chinese who, finding roast pork in the remains of a farm that had been destroyed by fire, spent several centuries burning down farms before they discovered less wasteful ways of producing the delicacy. We must become less obsessed with quantifiable methods of measuring value, and accept that the value that some things have for us is not reducible to anything else. If I understand him correctly, it is such a position that lies behind Dr. Leavis's attack on what he calls Neo-Benthamism, although I feel that on occasions his objections are aimed in the wrong directions. If we want literature to reveal its full potentiality to our pupils and students we must try to appreciate the practical implications of Henry James's point that relations end nowhere, and make of the study of literature a continuing and enriching process which does not end in the neatly quantifiable. In this we may perhaps be helped by a consideration of the educational possibilities contained in the dialectical method suggested by Allan Rodway and Lucien Goldmann. This might lead to a situation where the student was no longer capable of talking animatedly in pubs with his fellow-students about literature, and remaining silent and bored in seminar discussion. A dialectical method would aim to reject any feeling of finality being aimed for at any point in the study of literature. The student should never be encouraged to feel that there is an observable 'end' (Finals, for example), to which his reading must be subordinated.

These questions cannot, of course, be solved independently from other problems that our society faces, with which they are related. Everett Knight has commented upon the fact that the University mirrors the society of which it is a part, noting that

> The 'free choice' (the student) had been invited to make on the basis of information 'objectively' submitted to him by his teachers emerges as an aspect of the way in which *his* particular society functions.[2]

There is nothing to prevent our attempting simultaneously to change our society and aspects of our educational system, however, and at a time when social changes are manifesting themselves as much within the educational system as outside of it it would appear to be a logical way of proceeding. There can surely be no question that the academic institutional equivalent of formalism which seeks to purify the study of literature by studying it 'by itself' can and should be attacked in consort with a demonstration of the needs that our society has, as revealed, in part, by a study of literature. 'The one thing that we must resist at all costs is the student demand for "relevance"', announced a well-known professor of English at a conference I attended. There seems little doubt that whether or not such calls have the effect of rallying the academic clans, the student demand is going to make considerable headway, if only because teachers and academics have no answer to it beyond the mouthing of clichés about the purity of research. Of course, it may be feared that within the context of our own society, any achievement of 'relevance' might mean relevance to the needs of big-business, but the answer to such fears is to present alternatives, rather than to retreat into academic funk-holes. In his essay 'Criticism as a Humanist Discipline',[3] Graham Hough has noted that the great critical documents in our language are also political acts, implying quite correctly, I feel, a direct connection between their greatness as criticism and their involvement with the wider issues of their time. In comparison to this, the efforts of a British University to discipline one of its members at the present moment, because of his alleged introduction of politics into his lectures (and because of his extra-academic political commitment) strikes a sorry note. Behind accusations of bias (from which it is always left-wingers who suffer) there still lies that scientistic belief in the attainability of 'objectivity' in the study of literature. Try telling that to Johnson, or Coleridge, or Arnold, or Leavis, or any other great critic.

In this respect, in spite of occasional dogmatism, ignorance or over-simplification, student (and now pupil) demands for a greater relevance, commitment to the real world in the study of literature, have shown the way forward. The demand for student participation in course arrangement, and the decision-making machinery concerned with academic study, is not an isolated 'political' demand, but arises from the contradiction between the principles of equality assumed in academic discussion about literature, and the principles of authority encapsulated in the educational hierarchy in school and college—a contradiction as marked as that between the private ownership of property and the public cooperation necessary to produce it which is characteristic of capitalist society. It is necessary to change the framework within which literature is studied if we wish to make this study relevant and meaningful. In this respect, we must develop more democratic educational institutions, in which the study of literature follows the changing needs of those who study it as individuals and as a collective, and in which the identity of literature is regained by stressing, not by ignoring, its connections with the real world. This is not the place to go into details about such matters, but I would suggest that rather than the sterile study of the history of literary forms, divorced from social and historical life, the encapsulated 'Beowulf to Virginia Woolf' of the isolated academic, we should realise that there is no 'objective' continuum of English (or any other) literature, but a large body of work which can be approached in different ways which are more or less exclusive, and more or less rewarding at any particular time. The search for comprehensiveness, whether it be chronological, formalistic or what have you, is born of a belief in the existence of an objective and finite body of knowledge waiting to be known.

An adequate study of literature must leave things out, and should seek not to achieve an illusory comprehensiveness, but to stress the multiplicity of our relationships with literature. The pupil or student should be able to choose to study individual works in the context of a genre-study of literature, in the context of the study of a particular author, or in the context of a particular historical period, and from this to consider the significance that a work has for himself. Most importantly, he should be encouraged to tack dialectically between these different contexts, to perceive the dynamic of the literary process. The process of literary study should oscillate between the personal and the social; individual essays and group discussions should force the individual both to develop a response of his own, and to test and modify it in a social manner. Finally, and most importantly, the barriers between such study and the outside world should be broken down. Yeats's poem 'The Scholars' ironically contrasts the young poet creating his poem in the agonies of love-sickness with the Casaubon-type scholar examining it in sterile academic isolation. Much of our study of literature is in a similar way a denial of the life it contains and can communicate, and until we accept that it is the relationships with the real world that a literary work has which create and enrich its literary identity, we will not make of literary study a meaningful or worthwhile occupation.

If, finally, I return to the question I raised at the start of this book regarding the possibility of synthesising metacritical and intrinsic criticism, I would suggest that it is only when the work of literature is seen in as full and as dynamic a series of contexts as is possible that its identity, its 'thisness' as literature, can really be released and perceived. A great work of literature will only reveal its greatness if it is allowed to live in as many different contexts as are possible, if it really feeds on and is fed by the richness of the life and experience of those who read it. Just as a great man, as Caudwell shows in his essay on T. E. Lawrence, is not a thing *per se* but is great because of the relationships between his identity and his circumstances, so too a great work of art cannot maintain its greatness in a claustrophobic academic vacuum. We may be stuck with a number of Universities 'purpose built' on purpose as far away from urban life as possible in order to encourage 'pure' academic interest; there is no reason why we should similarly emasculate and starve of human contact the literature which is studied in these would-be ivory towers. Towards the end of *Seven Types of Ambiguity*, William Empson comments that no critical activity is final because as 'people are always reading an author, he is always being read differently', and it is this sense of literature both being about life and being life that ensures its movement, its dynamism. Empson concludes this particular argument with words which I feel should be pinned to the walls of all those engaged in teaching literature: 'It does not even satisfy the understanding to stop living in order to understand'.[4]

NOTES

[1] F. W. Bateson, *Essays in Critical Dissent*, London 1972, p. 201.
[2] *A Theory of the Classical Novel*, p. 2.
[3] *Contemporary Criticism*, p. 51.
[4] William Empson, *Seven Types of Ambiguity*, third edition, reprinted Harmondsworth 1965, p. 245.

BOOKS AND ARTICLES QUOTED AND REFERRED TO

Articles by a single author gathered together in one volume are not generally referred to individually. References are to the editions used, which are not necessarily the first editions.

Louis Althusser, *For Marx*, trans. Brewster (London, Allen Lane, 1969).

Aristotle, *Poetics*, The Oxford Aristotle, vol. XI (Oxford University Press).

Matthew Arnold, *Essays in Criticism* (*second series*) (London, Macmillan, 1888).

Irving Babbitt, 'Genius and Taste', *Five Approaches of Literary Criticism*, ed. Scott (London, Collier-Macmillan, 1962).

F. W. Bateson, *Essays in Critical Dissent* (London, Longman, 1972).

F. W. Bateson, 'Linguistics and Literary Criticism', *The Disciplines of Criticism*, ed. Demetz, Greene and Nelson (London, Yale University Press, 1968).

F. W. Bateson, *Wordsworth, A Reinterpretation* (London, Longman, 1963).

John Bayley, *The Characters of Love* (London, Chatto and Windus, 1968).

Monroe C. Beardsley, *Aesthetics* (New York, Harcourt Brace and World, 1958).

R. W. Beardsmore, *Art and Morality* (London, Macmillan, 1971).

Wayne C. Booth, *The Rhetoric of Fiction* (London, University of Chicago Press, 1966).

Cleanth Brooks, 'Keats' Sylvan Historian: History Without Footnotes', *Five Approaches of Literary Criticism* (London, Collier-Macmillan, 1962).

Cleanth Brooks, 'Literary Criticism: Poet, Poem, and Reader', *Perspectives in Contemporary Criticism*, ed. Grebstein (London, Harper and Row, 1968).

Cleanth Brooks, 'What Does Poetry Communicate?', *American Critical Essays*, ed. Beaver (Oxford University Press, 1959).

Calvin S. Brown, 'Difficulty and Surface Value', *The Disciplines of Criticism*, ed. Demetz, Greene and Nelson (London, Yale University Press, 1968).

W. C. Brownell, *Criticism* (Port Washington, Kennikat Press, 1967).

N. I. Bukharin, 'Poetry, Poetics and the Problems of Poetry in the

USSR', *Problems of Soviet Literature* (London, Martin Lawrence, n.d. ?1935).

Kenneth Burke, 'The Problem of the Intrinsic (as reflected in the Neo-Aristotelian School)', *Aristotle's Poetics and English Literature*, ed. Olson (London, University of Chicago Press, 1965).

J. M. Cameron, *Poetry and Dialectic* (Leeds, University of Leeds Press, 1961).

Christopher Caudwell, *Illusion and Reality* (London, Lawrence and Wishart, 1958).

Christopher Caudwell, *Romance and Realism* (Princeton University Press, 1970).

Christopher Caudwell, *Studies and Further Studies in a Dying Culture* (London, Monthly Review Press, 1971).

Maurice Cornforth, *Communism and Human Values* (London, Lawrence and Wishart, 1972).

R. S. Crane, ed., *Critics and Criticism* (London, University of Chicago Press, 1968).

Frederick C. Crews, *The Pooh Perplex* (London, Arthur Barker, 1967).

Peter Demetz, *Marx, Engels and the Poets* (London, University of Chicago Press, 1967).

Margaret Drabble, 'Crossing the Alps', *Penguin Modern Stories 3* (Harmondsworth, Penguin Books, 1969).

Richard Eberhart, 'Empson's Poetry', *Accent Anthology*, ed. Quinn and Shattuck (New York, Harcourt Brace and World, 1946).

T. S. Eliot, *On Poetry and Poets* (London, Faber and Faber, 1969).

T. S. Eliot, *Selected Essays* (revised edition) (London, Faber and Faber, 1965).

T. S. Eliot, *The Use of Poetry and the Use of Criticism* (London, Faber and Faber, 1968).

T. S. Eliot, *To Criticize the Critic* (London, Faber and Faber, 1965).

William Empson, *Collected Poems* (London, Chatto and Windus, 1962).

William Empson, sleeve notes to record of *William Empson Reading Selected Poems* (Hessle, Yorkshire, The Marvell Press, ?1959).

William Empson, 'Rhythm and Imagery in English Poetry', 'British Journal of Aesthetics', January 1962.

William Empson, *Seven Types of Ambiguity* (third edition) (Harmondsworth, Penguin Books, 1965).

Ernst Fischer, *The Necessity of Art*, trans. Bostock (Harmondsworth, Penguin Books, 1963).

E. M. Forster, *Aspects of the Novel* (Harmondsworth, Penguin Books, 1970).

Roger Fowler, *The Languages of Literature* (London, Routledge and Kegan Paul, 1971).

Roger Fowler, 'The Structure of Criticism and the Languages of Poetry', *Contemporary Criticism*, ed. Bradbury and Palmer (London, Edward Arnold, 1970).

Robert Frost, *The Poetry of Robert Frost*, ed. Lathem (London, Cape, 1969).

Helen Gardner, *The Business of Criticism* (Oxford University Press, 1966).

Lucien Goldmann, 'Criticism and Dogmatism in Literature', trans. Halberstadt, *The Dialectics of Liberation*, ed. Cooper (Harmondsworth, Penguin Books, 1968).

Lucien Goldmann, *The Hidden God*, trans. Thody (London, Routledge and Kegan Paul, 1964).

Lucien Goldmann, *The Human Sciences and Philosophy*, trans. White and Anchor (London, Cape Editions, 1969).

Lucien Goldmann, *Immanuel Kant*, trans. Black (London, New Left Books, 1971).

Lucien Goldmann, interview with Brigitte Devismes, 'VH 101' (Paris, Summer 1970).

Lucien Goldmann, 'Reflections on *History* and *Class Consciousness*', trans. France, *Aspects of History and Class Consciousness*, ed. Mészáros (London, Routledge and Kegan Paul, 1971).

Geoffrey Gorer, 'The Myth in Jane Austen', *Five Approaches of Literary Criticism*, ed. Scott (London, Collier-Macmillan, 1962).

Antonio Gramsci, *Selections from the Prison Notebooks of Antonio Gramsci*, ed. and trans. Hoare and Nowell Smith (London, Lawrence and Wishart, 1971).

Ian Gregor, 'Criticism as an Individual Activity: The Approach Through Reading', *Contemporary Criticism*, ed. Bradbury and Palmer (London, Edward Arnold, 1970).

Thom Gunn, review of *Collected Poems* by William Empson, 'The London Magazine', February 1956.

Thomas Hardy, *The Return of the Native* (London, Macmillan, 1878).

R. M. Hare, *The Language of Morals* (Oxford University Press, 1952).

W. J. Harvey, *Character and the Novel* (London, Chatto and Windus, 1970).

J. M. Hawthorn, 'The Strange Deaths of Sally, Ann, Lucy and others . . .', 'Trivium', vol. VI, 1971.

Geoffrey Hill, *King Log* (London, André Deutsch, 1968).

Richard Hoggart, 'Contemporary Cultural Studies', *Contemporary Criticism*, ed. Bradbury and Palmer (London, Edward Arnold, 1970).

Norman N. Holland, 'The "Unconscious" of Literature: The Psycho-analytic Approach', *Contemporary Criticism*, ed. Bradbury and Palmer (London, Edward Arnold, 1970).

Graham Hough, *An Essay on Criticism* (London, Duckworth, 1966).

Graham Hough, 'Criticism as a Humanist Discipline', *Contemporary Criticism*, ed. Bradbury and Palmer (London, Edward Arnold, 1970).

Henry James, *The Portrait of a Lady*, ed. Edel (London, The Bodley Head, 1968).

Walter Kerr, 'The Theater of Say It! Show It!', 'Dialogue', 11.3, 1969.

Everett Knight, *A Theory of the Classical Novel* (London, Routledge and and Kegan Paul, 1970).

Everett Knight, *The Objective Society* (London, Routledge and Kegan Paul, 1959).

Leszek Kolakowski, 'Althusser's Marx', *The Socialist Register 1971*, ed. Miliband and Saville (London, The Merlin Press, 1971).

Jan Kott, *Shakespeare Our Contemporary*, revised edition (London, Methuen, 1967).

F. R. Leavis, *The Common Pursuit* (Harmondsworth, Penguin Books, 1966).

Lee T. Lemon, *The Partial Critics* (Oxford University Press, 1965).

V. I. Lenin, *Collected Works*, vol. 38 (*Philosophical Notebooks*) (London, Lawrence and Wishart, 1961).

V. I. Lenin, 'Once Again on the Trade Unions, the Present Situation and the Mistakes of Comrades Trotsky and Bukharin', *Selected Works*, vol. 3 (London, Lawrence and Wishart, 1960).

Jack Lindsay, *Perspective for Poetry* (London, Fore Publications, 1944).

David Lodge, *The Language of Fiction* (London, Routledge and Kegan Paul, 1967).

Edgar Lohner, 'The Intrinsic Method: Some Reconsiderations', *The Disciplines of Criticism*, ed. Demetz, Greene and Nelson (London, Yale University Press, 1968).

György Lukács, *History and Class Consciousness*, trans. Livingstone (London, The Merlin Press, 1971).

György Lukács, *The Meaning of Contemporary Realism*, trans. J. and N. Mander (London, The Merlin Press, 1969).

György Lukács, 'On the Personality of Lenin', 'Marxism Today', September 1971.

György Lukács, *The Theory of the Novel*, trans. Bostock (London, The Merlin Press, 1971).

György Lukács, *Writer and Critic*, trans. Kahn (London, The Merlin Press, 1970).

G. M. Mathews, 'Othello and the Dignity of Man', *Shakespeare in a Changing World*, ed. Kettle (London, Lawrence and Wishart, 1964).

Karl Marx and Frederick Engels, *Literature and Art* (New York, International Publishers, 1947).

Karl Marx, *A Contribution to the Critique of Political Economy*, trans. Ryazanskaya (London, Lawrence and Wishart, 1971).

Karl Marx, *Capital*, vol. I (London, Lawrence and Wishart, n.d. ?1967).

István Mészáros, ed., *Aspects of History and Class Consciousness* (London, Routledge and Kegan Paul, 1971).

Jan Mukařovský, 'The Esthetics of Language', *A Prague School Reader on Esthetics, Literary Structure, and Style*, selected and trans. Garvin (Washington D.C., Georgetown University Press, 1964).

Lowry Nelson, Jr., 'The Fictive Reader and Literary Self-Reflexiveness', *The Disciplines of Criticism*, ed. Demetz, Greene and Nelson (London, Yale University Press, 1968).

Elder Olson, '"Sailing to Byzantium": Prolegomena to a Poetics of the Lyric', *Five Approaches of Literary Criticism*, ed. Scott (London, Collier-Macmillan, 1962).

Luigi Pirandello, *Six Characters in Search of an Author*, trans. May (London, Heinemann, 1971).

John Preston, *The Created Self* (London, Heinemann, 1970).

Herbert Read, 'What is Revolutionary Art?', *Five on Revolutionary Art*, ed. Rea (London, Wishart Books, 1935).

Jean Rhys, *Wide Sargasso Sea* (Harmondsworth, Penguin Books, 1968).

I. A. Richards, *Principles of Literary Criticism* (London, Routledge and Kegan Paul, 1961).

Allan Rodway, 'Generic Criticism', *Contemporary Criticism*, ed. Bradbury and Palmer (London, Edward Arnold, 1970).

J.-P. Sartre, *What is Literature?*, trans. Frechtman (London, Methuen, 1970).

Gitta Sereny, 'Colloquy With a Conscience', 'The Daily Telegraph Magazine', October 8th, 1971.

Stephen Spender, *World Within World* (London, Hamish Hamilton, 1951).

George Steiner, *Language and Silence* (London, Faber and Faber, 1967).

Wallace Stevens, *The Collected Poems of Wallace Stevens* (London, Faber and Faber, 1966).

Tom Stoppard, *Rosencrantz and Guildenstern are Dead* (London, Faber and Faber, 1971).

George Thomson, *Marxism and Poetry* (New York, International Publishers, 1946).

Julian Trevelyan, *Indigo Days* (London, Macgibbon and Kee, 1957).

Leon Trotsky, *Literature and Revolution*, trans. Strunsky (Michigan, Ann Arbor, 1960).

Various Authors, *Fundamentals of Marxism-Leninism* (Moscow, Foreign Languages Publishing House, n.d.).

Felix Vodička, 'The History of the Echo of Literary Works', *A Prague School Reader on Esthetics, Literary Structure, and Style*, selected and trans. Garvin (Washington D.C., Georgetown University Press, 1964).

Alick West, *Crisis and Criticism* (London, Lawrence and Wishart, 1937).

René Wellek and Austen Warren, *Theory of Literature* (Harmondsworth, Penguin Books, 1963).

Arnold Wesker, *The Four Seasons, New English Dramatists number four* (Harmondsworth, Penguin Books, 1970).

The Portable Walt Whitman, selected and ed. Van Doren (New York, The Viking Press, 1963).

Raymond Williams, *Culture and Society* (Harmondsworth, Penguin Books, 1966).

Raymond Williams, 'On and from any shore', 'Stand', vol. 12, no. 2.

W. K. Wimsatt, 'Battering the Object: The Ontological Approach', *Contemporary Criticism*, ed. Bradbury and Palmer (London, Edward Arnold, 1970).

W. K. Wimsatt, 'Genesis: A Fallacy Revisited', *The Disciplines of Criticism*, ed. Demetz, Greene and Nelson (London, Yale University Press, 1968).

W. K. Wimsatt, with Monroe C. Beardsley, *The Verbal Icon* (London, Methuen, 1970).

W. B. Yeats, *Collected Poems* (London, Macmillan, 1952).

Name Index

Subject Index